THE MERRY WIVES
OF WINDSOR

The RSC Shakespeare

Edited by Jonathan Bate and Eric Rasmussen

Chief Associate Editors: Jan Sewell and Will Sharpe

Associate Editors: Trey Jansen, Eleanor Lowe, Lucy Munro,
Dee Anna Phares, Héloïse Sénéchal

The Merry Wives of Windsor

Textual editing: Eric Rasmussen

Introduction and Shakespeare's Career in the Theater: Jonathan Bate

Commentary: Héloïse Sénéchal

Scene-by-Scene Analysis: Esme Miskimmin

In Performance: Clare Smout (RSC stagings) and Peter Kirwan (overview)

The Director's Cut (interviews by Jonathan Bate and Kevin Wright):
Bill Alexander and Rachel Kavanaugh
Playing Falstaff: Simon Callow

Editorial Advisory Board

The RSC Shakespeare

William Shakespeare

THE MERRY WIVES OF WINDSOR

Edited by Jonathan Bate and Eric Rasmussen

Introduction by Jonathan Bate

The Modern Library
New York

2011 Modern Library Paperback Edition

Copyright © 2007, 2011 by The Royal Shakespeare Company

Published in the United States by Modern Library, an imprint of
The Random House Publishing Group, a division of
Random House, Inc., New York.

The version of *The Merry Wives of Windsor* and the corresponding footnotes
that appear in this volume were originally published in *William Shakespeare:
Complete Works*, edited by Jonathan Bate and Eric Rasmussen, published
in 2007 by Modern Library, an imprint of The Random House
Publishing Group, a division of Random House, Inc.

ISBN 978-0-8129-6932-0

Printed in the United States of America

www.modernlibrary.com

2 4 6 8 9 7 5 3 1

CONTENTS

INTRODUCTION

WOMEN ON TOP?

In 1702 the poet and critic John Dennis rewrote *The Merry Wives of Windsor* with the title *The Comical Gallant: or, the Amours of Sir John Falstaff.* Dennis claimed that the original Shakespearean play was a particular favorite of Queen Elizabeth. Indeed, he reported, "This comedy was written at her command, and by her direction, and she was so eager to see it acted that she commanded it to be finished in fourteen days; and was afterward, as tradition tells us, very well pleased at the representation." A few years later, the story was elaborated in the biography appended to Nicholas Rowe's edition of Shakespeare: the Queen was so well pleased "with that admirable character of Falstaff in the two parts of Henry the Fourth" that she commanded Shakespeare "to continue it for one play more, and to show him in love."

We do not know whether the story is true, but there is great appeal in the idea of Falstaff reincarnated by royal command and transposed from tavern and battlefield to lady's chamber and linen basket. There is no doubt that the play's popularity on the eighteenth- and nineteenth-century stage owed much to its status as a vehicle for Falstaff. And at the end of the nineteenth century, the drama underwent another transposition as it was re-created in perhaps the greatest of all Shakespearean operas, Verdi and Boito's *Falstaff.* This afterlife, together with the sheer comic energy of the fat knight, means that it tends to be thought of as "his" play. So it is often forgotten that this is the only First Folio work named for its women. Or, to be more exact, the only one in which the women have the title to themselves: Juliet, Cleopatra, and Cressida have to share a billing with their lovers, while *The Shrew* is identified as object rather than subject (*The Taming of* clearly implies a tamer).

The play first appeared in print in a quarto-format text printed in 1602, with a title page listing a full roster of characters for promotional purposes: *A most pleasant and excellent conceited Comedy of Sir John Falstaff and the Merry Wives of Windsor. Intermixed with sundry variable and pleasing humours of Sir Hugh the Welsh Knight, Justice Shallow and his wise Cousin Master Slender. With the swaggering vein of Ancient Pistol and Corporal Nim. By William Shakespeare. As it hath been divers times acted by the right honourable my Lord Chamberlain's servants. Both before her Majesty and elsewhere* (the description of Slender as "wise" is a rare instance of wholesale irony on a title page). A payment to the King's Men for a 1613 court performance of "Sir John Falstaff" probably refers to the play, but in the First Folio ten years later the "Merry Wives" stood alone at the head of the text.

In 1656 an educational theorist called Philip King complained that it was ridiculous to suggest that "the condition of all our English women may be drawn out of Shakespeare's merry wives of Windsor." Eight years later, the leading English female intellectual of the age, Margaret Cavendish, Duchess of Newcastle, singled out those wives as particularly strong examples of Shakespeare's gift for representing women: "who could describe Cleopatra better than he hath done, and many other females to his own creating, as Nan Page, Mrs Page, Mrs Ford, the Doctor's Maid, Beatrice, Mrs Quickly, Doll Tearsheet, and others, too many to relate?" Though King disapproved and the duchess approved, they clearly agreed that *The Merry Wives* was one of Shakespeare's best plays for women.

Whereas Shakespeare's other comedies are courtship dramas that end with weddings or the promise of them, *The Merry Wives of Windsor* is more interested in how it is witty wives who sustain society. There is a courtship plot in which a handsome, if opportunistic, young gentleman named Master Fenton wins his girl, Anne Page, while his rivals, two comic suitors—the irascible French physician Dr. Caius and the country gentleman Master Abraham Slender, whose name reflects both his girth and his IQ—are tricked into eloping with boys. But the main focus is upon the girl's worldly-wise mother and her equally knowing friend Mistress Alice Ford, who has the misfortune to be married to a man of pathological jealousy. In later plays—*Othello, Cymbeline,* and *The Winter's Tale*—the husband's sexual insecurity has catastrophic consequences for the wife, but here Alice knows exactly how to deploy her hand.

The play is Shakespeare's nearest approach to farce or sitcom. People are forever rushing in and out of doors. One moment Falstaff is bundled into a stinking laundry basket and dunked in the Thames; the next he is dressed up as the old fat woman of Brentford, in whose garb he is heartily beaten. As a final indignity, he is persuaded to wear a pair of horns, and he finds himself pinched black and blue by a gaggle of children. The play tells some simple home truths about male jealousy (Ford's false fears) and vanity (Falstaff's ludicrous expectation that he will make his way into Alice's bed).

WHY WINDSOR?

"The Merry Wives" indicates that this is a play in which the women will be on top. "Of Windsor" promises a comedy of English town life. This is in sharp contrast to Shakespeare's other comedies of the late 1590s and early 1600s, with their courtly, continental, and often pastoral settings. Indeed, with the exception of the Eastcheap scenes in the *Henry IV* plays, Windsor is the closest Shakespeare comes to the one major dramatic genre of the age which he did not attempt: the comedy of London life. City comedy was the forte of the group of slightly younger dramatists who came onto the theater scene around the turn of the century—Ben Jonson, Thomas Dekker, and Thomas Middleton.

But Windsor is not London. Though the play includes several types familiar from city comedy—the jealous husband, the marriageable citizen's daughter, the simpleton up from the country—the setting is more provincial town than buzzing metropolis. The dramatist's own experience of life in Stratford-upon-Avon was probably a more formative influence on the creation of this play than any literary source of the kind that inspired most of his other comedies. The scene in which a cheeky boy called William is drilled in Latin grammar feels as close to autobiographical reminiscence as anything in Shakespeare.

Nor is Windsor a generic English town. The castle and the royal park made it synonymous with the monarchy. During the closing nocturnal scene in the park, Mistress Quickly in the role of Queen of the Fairies offers a good luck charm to Queen Elizabeth, whom the poet Edmund Spenser had immortalized a few years before under the guise of England's *Faerie Queene:*

> Search Windsor Castle, elves, within and out.
> Strew good luck, oafs, on every sacred room,
> That it may stand till the perpetual doom,
> In state as wholesome as in state 'tis fit,
> Worthy the owner and the owner it.

Quickly's speech goes on to make a series of very specific allusions to the Knights of the Garter, the most senior and oldest Order of English knighthood. Founded by Edward III in 1348, the Order of the Garter was reserved as the highest reward for loyalty and military merit. Membership was confined to the monarch and twenty-five knights; the founders had all served against the French at the battle of Crécy. The emblem of the Order was a blue garter. The story of its origin was that when King Edward was dancing with either his queen or the Countess of Salisbury (with whom he was in love), her garter slipped to the floor and he retrieved it and tied it to his own leg. In response to those watching, the King said "*Honi soit qui mal y pense*" ("Shame on him who thinks this evil"), which became the motto of the Order. Through such spectacles as her Accession Day tilts, Queen Elizabeth had revived many of Edward III's chivalric rites as a way of bolstering the cult of the monarchy. During the 1590s, particular emphasis was placed on the Order of the Garter. Its spiritual home was the Chapel of St. George in Windsor.

Many scholars suppose that *The Merry Wives of Windsor* was especially written for a Garter ceremony, perhaps in 1597. Whether or not that was the case, there is no doubt that the equation of Windsor and the Garter made for a strong allusion to the idea of true English knighthood and absolute loyalty to the crown. That one of the main locations of the play is the Garter Inn only highlights the connection. The offstage Knights of the Garter evoked by Fairy Queen

Quickly are clearly intended as an extreme contrast to the onstage figure of the debased and humiliated knight Sir John Falstaff.

WHICH FALSTAFF?

This opposition raises the question of when in Sir John's imaginary history the action of the play is supposed to take place. *The Merry Wives* was unquestionably written after *Henry IV Part I*, where Falstaff and company first appeared in their role as misleaders of Prince Hal. There is, however, a debate among scholars as to whether the comedy appeared before, during, or after the composition of *Henry IV Part II*. After the second history play seems more likely, since, like Falstaff himself, Justice Shallow, Bardolph, Pistol, and Mistress Quickly have the air of familiar comic characters brought back to the stage because of their popularity in an earlier work. The shift from chronicle to comedy means an abandonment of historical specificity: the play has a very contemporary feel, creating the illusion that Sir John and his friends have jumped from the age of Henry IV into that of Queen Elizabeth. Quickly, meanwhile, has become housekeeper to a French physician resident in Windsor instead of hostess of a London tavern. A reference in the past tense to Master Fenton having "kept company with the wild prince and Poins" suggests that we are supposed to imagine the action taking place after the transformation of riotous Prince Hal into heroic King Henry V.

At the end of *Henry IV Part II*, the newly crowned king banishes Falstaff from his company, but allows him "competence of life." Perhaps we are to suppose that the fat knight is now a "crown pensioner," one of a group of retired soldiers who resided at Windsor and were expected to pray twice a day for the king in return for clothing and a small annual allowance. They were popularly known as "poor knights of Windsor." There may be an allusion to them when Quickly, describing to Falstaff the arrival of the court at Windsor, erroneously—or teasingly—ranks "pensioners" above "earls." If *The Merry Wives* was written after *Henry IV Part II* the play may have been Shakespeare's compensation for his failure to deliver in *Henry V* on the promise that "our humble author will continue the story, with

Sir John in it" (epilogue to *Henry IV Part II*)—*Henry V* in fact features Bardolph, Nim, Pistol, and Quickly, but no Falstaff, only a report of his death.

The action of *The Merry Wives* begins with Shallow boasting of his status and pedigree as a Justice of the Peace in the county of Gloucester and a gentleman with a well-established coat of arms. He is in dispute with Falstaff and has come to Windsor to seek redress from the Star Chamber or the King's Council.

> FALSTAFF   Now, Master Shallow, you'll complain of me to the king?
>
> SHALLOW   Knight, you have beaten my men, killed my deer, and broke open my lodge.

This is the play's only reference to the king, and it is not made explicit whether Henry IV or Henry V is on the throne. The action soon veers away from the dispute: Shallow's principal role is his attempt to marry his kinsman Slender to Anne Page, while Falstaff turns his attention to Mistress Ford. This has not prevented the spilling of centuries of scholarly ink over the first scene's reference to deer-stealing and its wordplay on the "luces" in Shallow's coat of arms. There is a long tradition of reading the sequence in the light of the unsubstantiated story that Shakespeare left Stratford-upon-Avon because he had been caught stealing deer from the park of the local grandee, Sir Thomas Lucy of Charlecote. The link was first made in the late seventeenth century by a Gloucestershire clergyman called Richard Davies:

> William Shakespeare was born at Stratford upon Avon in Warwickshire about 1563–64. Much given to all unluckiness in stealing venison and rabbits particularly from Sir [ ] Lucy, who had him oft whipped and sometimes imprisoned and at last made him fly his native country to his great advancement, but his revenge was so great that he is his Justice Clodpate and calls him a great man and that in allusion to his name bore three louses rampant for his arms.

It appears that Lucy did not have a deer park at Charlecote, though there was a rabbit warren there, so perhaps Shakespeare was actually a "cony-catching rascal," as Slender accuses Bardolph, Nim, and Pistol of being. Whatever personal allusion there may or may not be, for an audience the purpose of the opening scenes is to reestablish the image, familiar from *Henry IV*, of Falstaff and his followers as rogues and chancers, living from hand to mouth on the far edge of the law.

Heavy-drinking Bardolph, bombastic Pistol, and filching Nim are no sooner introduced than Falstaff says he needs to dismiss them because he is short of money. They come and go without being fully integrated into the plot, strongly suggesting that Shakespeare brought them on because an audience would expect them in a Falstaff play, but that he then lost interest in them. In the list of roles in *Henry IV Part II*, they are described as "irregular humorists," "irregular" meaning "lawless" and "humorist" meaning a person subject to an excess of one of the four humors that made up the human temperament (melancholic, choleric, phlegmatic, sanguine). *The Merry Wives* has strong elements of the comedy of humoral types that Ben Jonson pioneered with his *Every Man in His Humour* and *Every Man out of His Humour* (1598–99). In particular, Doctor Caius is a case study in the humor of hot-blooded choler (explosive anger) and Ford's pathological jealousy is—as in a Jonson comedy—a deformation of character produced by an unbalanced temperament.

THE COMEDY OF ENGLISHNESS

Given its close relationship to the history plays and the fact that it is the only Shakespearean comedy with an English setting, *The Merry Wives* is inevitably interested in questions of Englishness. The comic treatment of honor and cozening, true and false knighthood, and the nature of gentility rearticulates some of the matter of the *Henry IV* plays in a new key, but the most sustained exploration of national identity takes place at the level of language. Shakespeare has always been so admired for his poetry that the language of *The Merry Wives* has often been underrated for the simple reason that of all his plays this is the one with the highest proportion of prose. Yet its command of the prose medium is unstoppable: from first to last there is a stream of wordplay, innuendo, and hilarious linguistic misapprehension. The comic suitors are the key here: the Welsh parson Sir Hugh Evans and the French doctor Caius are characterized by their abuse of the English language. Extraordinary mileage is obtained from Caius' verbal tics ("By gar," "vat is?") and such simple substitutions as Evans's "f" for "v" (thus in the Latin language lesson, the grammatical term "vocative" becomes the obscene-sounding "focative"). Verbal sparring stands in for physical. Whereas in the history plays national pride comes from prowess at arms, here it is a matter of prowess at words. When the Welshman and the Frenchman prepare to fight a duel over their rivalry for Anne, Shallow and Page remove their swords and the Host says "Let them keep their limbs whole and hack our English."

Comedy at the expense of foreigners for their abuse of the English tongue might be described as crudely patriotic or mildly xenophobic. A deeper patriotism and a richer form of comedy come from the capacity of the English language to turn adversity to advantage. That is the art of Falstaff, as it is in a more general sense the art of Shakespeare and his actors. Falstaff is repeatedly humiliated, but his mastery of the English language always gives him the last word. On discovering that he has been pinched and beaten not by real goblins but by Sir Hugh and his class of children, Falstaff magnificently retorts "Have I lived to stand at the taunt of one that makes fritters of English?" and then "I am not able to answer the Welsh flannel." He is physically humiliated ("dejected"), but his linguistic gift never fails. Like his creator, he can seemingly conjure anything into language. Again and again, a bodily battering is transformed into the opportunity for a verbal display in which a tone of feigned incredulity creates a unique combination of excess and humility, self-delusion and self-knowledge, that is irresistible to a theater audience:

But mark the sequel, Master Broom. I suffered the pangs of three several deaths: first, an intolerable fright, to be detected with a jealous rotten bell-wether: next, to be compassed, like a good bilbo in the circumference of a peck, hilt to point, heel to

head, and then, to be stopped in like a strong distillation with
stinking clothes that fretted in their own grease. Think of that,
a man of my kidney, think of that — that am as subject to heat
as butter — a man of continual dissolution and thaw: it was a
miracle to scape suffocation. And in the height of this bath,
when I was more than half stewed in grease like a Dutch dish,
to be thrown into the Thames, and cooled, glowing hot, in that
surge, like a horse-shoe. Think of that — hissing hot — think
of that, Master Broom.

By redescribing farcical action in words of mock-epic excess, verbally
reenacting the ducking from the point of view of the ducked, Falstaff embodies his creator's greatest achievement: the triumph of
the English language.

ABOUT THE TEXT

Shakespeare endures through history. He illuminates later times as well as his own. He helps us to understand the human condition. But he cannot do this without a good text of the plays. Without editions there would be no Shakespeare. That is why every twenty years or so throughout the last three centuries there has been a major new edition of his complete works. One aspect of editing is the process of keeping the texts up to date—modernizing the spelling, punctuation, and typography (though not, of course, the actual words), providing explanatory notes in the light of changing educational practices (a generation ago, most of Shakespeare's classical and biblical allusions could be assumed to be generally understood, but now they can't).

Because Shakespeare did not personally oversee the publication of his plays, with some plays there are major editorial difficulties. Decisions have to be made as to the relative authority of the early printed editions, the pocket format "Quartos" published in Shakespeare's lifetime and the elaborately produced "First Folio" text of 1623, the original "Complete Works" prepared for the press after his death by Shakespeare's fellow actors, the people who knew the plays better than anyone else. The *Merry Wives of Windsor* appeared in a Quarto of 1602 of dubious authority (reprinted in 1619), which was apparently a memorial report of a text adapted and shortened for performance, and in a much fuller form in the First Folio. The Quarto text omits much of Act 5, and shows evidence of theatrical adaptation in Acts 3 and 4 in its transposition of scenes and of dialogue. The Folio text was apparently prepared by Ralph Crane, the company scribe, and is unusually clear of profanity in accordance with the 1606 Parliamentary Act to Restrain the Abuses of Players, which forbade theater companies taking God's name in vain. As Crane's texts are often not so censorious, the nature of the copy from which he was working was possibly a post-1606 theatrical text that had itself been expurgated.

The following notes highlight various aspects of the editorial process and indicate conventions used in the text of this edition:

Lists of Parts are supplied in the First Folio for only six plays, not including *The Merry Wives of Windsor,* so the list here is editorially supplied. Capitals indicate that part of the name used for speech headings in the script (thus "Master FENTON, a young gentleman, in love with Anne Page").

Locations are provided by the Folio for only two plays, of which *The Merry Wives of Windsor* is not one. Eighteenth-century editors, working in an age of elaborately realistic stage sets, were the first to provide detailed locations ("*another part of the town*"). Given that Shakespeare wrote for a bare stage and often an imprecise sense of place, we have relegated locations to the explanatory notes at the foot of the page, where they are given at the beginning of each scene where the imaginary location is different from the one before. In the case of *The Merry Wives of Windsor,* the action is set entirely in the small Berkshire town of Windsor, situated at the foot of one of the oldest of the royal castles.

Act and Scene Divisions were provided in the Folio in a much more thoroughgoing way than in the Quartos. Sometimes, however, they were erroneous or omitted; corrections and additions supplied by editorial tradition are indicated by square brackets. Five-act division is based on a classical model, and act breaks provided the opportunity to replace the candles in the indoor Blackfriars playhouse which the King's Men used after 1608, but Shakespeare did not necessarily think in terms of a five-part structure of dramatic composition. The Folio convention is that a scene ends when the stage is empty. Nowadays, partly under the influence of film, we tend to consider a scene to be a dramatic unit that ends with either a change of imaginary location or a significant passage of time within the narrative. Shakespeare's fluidity of composition accords well with this convention, so in addition to act and scene numbers we provide a *running scene* count in the right margin at the beginning of each new scene, in the typeface used for editorial directions. Where there is a scene break caused by a momentary bare stage, but the location does not change and extra time does not pass, we use the convention *running scene continues*. There is inevitably a degree of editorial judgment in making such calls, but the system is very valuable in suggesting the pace of the plays.

Speakers' Names are often inconsistent in Folio. We have regularized speech headings, but retained an element of deliberate inconsistency in entry directions, in order to give the flavor of Folio. Thus ROBIN is always so-called in his speech headings, but is often referred to as "Page" in entry directions.

Verse is indicated by lines that do not run to the right margin and by capitalization of each line. The Folio printers sometimes set verse as prose, and vice versa (either out of misunderstanding or for reasons of space). We have silently corrected in such cases, although in some instances there is ambiguity, in which case we have leaned toward the preservation of Folio layout. Folio sometimes uses contraction ("turnd" rather than "turned") to indicate whether or not the final "-ed" of a past participle is sounded, an area where there is variation for the sake of the five-beat iambic pentameter rhythm. We use the convention of a grave accent to indicate sounding (thus "turnèd" would be two syllables), but would urge actors not to overstress. In cases where one speaker ends with a verse half line and the next begins with the other half of the pentameter, editors since the late eighteenth century have indented the second line. We have abandoned this convention, since the Folio does not use it, nor did actors' cues in the Shakespearean theater. An exception is made when the second speaker actively interrupts or completes the first speaker's sentence.

Spelling is modernized, but older forms are very occasionally maintained where necessary for rhythm or aural effect.

Punctuation in Shakespeare's time was as much rhetorical as grammatical. "Colon" was originally a term for a unit of thought in an argument. The semicolon was a new unit of punctuation (some of the Quartos lack them altogether). We have modernized punctuation throughout, but have given more weight to Folio punctuation than many editors, since, though not Shakespearean, it reflects the usage of his period. In particular, we have used the colon far more than many editors: it is exceptionally useful as a way of indicating how many Shakespearean speeches unfold clause by clause in a developing argument that gives the illusion of enacting the process of thinking in the moment. We have also kept in mind the origin of punctuation in classical times as a way of assisting the actor and orator: the comma suggests the briefest of pauses for breath, the colon a middling one, and a full stop or period a longer pause. Semicolons, by contrast, belong to an era of punctuation that was only just coming in during Shakespeare's time and that is coming to an end now: we have accordingly used them only where they occur in our copy texts (and not always then). Dashes are sometimes used for parenthetical interjections where the Folio has brackets. They are also used for interruptions and changes in train of thought. Where a change of addressee occurs within a speech, we have used a dash preceded by a period (or occasionally another form of punctuation). Often the identity of the respective addressees is obvious from the context. When it is not, this has been indicated in a marginal stage direction.

Entrances and Exits are fairly thorough in Folio, which has accordingly been followed as faithfully as possible. Where characters are omitted or corrections are necessary, this is indicated by square brackets (e.g. "[*and Attendants*]"). *Exit* is sometimes silently normalized to *Exeunt* and *Manet* anglicized to "remains." We trust Folio positioning of entrances and exits to a greater degree than most editors.

Editorial Stage Directions such as stage business, asides, indications of addressee and of characters' position on the gallery stage are used only sparingly in Folio. Other editions mingle directions of this kind with original Folio and Quarto directions, sometimes marking them by means of square brackets. We have sought to distinguish what could be described as *directorial* interventions of this kind from Folio-style directions (either original or supplied) by placing them in the right margin in a different typeface. There is a degree of subjectivity about which directions are of which kind, but the procedure is intended as a reminder to the reader and the actor that Shakespearean stage directions are often dependent upon editorial inference alone and are not set in stone. We also depart from editorial tradition in sometimes admitting uncertainty and thus printing permissive stage directions, such as an *Aside?* (often a line may be equally effective as an aside or as a direct address—it is for each production or reading to make its own decision) or a *may exit* or a piece of business placed between arrows to indicate that it may occur at various different moments within a scene.

Line Numbers in the left margin are editorial, for reference and to key the explanatory and textual notes.

Explanatory Notes at the foot of each page explain allusions and gloss obsolete and difficult words, confusing phraseology, occasional major textual cruces, and so on. Particular attention is given to nonstandard usage, bawdy innuendo, and technical terms (e.g. legal and military language). Where more than one sense is given, commas indicate shades of related meaning, slashes alternative or double meanings.

Textual Notes at the end of the play indicate major departures from the Folio. They take the following form: the reading of our text is given in bold and its source given after an equals sign with "Q" indicating a reading from the First Quarto of 1602, "Q3" a correction introduced in the Third Quarto of 1630, "F2" a correction that derives from the Second Folio of 1632, and "Ed" one that derives from the subsequent editorial tradition. The rejected Folio ("F") reading is then given. Thus for Act 1 Scene 3 line 46: "**1.3.46 legion** = Ed. Q = legians. F = legend" means that in the phrase "a legion of angels" we have adopted the editorial "legion" instead of the Quarto's "legians" or the Folio's "legend," possibly the result of a scribal or printing error.

KEY FACTS

MAJOR PARTS: (*with percentage of lines/number of speeches/scenes onstage*) Falstaff (17%/136/9), Mrs. Page (12%/101/9), Ford (12%/99/9), Mrs. Quickly (10%/74/9), Evans (8%/87/9), Mrs. Ford (6%/85/7), Page (6%/75/11), Slender (5%/56/7), Shallow (4%/59/7), Caius (4%/49/8), Host (4%/46/8), Fenton (4%/20/4), Pistol (2%/29/5), Simple (2%/25/5), Anne Page (1%/19/3).

LINGUISTIC MEDIUM: 10% verse, 90% prose. Highest proportion of prose in the *Complete Works*.

DATE: 1597–1601. Allusion to the Order of the Garter in the final scene has led to supposition that the play was performed at, or indeed commissioned for, the Garter Feast held at Whitehall in April 1597, when George Carey, Lord Chamberlain and patron of Shakespeare's acting company, was elected to the order, as (in absentia) was Frederick Duke of Württemberg (which may account for the allusions to a German duke in the scene involving the Host's horses). The 1597–98 winter season at court and the Garter festivities for 1599 have also been proposed as the occasion: the argument for the latter, when Henry Brooke, eighth Lord Cobham, was elected Knight of the Garter, is interwoven with the Brooke/Broom crux (see "Text," below). The argument against 1597 is that it would place the play before *2 Henry IV*, which seems counterintuitive: the relationship between Falstaff and Shallow, together with the retinue of "irregular humorists," is more likely to have been created in the history play and reanimated in the comedy than vice versa (though it has been suggested that *The Merry Wives* was dashed off when Shakespeare was halfway through the writing of *2 Henry IV*). The element of "humoral" comedy suggests a date after Ben Jonson introduced this vogue in *Every Man in His Humour* (1598). The argument against a special Garter commission is that a full-length comedy, as opposed to a shorter masque or entertainment of a more courtly kind, is unlikely to have been performed on such an occasion. It is possible that the Garter dimension is a vestige of an earlier commissioned work that was expanded into a comedy for the public stage. The play is not mentioned by Meres, suggesting late 1598 or 1599 as the earliest date for public performance. The 1602 Quarto title page clearly indicates performance both before the court and in the public theater. Quarto omits the speech alluding to the Order of the Garter and many other references to Windsor and the court. The major differences between Quarto and Folio texts (see below) suggest several stages of composition and probably performance in different versions.

SOURCES: No known source for the main plot, but the gallant who attempts to seduce another man's wife, is interrupted and hidden in a bizarre place, was a traditional comic motif, as was the clever wife who gets the upper hand (there is an example in one of the tales in Barnabe Riche's *Farewell to Military Profession*, a book that provided Shakespeare with the main source for *Twelfth Night*); the Anne Page plot of rival suitors for an attractive daughter also has many analogues. The horse-stealing episode may allude to the Duke of Württemberg's visit to England in 1592 and has parallels with a comic sequence in Marlowe's *Dr. Faustus*. Falstaff with his horns in the park combines the folktale of Herne the Hunter with the classical myth (from Ovid's *Metamorphoses*) of Actaeon. The pinching Fairies are themselves pinched from Act 4 Scene 3 of John Lyly's play *Endymion, the Man in the Moon* (published 1591).

TEXT: Published in Quarto in 1602, in a version that has the hallmarks of a "reported text" of a stage production. About half the length of the Folio, and with many textual corruptions, the Quarto was reprinted in 1619. The First Folio text of 1623 was set from a transcript by Ralph Crane, professional scribe to the King's Men, though it is not certain whether he worked from the playhouse "book" or an authorial manuscript.

The Quarto calls into question two significant details in the Folio. First, the name by which Ford calls himself when disguised: this is "Brooke" in Quarto but "Broom" in Folio. "Brooke" was clearly Shakespeare's original intention, being an aquatic variation on "Ford" and the occasion for at least one liquid pun ("Such Brooks are welcome to me, that o'erflows such liquor"—2.2.134). The change to "Broom" in Folio may well have been made in order to avoid offending the powerful family with whom Shakespeare had already been in trouble over a name in *1 Henry IV.* Lord Cobham had objected to the name Sir John Oldcastle, with the result that Shakespeare changed it to Sir John Falstaff. The Cobham family name was Brooke, so perhaps they intervened again, or the name was changed for fear that they might. We follow Folio's Broom, but in production it is probably best to revert to Brook, in order to make the watery jokes work. Falstaff does not, after all, hide in a broom cupboard: he is thrown into a brook.

The other issue is the color coding at the climactic moment of the play, when Anne's three suitors come on and take the fairy each of them supposes is her, while the children are singing their song and pinching Falstaff. In Folio, Master Page tells Slender that his daughter will be in white, but when Slender comes on with the humiliating news that he has grabbed and married a boy, he says that he took a fairy in green. With Caius, it is the other way around: Mistress Page tells him that Anne will be in green, but he takes a boy in white. Editors since the eighteenth century have reversed the colors in the dialogue at the end, to make them consistent with those of the initial plan. Since the inconsistency is much more likely to be the author's than the printer's, we have not done this, but attention is drawn to this issue in the gloss and the textual notes.

THE MERRY WIVES
OF WINDSOR

LIST OF PARTS

MISTRESS Margaret PAGE, of Windsor

Master George PAGE, her husband

ANNE Page, their daughter

WILLIAM Page, a boy, their son

MISTRESS Alice FORD, of Windsor

Master Frank FORD, her husband

Master FENTON, a young gentleman, in love with Anne Page

Sir John FALSTAFF

BARDOLPH ⎫
PISTOL ⎬ followers of Falstaff
NIM ⎭

ROBIN, Falstaff's pageboy

Robert SHALLOW, Esquire, a country justice ⎫
Master Abraham SLENDER, cousin to Shallow ⎬ up from the country
⎭

Peter SIMPLE, servant to Slender

Sir Hugh EVANS, a Welsh parson

HOST, of the Garter Inn

Doctor CAIUS, a French physician

John RUGBY, his servant

MISTRESS QUICKLY, his housekeeper

Servants; Children of Windsor playing Fairies

Act 1 Scene 1   *running scene 1*

Enter Justice Shallow, Slender [and] Sir Hugh Evans

SHALLOW   Sir Hugh, persuade me not. I will make a Star
          Chamber matter of it. If he were twenty Sir John Falstaffs, he
          shall not abuse Robert Shallow, esquire.

SLENDER   In the county of Gloucester, Justice of Peace and
5   Coram.

SHALLOW   Ay, cousin Slender, and Custalorum.

SLENDER   Ay, and Rato-lorum too; and a gentleman born,
          master parson, who writes himself *Armigero* in any bill,
          warrant, quittance or obligation, *Armigero*.

10   SHALLOW   Ay, that I do, and have done any time these three
          hundred years.

SLENDER   All his successors — gone before him — hath done't,
          and all his ancestors — that come after him — may. They
          may give the dozen white luces in their coat.

15   SHALLOW   It is an old coat.

EVANS   The dozen white louses do become an old coat well.
          It agrees well passant. It is a familiar beast to man, and
          signifies love.

SHALLOW   The luce is the fresh fish. The salt fish is an old coat.

20   SLENDER   I may quarter, coz.

1.1   Location: *the entire play is set in Windsor (twenty-five miles west of London),
moving between the streets, the homes of Page and Ford, the Garter Inn, a field
outside the town and, in the fifth act, the Great Park near Windsor Castle*   **Sir** the usual
title for a clergyman   **1 persuade** urge/argue with   **Star Chamber** court consisting of
most of the King's Privy Council, which met in a chamber with stars painted on its ceiling
5 Coram corruption of "quorum," a group of judges whose presence was required at a trial
6 cousin kinsman   **Custalorum** corruption of "custos rotulorum," the keeper of the shire
records and a justice of the peace   **7 Rato-lorum** i.e. "rotulorum"   **8 writes himself**
Armigero i.e. signs himself *armiger*, Latin for "esquire" (one entitled to bear arms/a gentleman)
bill legal document/document requiring the payment of debts   **9 warrant** document
authorizing a judicial sentence/the payment of debts between two parties   **quittance**
document certifying release from a debt or obligation   **obligation** contract binding a person to
an action or payment   **14 give** display (in a coat of arms)   **luces** pikes (freshwater fish)
coat coat of arms (Evans's **louses**—lice—plays on the sense of "garment")   **16 become** suit
17 passant (heraldic term for) walking/surpassingly   **familiar** well-known/overly intimate
19 coat Shallow plays on Evans's Welsh pronunciation of **coat** as "cod"   **20 quarter** add the
arms of another family to one's coat of arms (Evans understands "cut into four")   **coz** cousin
(i.e. kinsman)

SHALLOW   You may, by marrying.

EVANS   It is marring indeed, if he quarter it.

SHALLOW   Not a whit.

EVANS   Yes, py'r lady: if he has a quarter of your coat, there
25   is but three skirts for yourself, in my simple conjectures.
But that is all one: if Sir John Falstaff have committed
disparagements unto you, I am of the church, and will be glad
to do my benevolence, to make atonements and compromises
between you.

30   SHALLOW   The Council shall hear it, it is a riot.

EVANS   It is not meet the Council hear a riot: there is no fear
of Got in a riot. The Council, look you, shall desire to hear the
fear of Got, and not to hear a riot. Take your vizaments in that.

SHALLOW   Ha, o'my life, if I were young again, the sword should
35   end it.

EVANS   It is petter that friends is the sword, and end it. And
there is also another device in my prain, which peradventure
prings goot discretions with it. There is Anne Page, which is
daughter to Master Thomas Page, which is pretty virginity.

40   SLENDER   Mistress Anne Page? She has brown hair, and speaks
small like a woman.

EVANS   It is that fery person for all the 'orld, as just as you
will desire, and seven hundred pounds of moneys, and gold
and silver, is her grandsire upon his death's-bed — Got
45   deliver to a joyful resurrections! — give, when she is able to
overtake seventeen years old. It were a goot motion, if we

---

24 py'r lady by Our Lady (i.e. the Virgin Mary); Evans often substitutes "p" for "b"   **25 skirts**
separate sections forming the lower part of a coat   **28 do my benevolence** lend my help
atonements agreement/reconciliation (Evans often makes singular words into plurals)
compromises joint agreement/settlement made by an arbitrator   **30 Council** King's Privy
Council, which often heard cases of **riot**; Evans seems to think Shallow is referring to a
church council   **31 meet** fitting   **32 Got** God (Evans often substitutes "t" for "d")
33 Take . . . that take that into consideration   **vizaments** advisements   **36 friends . . .
sword** i.e. friendship is substituted for violence   **37 device** plan   **peradventure** perhaps/
most likely   **38 discretions** judgment   **39 Thomas** later named as George (presumably
Shakespeare's memory slip)   **41 small** in a high-pitched/light/quiet voice   **42 fery** very
(Evans often substitutes "f" for "v")   **'orld** world   **just** exact/exactly   **44 is** has   **45 give**
given (her)   **46 motion** suggestion

leave our pribbles and prabbles, and desire a marriage between Master Abraham and Mistress Anne Page.

SLENDER   Did her grandsire leave her seven hundred pound?

50   EVANS   Ay, and her father is make her a petter penny.

SLENDER   I know the young gentlewoman: she has good gifts.

EVANS   Seven hundred pounds, and possibilities, is goot gifts.

SHALLOW   Well, let us see honest Master Page. Is Falstaff there?

55   EVANS   Shall I tell you a lie? I do despise a liar as I do despise one that is false, or as I despise one that is not true. The knight, Sir John, is there, and I beseech you, be ruled by your well-willers. I will peat the door for Master Page.   *Knocks*
What, ho! Got pless your house here!

60   PAGE   Who's there?   *Speaks within and then enters*

EVANS   Here is Got's plessing, and your friend, and Justice Shallow, and here young Master Slender, that peradventures shall tell you another tale, if matters grow to your likings.

PAGE   I am glad to see your worships well. I thank you for
65   my venison, Master Shallow.

SHALLOW   Master Page, I am glad to see you: much good do it your good heart. I wished your venison better, it was ill killed. How doth good Mistress Page? And I thank you always with my heart, la — with my heart.

70   PAGE   Sir, I thank you.

SHALLOW   Sir, I thank you: by yea and no, I do.

PAGE   I am glad to see you, good Master Slender.

SLENDER   How does your fallow greyhound, sir? I heard say he was outrun on Cotsall.

75   PAGE   It could not be judged, sir.

SLENDER   You'll not confess, you'll not confess.

---

47 **pribbles and prabbles** petty squabbles   50 **is . . . penny** will give her more besides
51 **SLENDER** most editors reassign to **Shallow**, since Slender has already said he knows Anne
gifts qualities (Evans takes the word literally)   52 **possibilities** financial prospects
54 **honest** respectable/upright/sincere   58 **well-willers** well-wishers   63 **tell . . . tale** have
something else to say to you   67 **ill** clumsily/poorly/illegally (by Falstaff)   69 **la** an intensifier
equivalent to "indeed"   71 **by . . . no** a very mild oath   73 **fallow** light brown   74 **Cotsall**
the Cotswold hills, in central England   75 **judged** decided conclusively

SHALLOW	That he will not.—	
	'Tis your fault, 'tis your fault.— 'Tis a good	*Aside to Slender/*
	dog.	*To Page*
PAGE	A cur, sir.	

80 SHALLOW   Sir, he's a good dog, and a fair dog, can there be more said? He is good and fair. Is Sir John Falstaff here?

PAGE   Sir, he is within: and I would I could do a good office between you.

EVANS   It is spoke as a Christians ought to speak.

85 SHALLOW   He hath wronged me, Master Page.

PAGE   Sir, he doth in some sort confess it.

SHALLOW   If it be confessed, it is not redressed. Is not that so, Master Page? He hath wronged me, indeed he hath, at a word, he hath. Believe me: Robert Shallow esquire saith he is

90   wronged.

PAGE   Here comes Sir John.

[*Enter Falstaff, Bardolph, Nim and Pistol*]

FALSTAFF   Now, Master Shallow, you'll complain of me to the king?

SHALLOW   Knight, you have beaten my men, killed my deer,
95   and broke open my lodge.

FALSTAFF   But not kissed your keeper's daughter?

SHALLOW   Tut, a pin! This shall be answered.

FALSTAFF   I will answer it straight: I have done all this. That is now answered.

100 SHALLOW   The Council shall know this.

FALSTAFF   'Twere better for you if it were known in counsel. You'll be laughed at.

EVANS   *Pauca verba*, Sir John, goot worts.

---

78 'Tis your fault you (Slender) are to blame for teasing Page   **79 cur** dog (may or may not be contemptuous)   **82 would** wish   **office** service   **86 in some sort** partly/to some extent **88 at** in   *Pistol* pronounced to sound like "pizzle" ("penis")   **95 lodge** hunting lodge/ gamekeeper's cottage   **96 keeper's** gamekeeper's   **97 pin** i.e. a trifle   **answered** accounted for/responded to as a legal charge (Falstaff plays on the sense of "replied to")   **98 straight** straight away   **101 in counsel** in secret (puns on **Council**)   **103 *Pauca verba*** Latin for "few words"

FALSTAFF   Good worts? Good cabbage. Slender, I broke your
105   head. What matter have you against me?

SLENDER   Marry, sir, I have matter in my head against you,
and against your cony-catching rascals, Bardolph, Nim and
Pistol.

BARDOLPH   You Banbury cheese!

110   SLENDER   Ay, it is no matter.

PISTOL   How now, Mephostophilus?

SLENDER   Ay, it is no matter.

NIM   Slice, I say! *Pauca, pauca*. Slice, that's my humour.

SLENDER   Where's Simple, my man? Can you tell, cousin?

115   EVANS   Peace, I pray you. Now let us understand. There is
three umpires in this matter, as I understand; that is, Master
Page — *fidelicet* Master Page — and there is myself — *fidelicet*
myself — and the three party is — lastly and finally — mine
host of the Garter.

120   PAGE   We three to hear it and end it between them.

EVANS   Fery goot, I will make a prief of it in my note-book,
and we will afterwards 'ork upon the cause with as great
discreetly as we can.

FALSTAFF   Pistol!

125   PISTOL   He hears with ears.

EVANS   The tevil and his tam! What phrase is this? He hears
with ear? Why, it is affectations.

FALSTAFF   Pistol, did you pick Master Slender's purse?

SLENDER   Ay, by these gloves, did he, or I would I might never
130   come in mine own great chamber again else, of seven groats

---

104 worts plants of the cabbage family (a joke on Evans's pronunciation of "words")   **broke**
wounded   **105 matter** cause of complaint (Slender shifts the sense to "matter of significance,"
while playing on the sense of "pus from a wound")   **107 cony-catching** cheating (literally
"rabbit-catching")   **109 Banbury cheese** the Oxfordshire town was known for its thin
cheeses; Slender is being mocked for being pale and slight   **110 matter** importance (plays on
sense of "substance")   **111 Mephostophilus** a devil, well-known from Christopher Marlowe's
play *Doctor Faustus*   **113 Slice** i.e. gash him with a sword/slice him up like a cheese   *Pauca*
i.e. briefly (from **pauca verba**)   **humour** inclination/frame of mind   **117 *fidelicet*** Evans
means *videlicet* (Latin for "namely")   **118 three** third   **119 host** innkeeper   **Garter** perhaps
a reference to the Garter Inn in Windsor   **121 prief** brief/summary   **122 'ork** work
123 discreetly discretion   **126 tevil . . . tam** devil and his dam (i.e. mother)   **130 great
chamber** main room/hall   **groats** fourpenny coins

in mill-sixpences, and two Edward shovel-boards, that cost me two shilling and two pence apiece of Yead Miller, by these gloves.

FALSTAFF   Is this true, Pistol?

135   **EVANS**   No, it is false, if it is a pick-purse.

PISTOL   Ha, thou mountain-foreigner! Sir John and master mine,

I combat challenge of this latten bilbo.

Word of denial in thy labras here!

Word of denial: froth and scum, thou liest!

140   **SLENDER**   By these gloves, then, 'twas he.   *Points to Nim*

NIM   Be advised, sir, and pass good humours: I will say 'marry trap' with you, if you run the nuthook's humour on me. That is the very note of it.

SLENDER   By this hat, then, he in the red face had it: for

145   though I cannot remember what I did when you made me drunk, yet I am not altogether an ass.

FALSTAFF   What say you, Scarlet and John?

BARDOLPH   Why, sir, for my part, I say the gentleman had drunk himself out of his five sentences.

150   **EVANS**   It is his five senses. Fie, what the ignorance is!

BARDOLPH   And being fap, sir, was, as they say, cashiered: and so conclusions passed the careers.

---

131 mill-sixpences sixpences that had their designs impressed on them in a stamping mill **Edward shovel-boards** shillings made in the reign of Edward VI (used in the game of **shovel-board**)   **132 Yead** i.e. Ed (Edward)   **135 it is false** he is dishonest (Evans responds to "true, Pistol" as if it were "true Pistol"—i.e. "honest Pistol")   **136 mountain-foreigner** i.e. Welshman   **137 combat challenge** challenge combat (i.e. trial by combat)   **latten** brass/tin-plate/thinly hammered   **bilbo** sword (from Bilbao, Spanish town famed for sword manufacture)   **138 labras** lips (from either the Spanish *labros* or the Latin *labra*, both meaning "lips")   **141 Be advised** think carefully/take my advice   **pass good humours** be agreeable   **142 'marry trap'** contemptuous phrase of uncertain meaning, the general sense of which may be something like "be off with you/mind your own business/you've caught yourself out"   **marry** by the Virgin Mary   **run . . . me** behave like a constable   **nuthook** hooked stick used to pull nuts from trees; slang for "constable"   **143 very note** right tune (i.e. the truth); perhaps with a play on "nut"   **144 he . . . face** i.e. Bardolph   **147 Scarlet and John** Will Scarlet and Little John were two of Robin Hood's companions; **Scarlet** is applied to Bardolph because of his drunkard's red nose   **151 fap** drunk   **cashiered** dismissed/got rid of/thrown out of the tavern   **152 conclusions . . . careers** his conclusions about what had happened galloped beyond all bounds   **career** short gallop at full speed

SLENDER   Ay, you spake in Latin then too. But 'tis no matter. I'll
ne'er be drunk whilst I live again, but in honest, civil, godly
155   company, for this trick. If I be drunk, I'll be drunk with those
that have the fear of God, and not with drunken knaves.

EVANS   So Got 'udge me, that is a virtuous mind.

FALSTAFF   You hear all these matters denied, gentlemen, you
hear it.

[*Enter Anne, with wine*]

160   PAGE   Nay, daughter, carry the wine in: we'll drink within.

[*Exit Anne*]

SLENDER   O heaven, this is Mistress Anne Page!   *Aside?*

[*Enter Mistress Ford and Mistress Page*]

PAGE   How now, Mistress Ford?

FALSTAFF   Mistress Ford, by my troth, you are very well met.
By your leave, good mistress.   *Kisses her*

165   PAGE   Wife, bid these gentlemen welcome. Come, we have
a hot venison pasty to dinner. Come, gentlemen, I hope we
shall drink down all unkindness.

[*Exeunt all except Shallow, Slender and Evans*]

SLENDER   I had rather than forty shillings I had my book of
Songs and Sonnets here.

[*Enter Simple*]

170   How now, Simple, where have you been? I must wait on
myself, must I? You have not the *Book of Riddles* about you,
have you?

SIMPLE   *Book of Riddles?* Why, did you not lend it to Alice
Shortcake upon Allhallowmas last, a fortnight afore
175   Michaelmas?

SHALLOW   Come, coz. Come, coz, we stay for you. A word
with you, coz. Marry, this, coz: there is, as 'twere, a tender,

---

157 'udge judge   mind intention   164 leave permission   166 pasty to pie for
168 book . . . *Sonnets* probably *Songs and Sonnets*, a collection of poems, most of them about
love, published by Richard Tottel in 1557 and known as *Tottel's Miscellany*   171 *Book of
Riddles* unidentified; several Elizabethan collections of riddles existed   174 Allhallowmas All
Saints' Day, November 1   175 Michaelmas the feast of Saint Michael, September 29; Simple
is wrong in saying it is two weeks after Allhallowmas   176 stay wait   177 tender offer (i.e. of
marriage, made on behalf of Slender)

a kind of tender, made afar off by Sir Hugh here. Do you
understand me?

180 SLENDER   Ay, sir, you shall find me reasonable. If it be so, I
shall do that that is reason.

SHALLOW   Nay, but understand me.

SLENDER   So I do, sir.

EVANS   Give ear to his motions. Master Slender, I will
185   description the matter to you, if you be capacity of it.

SLENDER   Nay, I will do as my cousin Shallow says. I pray you
pardon me, he's a Justice of Peace in his country, simple
though I stand here.

EVANS   But that is not the question. The question is
190   concerning your marriage.

SHALLOW   Ay, there's the point, sir.

EVANS   Marry, is it: the very point of it, to Mistress Anne
Page.

SLENDER   Why, if it be so, I will marry her upon any reasonable
195   demands.

EVANS   But can you affection the 'oman? Let us command
to know that of your mouth or of your lips, for divers
philosophers hold that the lips is parcel of the mouth.
Therefore, precisely, can you carry your good will to the maid?

200 SHALLOW   Cousin Abraham Slender, can you love her?

SLENDER   I hope, sir, I will do as it shall become one that would
do reason.

EVANS   Nay, Got's lords and his ladies, you must speak
possitable, if you can carry her your desires towards her.

205 SHALLOW   That you must. Will you, upon good dowry, marry
her?

---

178 **afar off** indirectly/in a roundabout manner   181 **do . . . reason** i.e. behave in a
reasonable manner/cooperate   184 **motions** suggestions   185 **be capacity of** have the
capacity to understand   187 **country** district   **simple . . . here** as sure as I stand here/
although I seem humble/despite my own undistinguished status   195 **demands** requests
196 **'oman** woman   197 **divers** various   198 **parcel** part   199 **carry . . . to** feel inclination/
affection for (with a quibble on the slang sense of **will**—i.e. "sexual desire/penis")
204 **possitable** malapropism for "positively"   **carry her** convey/direct   205 **upon** providing
that she comes with/on the promise of

SLENDER   I will do a greater thing than that upon your
request, cousin, in any reason.

SHALLOW   Nay, conceive me, conceive me, sweet coz. What I do
210   is to pleasure you, coz. Can you love the maid?

SLENDER   I will marry her, sir, at your request. But if there be
no great love in the beginning, yet heaven may decrease it
upon better acquaintance, when we are married, and have
more occasion to know one another. I hope upon familiarity
215   will grow more contempt. But if you say 'Marry her', I will
marry her — that I am freely dissolved, and dissolutely.

EVANS   It is a fery discretion answer. Save the fall is in the
'ord 'dissolutely' — the 'ort is, according to our meaning,
'resolutely' — his meaning is good.

220   SHALLOW   Ay, I think my cousin meant well.

SLENDER   Ay, or else I would I might be hanged, la!

SHALLOW   Here comes fair Mistress Anne.

[*Enter Anne*]

Would I were young for your sake, Mistress Anne.

ANNE   The dinner is on the table, my father desires your
225   worships' company.

SHALLOW   I will wait on him, fair Mistress Anne.

EVANS   'Od's plessèd will! I will not be absence at the grace.
[*Exeunt Shallow and Evans*]

ANNE   Will't please your worship to come in, sir?

SLENDER   No, I thank you, forsooth, heartily. I am very well.

230   ANNE   The dinner attends you, sir.

SLENDER   I am not a-hungry, I thank you, forsooth.—   *To Simple*
Go, sirrah, for all you are my man, go wait upon my cousin
Shallow.   [*Exit Simple*]
A justice of peace sometime may be beholding to his friend
235   for a man. I keep but three men and a boy yet, till my mother
be dead: but what though, yet I live like a poor gentleman
born.

---

209 conceive understand   **212 decrease** malapropism for "increase"   **216 dissolved**
resolved   **dissolutely** malapropism for "resolutely"   **217 fall** i.e. error   **218 'ord** word
229 forsooth in truth   **230 attends** waits for   **232 sirrah** sir (authoritative)   **for all**
although   **234 beholding** indebted   **236 what though** what of it

ANNE   I may not go in without your worship: they will not sit till you come.

240 SLENDER   I'faith, I'll eat nothing. I thank you as much as though I did.

ANNE   I pray you, sir, walk in.

SLENDER   I had rather walk here, I thank you. I bruised my shin th'other day with playing at sword and dagger with a
245 master of fence— three veneys for a dish of stewed prunes— and, by my troth, I cannot abide the smell of hot meat since. Why do your dogs bark so? Be there bears i'th'town?

ANNE   I think there are, sir. I heard them talked of.

SLENDER   I love the sport well, but I shall as soon quarrel at it,
250 as any man in England. You are afraid if you see the bear loose, are you not?

ANNE   Ay, indeed, sir.

SLENDER   That's meat and drink to me, now. I have seen Sackerson loose twenty times, and have taken him by the
255 chain: but, I warrant you, the women have so cried and shrieked at it that it passed. But women, indeed, cannot abide 'em: they are very ill-favoured rough things.

[Enter Page]

PAGE   Come, gentle Master Slender, come: we stay for you.

SLENDER   I'll eat nothing, I thank you, sir.

260 PAGE   By cock and pie, you shall not choose, sir. Come, come.

SLENDER   Nay, pray you lead the way.

PAGE   Come on, sir.

SLENDER   Mistress Anne, yourself shall go first.

265 ANNE · Not I, sir, pray you, keep on.

---

245 fence fencing   **veneys** technical (French) term for each assault in a fencing match (from *venu*, "come"); pun (not intended by Slender) on "Venus," slang for prostitute
stewed prunes known to be a popular dish in brothels ("the stews")   **246 smell . . . meat** unintentionally suggesting whore's flesh   **249 the sport** bear-baiting, a popular Elizabethan pastime   **254 Sackerson** a well-known bear kept at Paris Garden in Southwark
255 warrant assure   **256 passed** was past belief   **257 ill-favoured** ugly   **260 cock and pie** a mild oath; either a literal reference to fowl and cooked pie or a corruption of "God" and an allusion to the Church rules concerning the celebration of Saints' days   **you . . . choose** polite way of saying "I insist/you have no choice"   **265 keep on** go ahead/carry on

SLENDER   Truly, I will not go first. Truly, la! I will not do you
that wrong.

ANNE   I pray you, sir.

SLENDER   I'll rather be unmannerly than   *Goes first*
270   troublesome. You do yourself wrong, indeed, la!   *Exeunt*

Act 1 Scene 2   *running scene 2*

Enter Evans and Simple

EVANS   Go your ways, and ask of Doctor Caius' house,
which is the way; and there dwells one Mistress Quickly,
which is in the manner of his nurse, or his dry nurse, or his
cook, or his laundry, his washer and his wringer.

5 SIMPLE   Well, sir.

EVANS   Nay, it is petter yet. Give her this letter.   *Gives letter*
For it is a 'oman that altogether's acquaintance with Mistress
Anne Page. And the letter is to desire and require her to
solicit your master's desires to Mistress Anne Page. I pray
10   you, be gone: I will make an end of my dinner, there's pippins
and cheese to come.   *Exeunt*

Act 1 Scene 3   *running scene 3*

Enter Falstaff, Host, Bardolph, Nim, Pistol [and] page [Robin]

FALSTAFF   Mine host of the Garter!

HOST   What says my bully rook? Speak scholarly and
wisely.

FALSTAFF   Truly, mine host, I must turn away some of my
5   followers.

HOST   Discard, bully Hercules, cashier. Let them wag. Trot,
trot.

1.2   1 of concerning   **3 nurse** housekeeper   **dry nurse** i.e. not a wet nurse, who would look
after a baby   **4 laundry** laundress   **wringer** one who wrings out clothes after they have been
washed   **7 altogether's acquaintance** is well acquainted   **9 solicit** urge/court favor for
10 pippins apples   **1.3   2 bully rook** jolly companion/old rogue   **6 bully Hercules** old mate
Hercules (the Greek hero)   **cashier** dismiss   **wag** move on

FALSTAFF   I sit at ten pounds a week.

HOST   Thou'rt an emperor: Caesar, Kaiser and Pheazar. I
10   will entertain Bardolph: he shall draw, he shall tap. Said I
well, bully Hector?

FALSTAFF   Do so, good mine host.

HOST   I have spoke. Let him follow.— Let me   *To Bardolph*
see thee froth and lime. I am at a word: follow.   [*Exit*]

15   FALSTAFF   Bardolph, follow him. A tapster is a good trade. An
old cloak makes a new jerkin: a withered servingman a fresh
tapster. Go, adieu.

BARDOLPH   It is a life that I have desired. I will thrive.

[*Exit Bardolph*]

PISTOL   O base Hungarian wight, wilt thou the spigot wield?

20   NIM   He was gotten in drink. Is not the humour conceited?

FALSTAFF   I am glad I am so acquit of this tinderbox. His thefts
were too open: his filching was like an unskilful singer, he
kept not time.

NIM   The good humour is to steal at a minute's rest.

25   PISTOL   'Convey', the wise it call. 'Steal?' Foh! A *fico* for the
phrase.

FALSTAFF   Well, sirs, I am almost out at heels.

PISTOL   Why then, let kibes ensue.

FALSTAFF   There is no remedy: I must cony-catch, I must shift.

30   PISTOL   Young ravens must have food.

FALSTAFF   Which of you know Ford of this town?

---

8 sit at live here at the cost of   **9 Kaiser** emperor   **Pheazar** vizier (chief minister to a ruler),
or possibly a nonsense word to rhyme with **Caesar** and **Kaiser**   **10 entertain** employ
draw . . . tap withdraw liquor from a cask in the manner of an innkeeper   **11 Hector** hero of
the Trojan War   **14 froth** make the beer froth up on top as a means of serving less   **lime**
flavor wine with lime in order to mask its sourness   **I . . . word** i.e. without further ado
15 tapster barman   **16 jerkin** close-fitting jacket   **19 Hungarian wight** thievish, beggarly
person (with a play on "hungry")   **spigot** peg used to stop the hole in a cask of liquor
20 gotten in drink conceived while his parents were drunk   **Is . . . conceited** isn't that an
ingenious/witty notion   **21 acquit** rid   **tinderbox** i.e. Bardolph, an inflammable and red-
faced man   **22 open** obvious   **24 good humour** best method/way to do it   **at . . . rest** in the
space of a minute (**rest** plays on the sense of "moment of silence within a piece of music")
25 fico "fig" (Italian; a contemptuous word, sometimes accompanied by the obscene gesture of
thrusting the thumb between two fingers)   **27 out at heels** out of money (literally, with shoes
or stockings worn through)   **28 kibes** chilblains   **29 shift** provide for myself/live by
deception/live on my wits

PISTOL	I ken the wight: he is of substance good.
FALSTAFF	My honest lads, I will tell you what I am about.
PISTOL	Two yards, and more.

35 FALSTAFF No quips now, Pistol! Indeed, I am in the waist
two yards about, but I am now about no waste: I am about
thrift. Briefly, I do mean to make love to Ford's wife. I spy
entertainment in her: she discourses, she carves, she gives
the leer of invitation. I can construe the action of her

40 familiar style, and the hardest voice of her behaviour — to
be Englished rightly — is, 'I am Sir John Falstaff's.'

PISTOL He hath studied her will, and translated her will,
out of honesty, into English.

NIM The anchor is deep. Will that humour pass?

45 FALSTAFF Now, the report goes she has all the rule of her
husband's purse: he hath a legion of angels.

PISTOL As many devils entertain. And 'To her, boy!' say I.

NIM The humour rises: it is good. Humour me the angels.

FALSTAFF I have writ me here a letter to her.   *Shows letters*

50 And here another to Page's wife, who even now gave me
good eyes too, examined my parts with most judicious
oeillades. Sometimes the beam of her view gilded my foot,
sometimes my portly belly.

PISTOL Then did the sun on dunghill shine.

55 NIM I thank thee for that humour.

---

32 **ken the wight** know the person   33 **am about** up to (Pistol interprets "measure about the
waist")   37 **make love to** court/woo   38 **entertainment** welcome/a pleasant reception (with
sexual connotations)   **carves** is a courteous and generous hostess/has sex   39 **leer** sideways
glance/sexually inviting look   **construe** interpret/translate/analyze grammatically   **action**
working/oratorical gesture (with sexual connotations)   40 **familiar** usual/plain/courteous/
overly intimate   **hardest voice** most severe expression/most difficult grammatical form to
translate   41 **Englished** translated into English   42 **will** inclination/sexual desire/legal
document   43 **honesty** chastity   44 **The . . . deep** probably "this idea (of Falstaff's) is firmly
entrenched"   **that humour pass** Falstaff's frame of mind change/Falstaff's inclination get
him anywhere/my neat expression gain approval   46 **legion of angels** great number of gold
coins (plays on the sense of "host of heavenly beings")   47 **As . . . entertain** employ just as
many devils   **To her** a cry of encouragement such as might be used to a hound pursuing prey
48 **The humour rises** the wit improves/(Falstaff's) inclination grows   **Humour . . . angels** let
your inclination lead to the acquisition of the money (**me** is emphatic)   49 **writ me** written
52 **oeillades** amorous looks   55 **humour** turn of phrase

FALSTAFF   O, she did so course o'er my exteriors with such a
greedy intention, that the appetite of her eye did seem to
scorch me up like a burning-glass. Here's another letter to
her. She bears the purse too: she is a region in Guiana, all gold
60   and bounty. I will be cheaters to them both, and they shall be
exchequers to me. They shall be my East and West Indies,
and I will trade to them both.— Go bear thou this   *To Nim*
letter to Mistress Page — and thou this to Mistress   *To Pistol*
Ford. We will thrive, lads, we will thrive.

65   PISTOL   Shall I Sir Pandarus of Troy become,
And by my side wear steel? Then Lucifer take all!   *Gives back*

NIM   I will run no base humour. Here, take the   *the letter*
humour-letter. I will keep the 'haviour of   *Gives the letter back*
reputation.

70   FALSTAFF   Hold, sirrah, bear you these letters tightly,   *To Robin*
Sail like my pinnace to these golden shores.
Rogues, hence, avaunt! Vanish like hailstones: go,
Trudge, plod away o'th'hoof, seek shelter, pack!
Falstaff will learn the humour of the age,
75   French thrift, you rogues, myself and skirted page.

[Exeunt Falstaff and Robin]

PISTOL   Let vultures gripe thy guts! For gourd and fullam
holds,
And high and low beguiles the rich and poor:

---

56 course run (her eyes)   **57 intention** intent observation/purpose   **58 burning-glass**
magnifying glass   **59 purse** plays on sense of "vagina"   **Guiana** country in South America
fabled for its great wealth   **60 cheaters** escheator, a district official who supervised escheats,
estates that returned to the monarch's possession in the absence of a valid heir (plays on sense
of "sexual cheat, deceiver")   **61 exchequers** treasuries   **62 trade** plays on sense of "have sex
with"   **65 Pandarus of Troy** in Greek legend, the go-between (or pander) in Troilus and
Cressida's love affair   **66 And . . . steel** i.e. and having stooped to such an unmanly
profession, still call myself a soldier   **67 run . . . humour** undertake no such low task
68 humour-letter having repeated **humour** so often, Nim's use of it has begun to become
meaningless; possibly he means "letter written out of fancy" or simply adds **humour** for
contemptuous emphasis   **'haviour of reputation** an honorable bearing/a reputable manner
70 tightly properly/well   **71 pinnace** small sailing vessel   **72 avaunt** be gone   **73 o'th'hoof**
on foot   **pack** be off   **74 humour** mood/fashion   **75 French thrift** economy, possibly a
French tendency to have only one page rather than several attendants   **skirted** wearing a
coat with a fully skirted lower section   **76 gripe** grip/afflict the bowels with pain   **gourd and
fullam** false or loaded dice   **holds** hold good/continue to be effective   **77 high and low** i.e.
dice loaded to produce either high or low numbers   **beguiles** deceives

Tester I'll have in pouch when thou shalt lack,
Base Phrygian Turk!

80   NIM   I have operations which be humours of revenge.

PISTOL   Wilt thou revenge?

NIM   By welkin and her star!

PISTOL   With wit or steel?

NIM   With both the humours, I. I will discuss the humour
85   of this love to Ford.

PISTOL   And I to Page shall eke unfold
How Falstaff, varlet vile,
His dove will prove, his gold will hold,
And his soft couch defile.

90   NIM   My humour shall not cool. I will incense Ford to
deal with poison. I will possess him with yellowness, for the
revolt of mine is dangerous. That is my true humour.

PISTOL   Thou art the Mars of malcontents. I second thee,
troop on.   *Exeunt*

Act 1 Scene 4   *running scene 4*

Enter Mistress Quickly, Simple and John Rugby

MISTRESS QUICKLY   What, John Rugby! I pray thee go to the
casement and see if you can see my master, Master Doctor
Caius, coming. If he do, i'faith, and find anybody in the
house, here will be an old abusing of God's patience and the
5   King's English.

RUGBY   I'll go watch.

MISTRESS QUICKLY   Go, and we'll have a posset for't soon at night,
in faith, at the latter end of a sea-coal fire.—   [*Exit Rugby*]

---

78 Tester sixpence   **pouch** (my) purse   **79 Phrygian Turk** i.e. base, barbarous person
Phrygia region in Asia Minor conquered by the Turks in the fifteenth century; now part of
modern Turkey   **80 operations** plans   **humours of** inclinations for   **82 welkin** sky   **83 wit
or steel** intelligence/ingenuity or violence (the sword)   **84 humours** methods   **discuss** make
known   **humour** nature   **86 eke** also   **88 prove** put to the test (sexually)   **91 yellowness**
i.e. jealousy   **92 revolt** i.e. against Falstaff   **93 Mars of malcontents** most warlike of rebels
Mars god of war   **1.4**   **4 old** great   **7 posset** hot drink made with milk, liquor, and spices
soon at night before the night is too far advanced   **8 sea-coal** superior type of coal
transported by sea from the north of England

An honest, willing, kind fellow, as ever servant shall come in
10   house withal, and, I warrant you, no tell-tale nor no breed-
bate. His worst fault is that he is given to prayer, he is
something peevish that way, but nobody but has his fault.
But let that pass. Peter Simple you say your name is?

SIMPLE   Ay, for fault of a better.

15   MISTRESS QUICKLY   And Master Slender's your master?

SIMPLE   Ay, forsooth.

MISTRESS QUICKLY   Does he not wear a great round beard, like a
glover's paring-knife?

SIMPLE   No, forsooth, he hath but a little wee face, with a
20   little yellow beard: a Cain-coloured beard.

MISTRESS QUICKLY   A softly-sprighted man, is he not?

SIMPLE   Ay, forsooth, but he is as tall a man of his hands as
any is between this and his head. He hath fought with a
warrener.

25   MISTRESS QUICKLY   How say you? O, I should remember him:
does he not hold up his head, as it were, and strut in his gait?

SIMPLE   Yes, indeed, does he.

MISTRESS QUICKLY   Well, heaven send Anne Page no worse
fortune. Tell Master Parson Evans I will do what I can for
30   your master. Anne is a good girl, and I wish—

RUGBY   Out, alas! Here comes my master.   *Within*

MISTRESS QUICKLY   We shall all be shent. Run in here,   *To Simple*
good young man, go into this closet. He will not stay long.
What, John Rugby? John! What, John, I say?   *Simple goes into*
[*Enter Rugby*]   *the closet*

35   Go, John, go inquire for my master. I doubt he be not well,
that he comes not home.   [*Exit Rugby*]

And down, down, adown-a, etc.   *She sings*

---

10 withal with   **breed-bate** troublemaker   **12 peevish** foolish/perverse   **14 fault** i.e. lack
18 glover glove maker   **paring-knife** knife used for trimming leather   **20 Cain-coloured**
reddish yellow   **Cain** in the Bible, the world's first murderer   **21 softly-sprighted** gentle/
mild in spirit   **22 as . . . hands** as brave (**tall**) a fighter   **23 between . . . head** in these parts
24 warrener gamekeeper/one in charge of an enclosure for breeding rabbits   **31 Out, alas!**
exclamation of dismay   **32 shent** blamed/rebuked   **33 closet** private room   **35 doubt** fear
37 And . . . adown-a the refrain of a song

[*Enter Caius*]

CAIUS   Vat is you sing? I do not like des toys. Pray you, go
               and vetch me in my closet *une boîtie en vert*: a box, a green-a
40   box. Do intend vat I speak? A green-a box.

MISTRESS QUICKLY   Ay, forsooth, I'll fetch it you.— I am   *Aside*
               glad he went not in himself. If he had found the young man,
               he would have been horn-mad.   *She goes into the closet*

CAIUS   *Fe, fe, fe, fe, ma foi, il fait fort chaud. Je m'en vais voir à*
45   *le* Court *la grande affaire.*

[*Enter Mistress Quickly with a box*]

MISTRESS QUICKLY   Is it this, sir?

CAIUS   *Oui, mette-le au mon* pocket. *Dépêche*, quickly. Vere is
               dat knave Rugby?

MISTRESS QUICKLY   What, John Rugby? John?

[*Enter Rugby*]

50   RUGBY   Here, sir!

CAIUS   You are John Rugby, and you are Jack Rugby. Come,
               take-a your rapier, and come after my heel to the court.

RUGBY   'Tis ready, sir, here in the porch.

CAIUS   By my trot, I tarry too long. Od's me, *que ai-je oublié*.
55   Dere is some simples in my closet dat I vill not for the varld I
               shall leave behind.   *He goes into the closet*

MISTRESS QUICKLY   Ay me, he'll find the young man there and
               be mad.

CAIUS   O *diable, diable*! Vat is in my closet? Villain, *larron*!
60   Rugby, my rapier!   *Within/Pulls Simple out*

MISTRESS QUICKLY   Good master, be content.

CAIUS   Wherefore shall I be content-a?

MISTRESS QUICKLY   The young man is an honest man.

---

38 toys trifles (i.e. songs)   **39 *une boîtie en vert*** French for "a green box" (*boîtie* may also
mean "surgeon's instrument case")   **40 Do intend** i.e. do you hear (from the French *entendre*)
43 horn-mad wildly enraged, like a horned beast/madly jealous like a cuckold (horned
husband of an unfaithful wife)   **44 *ma . . . affaire*** by my faith, it's very hot. I'm going to see
the great business at the Court   **47 *Oui . . . Dépêche*** "yes; put it in my pocket: hurry up"
54 trot troth (faith)   **Od's me** God save me   ***que ai-je oublié*** "what have I forgotten"
55 simples medicinal herbs   **59 *diable*** devil   ***larron*** thief

CAIUS   What shall de honest man do in my closet? Dere is
65   no honest man dat shall come in my closet.

MISTRESS QUICKLY   I beseech you be not so phlegmatic. Hear the
truth of it: he came of an errand to me, from Parson Hugh.

CAIUS   Vell.

SIMPLE   Ay, forsooth, to desire her to—

70   MISTRESS QUICKLY   Peace, I pray you.

CAIUS   Peace-a your tongue. Speak-a   *To Mistress Quickly/*
your tale.   *To Simple*

SIMPLE   To desire this honest gentlewoman, your maid, to
speak a good word to Mistress Anne Page for my master in
75   the way of marriage.

MISTRESS QUICKLY   This is all, indeed, la! But I'll ne'er put my
finger in the fire, and need not.

CAIUS   Sir Hugh send-a you? Rugby, *baillez* me some paper.
Tarry you a little-a while.   *Rugby brings paper. Caius writes*

80   MISTRESS QUICKLY   I am glad he is so quiet. If he   *Aside to Simple*
had been throughly moved, you should have heard him so
loud and so melancholy. But notwithstanding, man, I'll do
you your master what good I can: and the very yea and the
no is, the French doctor, my master — I may call him my
85   master, look you, for I keep his house, and I wash, wring,
brew, bake, scour, dress meat and drink, make the beds and
do all myself—

SIMPLE   'Tis a great charge to come under one   *Aside to*
body's hand.   *Mistress Quickly*

90   MISTRESS QUICKLY   Are you avised o'that? You   *Aside to Simple*
shall find it a great charge, and to be up early and down late.
But notwithstanding — to tell you in your ear, I would have
no words of it — my master himself is in love with Mistress

---

66 phlegmatic dull/cold; presumably Quickly means "choleric"—i.e. "angry/hot"   **67 of** on
76 ne'er . . . not never burn my fingers (i.e. meddle) unnecessarily   **78 *baillez*** bring
82 melancholy introspective/sullen/broodingly angry; perhaps another error for "choleric"
83 you since you ask; or simply emphatic   **yea . . . no** truth   **86 dress meat** prepare food
88 charge responsibility/burden   **90 avised** aware/informed   **You . . . it** i.e. it certainly is/let
me assure you it is   **92 I . . . it** I wouldn't wish any word of it to get out

Anne Page. But notwithstanding that, I know Anne's mind
95   — that's neither here nor there.

CAIUS   You jack'nape, give-a this letter to   *Gives a letter*
Sir Hugh. By gar, it is a shallenge. I will cut his   *to Simple*
troat in de park, and I will teach a scurvy jack-a-nape priest
to meddle or make.— You may be gone. It is not   *To Simple*
100   good you tarry here.— By gar, I will cut all his two stones. By
gar, he shall not have a stone to throw at his dog.

[*Exit Simple*]

MISTRESS QUICKLY   Alas, he speaks but for his friend.

CAIUS   It is no matter-a ver dat: do not you tell-a me dat I
shall have Anne Page for myself? By gar, I vill kill de Jack
105   priest: and I have appointed mine host of de Jarteer to
measure our weapon. By gar, I will myself have Anne Page.

MISTRESS QUICKLY   Sir, the maid loves you, and all shall be well.
We must give folks leave to prate. What the good-year!

CAIUS   Rugby, come to the court with me.—   *To Mistress*
110   By gar, if I have not Anne Page, I shall turn your   *Quickly*
head out of my door. Follow my heels, Rugby.

MISTRESS QUICKLY   You shall have An—

[*Exeunt Caius and Rugby*]

fool's-head of your own. No, I know Anne's mind for that:
never a woman in Windsor knows more of Anne's mind than
115   I do, nor can do more than I do with her, I thank heaven.

FENTON   Who's within there, ho?   *Within*

MISTRESS QUICKLY   Who's there, I trow? Come near the house, I
pray you.

[*Enter Fenton*]

FENTON   How now, good woman? How dost thou?

---

96 jack'nape ape (hence "fool/upstart")   **97 gar** God   **98 park** enclosed hunting ground
99 meddle or make interfere   **100 stones** testicles   **103 ver** for   **104 Jack** knavish
105 Jarteer Garter   **106 measure our weapon** swords were measured before a duel to ensure
that they were of equal length (**weapon** has phallic connotations)   **108 prate** chatter/gossip
What the good-year what the devil   **112 An** puns on "Anne" (whom Caius will be a **fool** to
woo)   **117 trow** wonder   **near** in

120 MISTRESS QUICKLY   The better that it pleases your good worship
         to ask.

     FENTON   What news? How does pretty Mistress Anne?

     MISTRESS QUICKLY   In truth, sir, and she is pretty, and honest,
         and gentle, and one that is your friend— I can tell you that
125   by the way — I praise heaven for it.

     FENTON   Shall I do any good, thinkest thou? Shall I not lose
         my suit?

     MISTRESS QUICKLY   Troth, sir, all is in his hands above: but
         notwithstanding, Master Fenton, I'll be sworn on a book she
130   loves you. Have not your worship a wart above your eye?

     FENTON   Yes, marry, have I. What of that?

     MISTRESS QUICKLY   Well, thereby hangs a tale: good faith, it is
         such another Nan —but, I detest, an honest maid as ever
         broke bread. We had an hour's talk of that wart. I shall
135   never laugh but in that maid's company. But, indeed, she is
         given too much to allicholy and musing. But for you — well,
         go to—

     FENTON   Well, I shall see her today. Hold, there's money for
         thee: let me have thy voice in my behalf. If thou see'st her
140   before me, commend me—

     MISTRESS QUICKLY   Will I? I'faith, that we will. And I will tell your
         worship more of the wart the next time we have confidence,
         and of other wooers.

     FENTON   Well, farewell, I am in great haste now.

145 MISTRESS QUICKLY   Farewell to your worship.   [*Exit Fenton*]
         Truly, an honest gentleman. But Anne loves him not. For I
         know Anne's mind as well as another does. Out upon't, what
         have I forgot?   *Exit*

---

123 **honest** chaste   124 **friend** sympathizer/favorer (with a play on the sense of "lover")
129 **book** i.e. Bible   132 **it . . . Nan** what an extraordinary girl she is   **Nan** diminutive of
"Anne"   133 **detest** malapropism for "protest" (i.e. declare)   136 **allicholy** malapropism for
"melancholy"   137 **go to** expression of impatient dismissal   139 **voice** support
142 **confidence** malapropism for "conference"; Quickly means "private conversation"
147 **Out upon't** expression of irritation

Act 2 Scene 1

Enter Mistress Page   With a letter

MISTRESS PAGE   What, have I scaped love-letters in the holiday-
time of my beauty, and am I now a subject for them? Let me
see: 'Ask me no reason why I love you, for though   Reads
Love use Reason for his precisian, he admits him not for his
5   counsellor. You are not young, no more am I: go to then,
there's sympathy. You are merry, so am I: ha, ha, then there's
more sympathy. You love sack, and so do I: would you desire
better sympathy? Let it suffice thee, Mistress Page, at the
least if the love of soldier can suffice, that I love thee. I will
10   not say, pity me — 'tis not a soldier-like phrase — but I say,
love me. By me,
            Thine own true knight,
            By day or night,
            Or any kind of light,
15   With all his might
            For thee to fight,
                    John Falstaff.'
What a Herod of Jewry is this? O wicked, wicked world! One
that is well-nigh worn to pieces with age, to show himself a
20   young gallant? What an unweighed behaviour hath this
Flemish drunkard picked — with the devil's name — out of
my conversation, that he dares in this manner assay me?
Why, he hath not been thrice in my company! What should I
say to him? I was then frugal of my mirth — heaven forgive
25   me! Why, I'll exhibit a bill in the parliament for the putting

---

2.1   1 scaped escaped   **holiday-time** best time/heyday   **4 precisian** puritan/strict spiritual
adviser (some editors emend to "physician")   **5 counsellor** adviser/confidant   **6 sympathy**
agreement/affinity (between us)   **7 sack** Spanish white wine   **18 Herod of Jewry** i.e.
ranting villain; in the Bible, Herod of Judaea ordered the deaths of John the Baptist and the
infant Jesus; he was presented in morality plays as both evil and absurdly boastful   **20 gallant**
fashionable young gentleman/one who woos ladies   **unweighed** unconsidered   **21 Flemish**
from the Netherlands; the Flemish were proverbially heavy drinkers   **23 should I say** could I
have said   **25 putting down** suppression (perhaps with sexual connotations)

down of men. How shall I be revenged on him? For revenged
I will be, as sure as his guts are made of puddings.

[*Enter Mistress Ford*]

MISTRESS FORD   Mistress Page, trust me, I was going to your
house.

30   **MISTRESS PAGE**   And, trust me, I was coming to you. You look
very ill.

MISTRESS FORD   Nay, I'll ne'er believe that; I have to show to the
contrary.

MISTRESS PAGE   Faith, but you do, in my mind.

35   **MISTRESS FORD**   Well, I do then: yet I say I could show you to the
contrary. O Mistress Page, give me some counsel!

MISTRESS PAGE   What's the matter, woman?

MISTRESS FORD   O woman, if it were not for one trifling respect,
I could come to such honour!

40   **MISTRESS PAGE**   Hang the trifle, woman, take the honour. What
is it? Dispense with trifles: what is it?

MISTRESS FORD   If I would but go to hell for an eternal moment
or so, I could be knighted.

MISTRESS PAGE   What? Thou liest! Sir Alice Ford? These knights
45   will hack, and so thou shouldst not alter the article of thy
gentry.

MISTRESS FORD   We burn daylight. Here, read,   *Gives letter to*
read. Perceive how I might be knighted. I shall   *Mistress Page*
think the worse of fat men, as long as I have an eye to make
50   difference of men's liking. And yet he would not swear,
praised women's modesty, and gave such orderly and well-
behaved reproof to all uncomeliness, that I would have
sworn his disposition would have gone to the truth of his
words. But they do no more adhere and keep place together

---

27 **puddings** sausages (also used to refer to the human guts)   28 **trust me** believe me/depend
upon it   31 **ill** unwell/out of sorts (Mistress Ford responds to the sense of "ugly")   32 **have**
have something (i.e. the letter)   38 **respect** consideration   42 **go to hell** i.e. by committing
adultery with Falstaff   45 **hack** strike repeatedly with a sword/have sex/make a whore of a
woman   **article . . . gentry** nature of your social rank   47 **burn daylight** i.e. waste time
49 **make . . . liking** discriminate between men's physiques   52 **uncomeliness** unseemly
behavior   53 **gone . . . of** accorded with

55　　than the hundred Psalms to the tune of 'Greensleeves'.
　　　What tempest, I trow, threw this whale — with so many tuns
　　　of oil in his belly — ashore at Windsor? How shall I be
　　　revenged on him? I think the best way were to entertain him
　　　with hope, till the wicked fire of lust have melted him in his
60　　own grease. Did you ever hear the like?

MISTRESS PAGE　　Letter for letter, but that the name of Page and
　　　Ford differs. To thy great comfort in this mystery of ill
　　　opinions, here's the twin-brother of thy letter.　　*Shows her*
　　　But let thine inherit first, for I protest mine never　　*own letter*
65　　shall. I warrant he hath a thousand of these letters, writ
　　　with blank space for different names — sure, more — and
　　　these are of the second edition. He will print them, out of
　　　doubt, for he cares not what he puts into the press, when he
　　　would put us two. I had rather be a giantess, and lie under
70　　Mount Pelion. Well, I will find you twenty lascivious turtles
　　　ere one chaste man.

MISTRESS FORD　　Why, this is the very same: the　　*Compares the*
　　　very hand, the very words. What doth he think　　*two letters*
　　　of us?

75　MISTRESS PAGE　　Nay, I know not. It makes me almost ready to
　　　wrangle with mine own honesty. I'll entertain myself like
　　　one that I am not acquainted withal: for, sure, unless he
　　　know some strain in me that I know not myself, he would
　　　never have boarded me in this fury.

80　MISTRESS FORD　　'Boarding', call you it? I'll be sure to keep him
　　　above deck.

---

55 'Greensleeves' a popular love song, here incongruously juxtaposed with the sacred tunes of the **Psalms** (some editors emend **hundred** to "hundredth," suggesting specific allusion to Psalm 100, "All people that on earth do dwell/Sing to the Lord with cheerful voice")　　**56 tuns** barrels/tons　　**58 entertain** receive/welcome/occupy his attention　　**62 ill opinions** Falstaff's poor opinions of the women's virtue　　**64 inherit** take possession (of Falstaff's offer)　　**68 into the press** into the printing press/under pressure of his weight during sex　　**70 Mount Pelion** in Greek mythology, warring giants piled Pelion on top of Mount Ossa in an attempt to reach Olympus, home of the gods　　**turtles** turtledoves, proverbially faithful birds　　**71 ere** before　　**73 hand** handwriting　　**76 wrangle . . . honesty** quarrel with my own virtue　　**entertain** treat/consider　　**78 strain** quality　　**79 boarded** accosted/wooed (Mistress Ford picks up on the sense of "have sex with")　　**fury** fierce passion　　**81 above deck** i.e. above the waist

MISTRESS PAGE   So will I: if he come under my hatches, I'll never
to sea again. Let's be revenged on him. Let's appoint him a
meeting, give him a show of comfort in his suit and lead him
85   on with a fine-baited delay, till he hath pawned his horses to
mine host of the Garter.

MISTRESS FORD   Nay, I will consent to act any villainy against
him that may not sully the chariness of our honesty. O, that
my husband saw this letter! It would give eternal food to his
90   jealousy.

MISTRESS PAGE   Why, look where he comes, and my good man
too: he's as far from jealousy as I am from giving him cause,
and that — I hope — is an unmeasurable distance.

MISTRESS FORD   You are the happier woman.

95 MISTRESS PAGE   Let's consult together against this greasy knight.
Come hither.   *They withdraw*

[*Enter Ford with Pistol, and Page with Nim*]

FORD   Well, I hope it be not so.

PISTOL   Hope is a curtal dog in some affairs.
Sir John affects thy wife.

100 FORD   Why, sir, my wife is not young.

PISTOL   He woos both high and low, both rich and poor,
Both young and old, one with another, Ford.
He loves the gallimaufry, Ford, perpend.

FORD   Love my wife?

105 PISTOL   With liver burning hot. Prevent,
Or go thou like Sir Actaeon, he
With Ringwood at thy heels.
O, odious is the name!

FORD   What name, sir?

---

82 come plays on the sense of "have an orgasm"   **hatches** with vaginal connotations
84 comfort . . . suit encouragement in his courtship   **85 fine-baited** tempting/alluring/
skillfully baited   **88 chariness** careful preservation   **98 curtal** with a tail docked or cut off
99 affects aims at/loves   **103 gallimaufry** mixture (literally, stew made from a variety of odds
and ends)   **perpend** consider   **105 liver** thought to be the seat of the passions   **Prevent** i.e.
act now to stop Falstaff   **106 Actaeon** in Greek mythology, the goddess Diana turned
Actaeon into a stag after he had seen her bathing; he was then killed by his own hounds
107 Ringwood one of Actaeon's hounds   **thy** some editors emend to "his"   **108 the name**
i.e. of cuckold (Actaeon's horns made him a symbol of cuckoldry)

110   PISTOL   The horn, I say. Farewell.

Take heed, have open eye, for thieves do foot by night.

Take heed, ere summer comes, or cuckoo-birds do sing.

Away, Sir Corporal Nim!

Believe it, Page, he speaks sense.   [*Exit*]

115   FORD   I will be patient. I will find out this.   *Aside*

NIM   And this is true, I like not the humour   *To Page*
of lying. He hath wronged me in some humours: I should
have borne the humoured letter to her, but I have a sword,
and it shall bite upon my necessity. He loves your wife:

120   there's the short and the long. My name is Corporal Nim. I
speak and I avouch 'tis true: my name is Nim, and Falstaff
loves your wife. Adieu. I love not the humour of bread and
cheese. Adieu.   [*Exit*]

PAGE   'The humour of it', quoth a! Here's a fellow frights

125   English out of his wits.

FORD   I will seek out Falstaff.

PAGE   I never heard such a drawling, affecting rogue.

FORD   If I do find it — well.

PAGE   I will not believe such a Cataian, though the priest

130   o'th'town commended him for a true man.

FORD   'Twas a good sensible fellow — well.

PAGE   How now, Meg?   *Mistress Page and Mistress*

MISTRESS PAGE   Whither go you, George?   *Ford come forward*
Hark you.

135   MISTRESS FORD   How now, sweet Frank, why art thou melancholy?

FORD   I melancholy? I am not melancholy. Get you
home, go.

MISTRESS FORD   Faith, thou hast some crotchets in thy head
now.— Will you go, Mistress Page?

---

111 foot walk   **112 cuckoo-birds** known for laying their eggs in other birds' nests; they were
associated with cuckolds because of their name, and their call was considered a warning to
married men   **113 Away** come away   **117 should have borne** was to have carried
119 upon my necessity when I need it   **122 bread and cheese** i.e. basic rations (perhaps
those received in the service of Falstaff)   **124 quoth a** said he   **125 his** its   **127 affecting**
affected   **128 it** i.e. it to be true   **129 Cataian** person from Cathay (China), used to mean
"scoundrel"   **though** even if   **138 crotchets** whims/peculiar ideas

140　MISTRESS PAGE   Have with you.— You'll come to dinner,
George?—

Look who comes yonder: she shall be our messenger to this
paltry knight.   *Aside to Mistress Ford*

[*Enter Mistress Quickly*]

MISTRESS FORD   Trust me, I thought on her: she'll fit it.   *Aside to*

145　MISTRESS PAGE   You are come to see my daughter   *Mistress Page*
Anne?

MISTRESS QUICKLY   Ay, forsooth, and I pray how does good
Mistress Anne?

MISTRESS PAGE   Go in with us and see. We have an hour's talk
150　with you.

[*Exeunt Mistress Page, Mistress Ford and Mistress Quickly*]

PAGE   How now, Master Ford?

FORD   You heard what this knave told me, did you not?

PAGE   Yes, and you heard what the other told me?

FORD   Do you think there is truth in them?

155　PAGE   Hang 'em, slaves! I do not think the knight would
offer it. But these that accuse him in his intent towards our
wives are a yoke of his discarded men: very rogues, now they
be out of service.

FORD   Were they his men?

160　PAGE   Marry, were they.

FORD   I like it never the better for that. Does he lie at the
Garter?

PAGE   Ay, marry, does he. If he should intend this voyage
toward my wife, I would turn her loose to him, and what he
165　gets more of her than sharp words, let it lie on my head.

FORD   I do not misdoubt my wife, but I would be loath to
turn them together. A man may be too confident. I would
have nothing lie on my head. I cannot be thus satisfied.

---

140 **Have with you** I'll come with you/let's go   144 **fit it** suit the part   156 **offer** attempt
157 **yoke** pair   161 **lie** lodge   163 **voyage** sexual advances   165 **lie on my head** be my
responsibility/fault (in his response, Ford plays on the idea of wearing a cuckold's horns on
one's head)   166 **misdoubt** mistrust/doubt   167 **turn them** release them (language used of
cattle)

PAGE   Look where my ranting host of the Garter comes:
170   there is either liquor in his pate or money in his purse, when
he looks so merrily.

[*Enter Host*]

How now, mine host?

HOST   How now, bully-rook? Thou'rt a gentleman.

[*Enter Shallow*]

Cavaliero Justice, I say!

175 SHALLOW   I follow, mine host, I follow. Good even and twenty,
good Master Page. Master Page, will you go with us? We have
sport in hand.

HOST   Tell him, Cavaliero Justice: tell him, bully-rook.

SHALLOW   Sir, there is a fray to be fought between Sir Hugh the
180   Welsh priest and Caius the French doctor.

FORD   Good mine host o'th'Garter, a word   *They speak apart*
with you.

HOST   What sayst thou, my bully-rook?

SHALLOW   Will you go with us to behold it? My merry   *To Page*
185   host hath had the measuring of their weapons, and, I think,
hath appointed them contrary places, for, believe me, I hear
the parson is no jester. Hark, I will tell you what our sport
shall be.   *They speak apart*

HOST   Hast thou no suit against my knight, my guest-
190   cavalier?

FORD   None, I protest. But I'll give you a pottle of burned
sack to give me recourse to him, and tell him my name is
Broom, only for a jest.

---

169 ranting jovial/boisterous/verbally extravagant   **170 pate** head   **174 Cavaliero** knight/
courtly gentleman (from the Spanish *caballero* or the Italian *cavaliere*)   **175 Good . . . twenty**
good day, many times over   **186 contrary** different/opposing   **187 no jester** i.e. Evans is
skilled at swordsmanship/Evans is deadly serious   **189 my guest-cavalier** i.e. Falstaff, who is a
guest at the Host's inn   **191 protest** declare   **pottle** drinking vessel containing half a gallon
(about four pints)   **burned sack** mulled wine/wine containing burnt sugar   **192 recourse**
access

HOST   My hand, bully. Thou shalt have egress and regress
195   — said I well? — and thy name shall be Broom. It is a merry
knight.— Will you go, An-heires?   *To Shallow and Page*

SHALLOW   Have with you, mine host.

PAGE   I have heard the Frenchman hath good skill in his
rapier.

200 SHALLOW   Tut, sir, I could have told you more. In these times
you stand on distance: your passes, stoccadoes, and I know
not what. 'Tis the heart, Master Page, 'tis here, 'tis here. I
have seen the time, with my long sword, I would have made
you four tall fellows skip like rats.

205 HOST   Here, boys, here, here! Shall we wag?

PAGE   Have with you. I had rather hear them scold than
fight.   [*Exeunt Host, Shallow and Page*]

FORD   Though Page be a secure fool, and stands so firmly
on his wife's frailty, yet I cannot put off my opinion so easily.
210   She was in his company at Page's house, and what they
made there I know not. Well, I will look further into't, and I
have a disguise to sound Falstaff. If I find her honest, I lose
not my labour: if she be otherwise, 'tis labour well bestowed.
      Exit

Act 2 Scene 2   *running scene 6*

Enter Falstaff [and] Pistol

FALSTAFF   I will not lend thee a penny.

PISTOL   Why, then the world's mine oyster, which I with
sword will open.

---

194 egress and regress right of exit and entry (legal terms)   **196 An-heires** of unclear
meaning; possibly a partly Anglicized version of the Dutch *mynheers* ("gentlemen") or a
corruption of *ameers* or "emirs" (Arab princes or military commanders)   **201 stand on
distance** attach importance to the prescribed distance between the two duelists   **passes,
stoccadoes** thrusts (technical terms used in fencing)   **202 heart** courage/spirit   **203 long
sword** heavier weapon (the lighter rapier was now more fashionable)   **204 tall** brave/skillful
with weapons   **205 wag** go   **206 scold** quarrel/wrangle   **208 secure** overconfident
stands . . . frailty relies so firmly on what is in fact his wife's moral weakness   **210 his** i.e.
Falstaff's   **211 made** did   **212 sound** sound the depth of/examine/make trial of

FALSTAFF   Not a penny. I have been content, sir, you should
5   lay my countenance to pawn. I have grated upon my good
       friends for three reprieves for you and your coach-fellow
       Nim, or else you had looked through the grate, like a gemini
       of baboons. I am damned in hell for swearing to gentlemen
       my friends you were good soldiers and tall fellows. And when
10   Mistress Bridget lost the handle of her fan, I took't upon
       mine honour thou hadst it not.

PISTOL   Didst not thou share? Hadst thou not fifteen pence?

FALSTAFF   Reason, you rogue, reason. Think'st thou I'll
       endanger my soul gratis? At a word, hang no more about
15   me, I am no gibbet for you. Go — a short knife and a throng
       — to your manor of Picked-hatch, go! You'll not bear a letter
       for me, you rogue. You stand upon your honour. Why, thou
       unconfinable baseness, it is as much as I can do to keep the
       terms of my honour precise. Ay, ay, I myself sometimes,
20   leaving the fear of heaven on the left hand, and hiding mine
       honour in my necessity, am fain to shuffle, to hedge and to
       lurch: and yet, you rogue, will ensconce your rags, your cat-
       a-mountain looks, your red-lattice phrases, and your bold-
       beating oaths, under the shelter of your honour? You will
25   not do it? You?

PISTOL   I do relent. What would thou more of man?

[*Enter Robin*]

ROBIN   Sir, here's a woman would speak with you.

2.2   5 countenance to pawn borrow money on the strength of being in my service
countenance standing/reputation   **grated upon** harassed with demands   **6 coach-fellow**
companion (literally, one of a pair of horses harnessed to a coach)   **7 grate** prison bars (plays
on **grated**)   **gemini** pair   **10 handle . . . fan** these were often made of precious material such
as ivory or silver   **took't upon** swore by   **12 share** have a share in it   **13 Reason** with good
reason   **14 gratis** for nothing   **hang . . . me** cease to be a burden to me (**hang** plays on
the sense of "put to death")   **15 a . . . throng** i.e. go and find a crowd where you may cut
people's purse strings with a short knife   **16 Picked-hatch** a brothel or a disreputable part of
London (literally, the half-door surmounted by spikes that may have characterized a brothel)
18 unconfinable limitless/infinite   **19 precise** pure/scrupulously observed   **20 on . . . hand**
disregarded/to one side   **21 fain . . . lurch** obliged to deceive, dodge, and cheat   **22 ensconce**
hide, as in a small fort (sconce)   **cat-a-mountain** wildcat   **23 red-lattice** alehouse (wooden
lattices painted red characterized a tavern)   **bold-beating** excessively presumptuous/
repeatedly coarse   **26 relent** yield

FALSTAFF   Let her approach.

[*Enter Mistress Quickly*]

MISTRESS QUICKLY   Give your worship good morrow.

30   **FALSTAFF**   Good morrow, good wife.

MISTRESS QUICKLY   Not so, an't please your worship.

FALSTAFF   Good maid, then.

MISTRESS QUICKLY   That I am, I'll be sworn,

As my mother was the first hour I was born.

35   **FALSTAFF**   I do believe the swearer. What with me?

MISTRESS QUICKLY   Shall I vouchsafe your worship a word or two?

FALSTAFF   Two thousand, fair woman, and I'll vouchsafe thee the hearing.

MISTRESS QUICKLY   There is one Mistress Ford, sir — I pray come

40   a little nearer this ways— I myself dwell with master Doctor Caius—

FALSTAFF   Well, on. Mistress Ford, you say—

MISTRESS QUICKLY   Your worship says very true. I pray your worship come a little nearer this ways.

45   **FALSTAFF**   I warrant thee nobody hears. Mine   *Gestures toward* own people, mine own people.   *Pistol and Robin*

MISTRESS QUICKLY   Are they so? Heaven bless them, and make them his servants.

FALSTAFF   Well, Mistress Ford: what of her?

50   **MISTRESS QUICKLY**   Why, sir, she's a good creature. Lord, lord, your worship's a wanton! Well, heaven forgive you, and all of us, I pray—

FALSTAFF   Mistress Ford, come, Mistress Ford.

MISTRESS QUICKLY   Marry, this is the short and the long of it: you

55   have brought her into such a canaries as 'tis wonderful. The best courtier of them all — when the court lay at Windsor — could never have brought her to such a canary. Yet there has

---

29 Give God give   **31 Not so** i.e. I am not a **wife**   **34 As . . . born** Quickly means "just as much of an innocent maid as I was when I was born, like my mother was before me," but actually says "just as much of a virgin as my mother was in childbirth"   **37 vouchsafe** permit (Quickly means something like "entreat")   **40 ways** way   **42 on** go on   **51 wanton** seducer/ lewd person/unruly one   **55 canaries** malapropism for "quandary"; a canary was either a dance or a wine   **wonderful** astonishing

been knights, and lords, and gentlemen, with their coaches,
I warrant you —coach after coach, letter after letter, gift
60   after gift, smelling so sweetly, all musk, and so rushling, I
warrant you, in silk and gold, and in such alligant terms, and
in such wine and sugar of the best and the fairest that would
have won any woman's heart: and, I warrant you, they
could never get an eye-wink of her. I had myself twenty
65   angels given me this morning, but I defy all angels — in any
such sort, as they say — but in the way of honesty: and, I
warrant you, they could never get her so much as sip on a
cup with the proudest of them all. And yet there has been
earls, nay, which is more, pensioners, but, I warrant you, all
70   is one with her.

FALSTAFF   But what says she to me? Be brief, my good she-
Mercury.

MISTRESS QUICKLY   Marry, she hath received your letter, for the
which she thanks you a thousand times; and she gives you to
75   notify that her husband will be absence from his house
between ten and eleven.

FALSTAFF   Ten and eleven.

MISTRESS QUICKLY   Ay, forsooth, and then you may come and see
the picture, she says, that you wot of. Master Ford, her
80   husband, will be from home. Alas, the sweet woman leads an
ill life with him: he's a very jealousy man. She leads a very
frampold life with him, good heart.

FALSTAFF   Ten and eleven. Woman, commend me to her. I will
not fail her.

85   MISTRESS QUICKLY   Why, you say well. But I have another
messenger to your worship. Mistress Page hath her hearty
commendations to you too: and let me tell you in your ear,

---

60 rushling Quickly means "rustling"   **61 alligant** Quickly means "elegant"; **alligant** was a
form of "alicant," a Spanish wine   **64 eye-wink of** glance from   **65 angels** i.e. as a bribe for
her help from one of the suitors   **66 sort** manner/way   **69 pensioners** "poor knights of
Windsor," who prayed for the king in return for an annuity   **71 she-Mercury** female Mercury,
the messenger of the gods   **75 notify** understand/take note   **79 wot** know   **82 frampold**
sour-tempered   **86 messenger** Quickly means "message"

she's as fartuous a civil modest wife, and one, I tell you, that
will not miss you morning nor evening prayer, as any is in
90 Windsor, whoe'er be the other: and she bade me tell your
worship that her husband is seldom from home, but she
hopes there will come a time. I never knew a woman so dote
upon a man. Surely I think you have charms, la. Yes, in truth.

FALSTAFF   Not I, I assure thee. Setting the attraction of my
95 good parts aside, I have no other charms.

MISTRESS QUICKLY   Blessing on your heart for't!

FALSTAFF   But I pray thee tell me this: has Ford's wife and
Page's wife acquainted each other how they love me?

MISTRESS QUICKLY   That were a jest indeed! They have not so little
100 grace, I hope — that were a trick indeed! But Mistress Page
would desire you to send her your little page, of all loves. Her
husband has a marvellous infection to the little page, and
truly Master Page is an honest man. Never a wife in Windsor
leads a better life than she does: do what she will, say what
105 she will, take all, pay all, go to bed when she list, rise when
she list, all is as she will, and truly she deserves it, for if there
be a kind woman in Windsor, she is one. You must send her
your page, no remedy.

FALSTAFF   Why, I will.

110 MISTRESS QUICKLY   Nay, but do so, then, and, look you, he may
come and go between you both: and in any case have a nay-
word, that you may know one another's mind, and the boy
never need to understand anything, for 'tis not good that
children should know any wickedness. Old folks, you know,
115 have discretion, as they say, and know the world.

FALSTAFF   Fare thee well, commend me to them both. There's
my purse: I am yet thy debtor.— Boy, go along with this
woman.   [*Exeunt Mistress Quickly and Robin*]
This news distracts me.

---

88 fartuous Quickly means "virtuous"   **civil modest** decent and proper   **89 miss you** miss
(**you** is emphatic)   **93 charms** magic spells   **95 parts** personal qualities/physical features
100 grace decency   **101 of all loves** for the sake of love   **102 infection to** Quickly means
"affection for"   **105 list** pleases   **107 kind** plays on the sense of "sexually willing"
111 nay-word code word   **119 distracts** bewilders

120 PISTOL   This punk is one of Cupid's carriers.
            Clap on more sails, pursue, up with your fights,
            Give fire. She is my prize, or ocean whelm them all!   [*Exit*]

FALSTAFF   Say'st thou so, old Jack? Go thy ways: I'll make more
            of thy old body than I have done. Will they yet look after
125   thee? Wilt thou, after the expense of so much money, be now
            a gainer? Good body, I thank thee. Let them say 'tis grossly
            done, so it be fairly done, no matter.

[*Enter Bardolph, with a goblet*]

BARDOLPH   Sir John, there's one Master Broom below would
            fain speak with you and be acquainted with you, and hath
130   sent your worship a morning's draught of sack.

FALSTAFF   Broom is his name?

BARDOLPH   Ay, sir.

FALSTAFF   Call him in.   [*Exit Bardolph*]
            Such Brooms are welcome to me, that o'erflows such liquor.
135   Aha, Mistress Ford and Mistress Page, have I encompassed
            you? Go to, *via*!

[*Enter Bardolph, with Ford disguised, carrying a bag of money*]

FORD   Bless you, sir.

FALSTAFF   And you, sir. Would you speak with me?

FORD   I make bold to press with so little preparation upon
140   you.

FALSTAFF   You're welcome. What's your will? Give us leave,
            drawer.   [*Exit Bardolph*]

FORD   Sir, I am a gentleman that have spent much: my
            name is Broom.

145 FALSTAFF   Good Master Broom, I desire more acquaintance
            of you.

---

120 punk prostitute   **carriers** messengers   **121 Clap** put (promptly)   **fights** screens used during a sea battle to protect the crew   **122 prize** treasure/captured vessel   **whelm** capsize/sink   **123 Say'st . . . Jack?** i.e. is that how things are (Falstaff is talking to himself) **124 look after** look at (desirously)   **126 grossly** clumsily/coarsely (puns on the sense of "fat") **127 so** as long as   **fairly** fully/well (puns on the sense of "handsome")   **129 fain** eagerly **135 encompassed** got hold of/got around (plays on the sense of "embraced")   **136 *via*** Italian exclamation of encouragement to action   **139 make bold** am presumptuous   **preparation** advance warning   **141 Give us leave** leave us please   **142 drawer** one who draws liquor/a tapster

FORD   Good Sir John, I sue for yours: not to charge you, for I must let you understand I think myself in better plight for a lender than you are, the which hath something emboldened
150   me to this unseasoned intrusion. For they say, if money go before, all ways do lie open.

FALSTAFF   Money is a good soldier, sir, and will on.

FORD   Troth, and I have a bag of money here troubles me. If you will help to bear it, Sir John, take all, or   *Sets it down*
155   half, for easing me of the carriage.

FALSTAFF   Sir, I know not how I may deserve to be your porter.

FORD   I will tell you, sir, if you will give me the hearing.

FALSTAFF   Speak, good Master Broom: I shall be glad to be your servant.

160   FORD   Sir, I hear you are a scholar — I will be brief with you — and you have been a man long known to me, though I had never so good means as desire to make myself acquainted with you. I shall discover a thing to you, wherein I must very much lay open mine own imperfection. But,
165   good Sir John, as you have one eye upon my follies, as you hear them unfolded, turn another into the register of your own, that I may pass with a reproof the easier, sith you yourself know how easy it is to be such an offender.

FALSTAFF   Very well, sir, proceed.

170   FORD   There is a gentlewoman in this town, her husband's name is Ford.

FALSTAFF   Well, sir.

FORD   I have long loved her, and, I protest to you, bestowed much on her: followed her with a doting observance,
175   engrossed opportunities to meet her, fee'd every slight occasion that could but niggardly give me sight of her: not only bought many presents to give her, but have given largely to many to know what she would have given. Briefly, I have

---

147 sue beg   **charge** burden—i.e. with expense   **148 plight** condition/health
150 unseasoned unseasonable/ill-timed   **152 on** go forward   **155 carriage** carrying (of it)
163 discover reveal   **166 register** record   **167 sith** since   **174 observance** attentiveness/
dutiful service   **175 engrossed** gathered   **fee'd** employed   **177 largely** generously
178 would have given would like to have given to her

pursued her as love hath pursued me, which hath been on the
180   wing of all occasions. But whatsoever I have merited, either
in my mind or in my means, meed I am sure I have received
none, unless experience be a jewel that I have purchased at an
infinite rate, and that hath taught me to say this:
      'Love like a shadow flies when substance love pursues,
185   Pursuing that that flies, and flying what pursues.'

FALSTAFF   Have you received no promise of satisfaction at her
            hands?

FORD   Never.

FALSTAFF   Have you importuned her to such a purpose?

190   FORD   Never.

FALSTAFF   Of what quality was your love, then?

FORD   Like a fair house built on another man's ground, so
        that I have lost my edifice by mistaking the place where I
        erected it.

195   FALSTAFF   To what purpose have you unfolded this to me?

FORD   When I have told you that, I have told you all.
        Some say that though she appear honest to me, yet in other
        places she enlargeth her mirth so far that there is shrewd
        construction made of her. Now, Sir John, here is the heart of
200   my purpose: you are a gentleman of excellent breeding,
        admirable discourse, of great admittance, authentic in your
        place and person, generally allowed for your many war-like,
        court-like and learned preparations.

FALSTAFF   O, sir!

205   FORD   Believe it, for you know it. There is   *Points to the bag*
        money: spend it, spend it, spend more, spend all I have, only
        give me so much of your time in exchange of it, as to lay an
        amiable siege to the honesty of this Ford's wife. Use your art

---

181 means methods/resources/wealth   **meed** reward   **184 flies** flees   **substance** wealth/
body (as opposed to **shadow**)   **185 that flies** which runs away from it (**love**)   **186 satisfaction**
payment/sexual gratification   **189 importuned** urged   **194 erected** plays on the idea of
penile erection   **197 honest** chaste   **198 mirth** enjoyment of pleasure/merriment   **shrewd
construction** malicious judgment   **201 great admittance** i.e. widely received by society/
admitted by the best persons   **authentic** respectable   **202 generally allowed** approved of by
all   **203 preparations** accomplishments   **208 amiable** amorous

of wooing, win her to consent to you. If any man may, you
210   may as soon as any.

FALSTAFF   Would it apply well to the vehemency of your
affection that I should win what you would enjoy? Methinks
you prescribe to yourself very preposterously.

FORD   O, understand my drift: she dwells so securely on
215   the excellency of her honour that the folly of my soul dares
not present itself. She is too bright to be looked against. Now,
could I come to her with any detection in my hand, my
desires had instance and argument to commend themselves:
I could drive her then from the ward of her purity, her
220   reputation, her marriage-vow, and a thousand other her
defences, which now are too too strongly embattled against
me. What say you to't, Sir John?

FALSTAFF   Master Broom, I will first make bold with your
money. Next, give me your hand. And last, as   *Takes the bag*
225   I am a gentleman, you shall, if you will, enjoy Ford's wife.

FORD   O, good sir!

FALSTAFF   I say you shall.

FORD   Want no money, Sir John: you shall want none.

FALSTAFF   Want no Mistress Ford, Master Broom, you shall
230   want none. I shall be with her, I may tell you, by her own
appointment. Even as you came in to me, her assistant or go-
between parted from me. I say I shall be with her between ten
and eleven, for at that time the jealous rascally knave her
husband will be forth. Come you to me at night: you shall
235   know how I speed.

FORD   I am blest in your acquaintance. Do you know
Ford, sir?

FALSTAFF   Hang him, poor cuckoldly knave, I know him not.
Yet I wrong him to call him poor: they say the jealous

---

211 **apply well to** be appropriate to/fit in with   213 **preposterously** perversely/irrationally/
foolishly   214 **drift** plan   215 **folly** lewdness/foolishness   216 **against** at directly (as if she
were the sun)   217 **detection** accusation/exposure   218 **instance** evidence   219 **ward**
protection/defensive posture (a fencing term)   220 **her** of her   228 **Want** lack   234 **forth**
away from home   235 **speed** get on/succeed

240   wittolly knave hath masses of money, for the which his wife
        seems to me well-favoured. I will use her as the key of the
        cuckoldly rogue's coffer, and there's my harvest-home.

FORD   I would you knew Ford, sir, that you might avoid
        him if you saw him.

245 FALSTAFF   Hang him, mechanical salt-butter rogue! I will stare
        him out of his wits, I will awe him with my cudgel. It shall
        hang like a meteor o'er the cuckold's horns. Master Broom,
        thou shalt know I will predominate over the peasant, and
        thou shalt lie with his wife. Come to me soon at night. Ford's
250   a knave, and I will aggravate his style. Thou, Master Broom,
        shalt know him for knave and cuckold. Come to me soon at
        night.   [Exit]

FORD   What a damned Epicurean rascal is this? My heart is
        ready to crack with impatience. Who says this is improvident
255   jealousy? My wife hath sent to him, the hour is fixed, the
        match is made. Would any man have thought this? See the
        hell of having a false woman: my bed shall be abused, my
        coffers ransacked, my reputation gnawn at, and I shall not
        only receive this villainous wrong, but stand under the
260   adoption of abominable terms, and by him that does me this
        wrong. Terms, names! Amaimon sounds well: Lucifer, well:
        Barbason, well: yet they are devils' additions, the names of
        fiends. But Cuckold? Wittol? Cuckold? The devil himself hath
        not such a name. Page is an ass, a secure ass. He will trust his
265   wife, he will not be jealous. I will rather trust a Fleming with
        my butter, Parson Hugh the Welshman with my cheese, an
        Irishman with my aqua-vitae bottle, or a thief to walk my

---

240 wittolly contentedly cuckolded   **the which** which reason   **241 well-favoured**
good-looking   **242 harvest-home** harvest gathered in/celebratory harvest festival
245 mechanical base, coarse (from the word for a manual worker)   **salt-butter** cheap
247 meteor considered to be a bad omen   **248 predominate** have ascendancy (an astrological
term)   **250 aggravate his style** add to his title (by calling him **cuckold** and **knave**)
253 Epicurean pleasure-loving/sensual   **254 improvident** unwary/rash   **257 false**
unfaithful/dishonest   **259 stand . . . terms** have to put up with being called offensive names
261 Amaimon . . . Barbason names of devils   **262 additions** names/titles   **264 secure** over-
confident/unsuspecting   **265 Fleming** person from Flanders (a country in the Netherlands,
whose inhabitants were supposedly very fond of **butter**)   **267 aqua-vitae** strong spirits such
as whiskey   **walk** exercise

ambling gelding, than my wife with herself. Then she plots,
then she ruminates, then she devises: and what they think in
270 their hearts they may effect — they will break their hearts
but they will effect. Heaven be praised for my jealousy!
Eleven o'clock the hour. I will prevent this, detect my wife, be
revenged on Falstaff, and laugh at Page. I will about it. Better
three hours too soon than a minute too late. Fie, fie, fie!
275 Cuckold, cuckold, cuckold!   *Exit*

Act 2 Scene 3   *running scene 7*

Enter Caius and Rugby

CAIUS	Jack Rugby!
RUGBY	Sir?
CAIUS	Vat is the clock, Jack?
RUGBY	'Tis past the hour, sir, that Sir Hugh promised to
5		meet.
CAIUS	By gar, he has save his soul, dat he is no come. He
	has pray his Pible well, dat he is no come. By gar, Jack Rugby,
	he is dead already, if he be come.
RUGBY	He is wise, sir. He knew your worship would kill
10		him, if he came.
CAIUS	By gar, de herring is no dead, so as I vill kill *Draws*
	him. Take your rapier, Jack. I vill tell you how I vill kill him.
RUGBY	Alas, sir, I cannot fence.
CAIUS	Villainy, take your rapier.
15 | RUGBY | Forbear. Here's company.   *Caius sheathes his sword* |

[*Enter Host, Shallow, Slender and Page*]

HOST	Bless thee, bully doctor.
SHALLOW	'Save you, Master Doctor Caius.
PAGE	Now, good master doctor.
SLENDER	Give you good morrow, sir.
20 | CAIUS | Vat be all you, one, two, tree, four, come for? |

---

268 ambling gelding easily ridden horse   **2.3   11 no . . . as** not so dead as he will be when
14 Villainy i.e. villain   **17 'Save** God save

HOST   To see thee fight, to see thee foin, to see thee traverse,
to see thee here, to see thee there, to see thee pass thy punto,
thy stock, thy reverse, thy distance, thy montant. Is he dead,
my Ethiopian? Is he dead, my Francisco? Ha, bully! What says
25   my Aesculapius, my Galen, my heart of elder? Ha? Is he dead,
bully stale? Is he dead?

CAIUS   By gar, he is de coward Jack-priest of de vorld. He is
not show his face.

HOST   Thou art a Castalion king-urinal. Hector of Greece,
30   my boy!

CAIUS   I pray you bear witness that me have stay, six or
seven, two, tree hours for him, and he is no come.

SHALLOW   He is the wiser man, Master Doctor: he is a curer of
souls, and you a curer of bodies. If you should fight, you go
35   against the hair of your professions. Is it not true, Master
Page?

PAGE   Master Shallow, you have yourself been a great
fighter, though now a man of peace.

SHALLOW   Bodykins, Master Page, though I now be old and of
40   the peace, if I see a sword out, my finger itches to make one.
Though we are justices and doctors and churchmen, Master
Page, we have some salt of our youth in us. We are the sons
of women, Master Page.

PAGE   'Tis true, Master Shallow.

45   SHALLOW   It will be found so, Master Page.— Master Doctor
Caius, I am come to fetch you home. I am sworn of the peace.
You have showed yourself a wise physician, and Sir Hugh

---

21 foin thrust/lunge with a sword   **traverse** pierce with a sword/move from side to side in fencing   **22 punto, thy stock** thrust with the point of the sword   **23 reverse** backhanded thrust or "punto reverso"   **distance** (awareness of) the distance that must be kept from the opponent   **montant** upward thrust   **24 Ethiopian** i.e. person of dark hair and complexion   **Francisco** i.e. Frenchman   **25 Aesculapius** Greek god of medicine   **Galen** famous second-century Greek physician   **heart of elder** i.e. as opposed to the firm "heart of oak" that denoted courage; the elder tree is low and has soft wood   **26 bully stale** my old laughing-stock/my old inspector of urine (i.e. doctor)   **29 Castalion** perhaps suggesting Spanish (from Castile)   **king-urinal** ruler over urine diagnosis   **Hector of Greece** the famed warrior was in fact from Troy   **35 against the hair** contrary to/against the grain   **39 Bodykins** by God's dear body   **40 make one** join in   **42 salt** savor/liveliness

hath shown himself a wise and patient churchman. You
must go with me, Master Doctor.

50 **HOST**   Pardon, guest-justice. A word, Monsieur Mockwater.

CAIUS   Mock-vater? Vat is dat?

HOST   Mockwater, in our English tongue, is valour, bully.

CAIUS   By gar, then I have as much mock-vater as de
Englishman. Scurvy Jack-dog priest! By gar, me vill cut his
55 ears.

HOST   He will clapper-claw thee tightly, bully.

CAIUS   Clapper-de-claw? Vat is dat?

HOST   That is, he will make thee amends.

CAIUS   By gar, me do look he shall clapper-de-claw me, for,
60 by gar, me vill have it.

HOST   And I will provoke him to't, or let him wag.

CAIUS   Me tank you for dat.

HOST   And, moreover, bully— but first,   *Speaks aside*
Master guest, and Master Page, and eke   *with Shallow,*
65 Cavaliero Slender, go you through the   *Page and Slender*
town to Frogmore.

PAGE   Sir Hugh is there, is he?

HOST   He is there. See what humour he is in. And I will
bring the doctor about by the fields. Will it do well?

70 **SHALLOW**   We will do it.

PAGE, SHALLOW and **SLENDER**   Adieu, good Master Doctor.

[*Exeunt Page, Shallow and Slender*]

CAIUS   By gar, me vill kill de priest, for he speak for a jack-
an-ape to Anne Page.

HOST   Let him die. Sheathe thy impatience, throw cold
75 water on thy choler. Go about the fields with me through
Frogmore. I will bring thee where Mistress Anne Page is, at a
farmhouse a-feasting, and thou shalt woo her. Cried game,
said I well?

---

50 guest-justice like Falstaff, Shallow is also staying at the Garter Inn   **Mockwater** i.e. one
who analyzes urine, perhaps with "mock" suggesting a degree of quackery (plays on "make
water"—i.e. urinate from fear)   **54 Jack-dog** male dog/mongrel/knavish dog   **56 clapper-
claw** beat/thrash   **66 Frogmore** small village near Windsor   **72 for a jack-an-ape** on behalf
of an ape (i.e. Slender)   **77 Cried game** probably a sporting exclamation

CAIUS	By gar, me dank you vor dat. By gar, I love you, and
80		I shall procure-a you de good guest: de earl, de knight, de
		lords, de gentlemen, my patients.
HOST	For the which I will be thy adversary toward Anne
		Page. Said I well?
CAIUS	By gar, 'tis good, vell said.
85	HOST	Let us wag, then.
CAIUS	Come at my heels, Jack Rugby. *Exeunt*

Act 3 Scene 1   *running scene 8*

Enter Evans and Simple.   *Evans with a sword in one hand and a book in the*
other, Simple carrying Evans' gown

EVANS   I pray you now, good master Slender's serving-man,
and friend Simple by your name, which way have you looked
for Master Caius, that calls himself doctor of physic?

SIMPLE   Marry, sir, the Petty-ward, the Park-ward, every
5   way: Old Windsor way, and every way but the town way.

EVANS   I most fehemently desire you, you will also look
that way.

SIMPLE   I will, sir.   *Steps aside and keeps watch*

EVANS   Pless my soul, how full of chollors I am, and
10   trempling of mind! I shall be glad if he have deceived me.
How melancholies I am! I will knog his urinals about his
knave's costard when I have good opportunities for the 'ork.
Pless my soul!
To shallow rivers, to whose falls   *Sings*
15   Melodious birds sings madrigals.

---

82 adversary the Host knows that Caius will misunderstand and take the word to mean
something like "advocate"   **3.1   3 physic** medicine   **4 Petty-ward** i.e. toward Windsor
Little ("petit") Park   **Park-ward** toward Windsor Great Park   **5 Old Windsor** village near
Windsor, south of **Frogmore   9 chollors** choler (i.e. bile/anger)   **11 knog** knock (possibly
"knot")   **urinals** vessel containing urine for medical inspection (possibly Evans confusedly
intends "testicles")   **12 costard** head (literally, large apple)   **14 To shallow rivers** throughout
the following two stanzas, Evans sings parts of Christopher Marlowe's well-known poem
"Come live with me and be my love"   **falls** cascades/waterfalls   **15 madrigals** songs for
several voices (more generally, pastoral or love songs)

There will we make our peds of roses,
And a thousand fragrant posies.
To shallow—
Mercy on me! I have a great dispositions to cry.

20   Melodious birds sing madrigals.   *Sings*
When as I sat in Pabylon
— And a thousand vagram posies.
To shallow, etc.

SIMPLE   Yonder he is coming, this way, Sir Hugh.

25 EVANS   He's welcome.
To shallow rivers, to whose falls—   *Sings*
Heaven prosper the right! What weapons is he?

SIMPLE   No weapons, sir. There comes my master, Master
Shallow, and another gentleman, from Frogmore, over the
30   stile, this way.

Enter Page, Shallow and Slender

EVANS   Pray you give me my gown, or else keep it in your
arms.   *Reads his Bible*

SHALLOW   How now, Master Parson? Good morrow, good Sir
Hugh. Keep a gamester from the dice, and a good student
35   from his book, and it is wonderful.

SLENDER   Ah, sweet Anne Page!   *Aside?*

PAGE   'Save you, good Sir Hugh!

EVANS   'Pless you from his mercy sake, all of you!

SHALLOW   What, the sword and the word? Do you study them
40   both, Master Parson?

PAGE   And youthful still: in your doublet and hose, this
raw rheumatic day?

EVANS   There is reasons and causes for it.

PAGE   We are come to you to do a good office, Master
45   Parson.

EVANS   Fery well: what is it?

---

21 **When . . . Pabylon** Evans inserts a line from the metrical version of Psalm 137   **Pabylon**
Babylon   22 **vagram** vagrant (malapropism for "fragrant")   24 **he** i.e. Caius   28 **No
weapons** presumably Simple means that, unlike Evans, Caius has not yet drawn his sword
38 **from** Evans means "for"   39 **word** i.e. scripture   41 **doublet and hose** close-fitting jacket
and breeches (without his **gown**)

PAGE   Yonder is a most reverend gentleman, who, belike, having received wrong by some person, is at most odds with his own gravity and patience that ever you saw.

50 SHALLOW   I have lived fourscore years and upward: I never heard a man of his place, gravity and learning so wide of his own respect.

EVANS   What is he?

PAGE   I think you know him: Master Doctor Caius, the
55 renowned French physician.

EVANS   Got's will, and his passion of my heart, I had as lief you would tell me of a mess of porridge.

PAGE   Why?

EVANS   He has no more knowledge in Hibocrates and
60 Galen, and he is a knave besides — a cowardly knave as you would desires to be acquainted withal.

PAGE   I warrant you, he's the man should fight   *To Shallow*
with him.

SLENDER   O sweet Anne Page!   *Aside?*

65 SHALLOW   It appears so by his weapons. Keep them asunder: here comes Doctor Caius.

[*Enter Host, Caius and Rugby*]   *Evans and Caius prepare to fight*

PAGE   Nay, good Master Parson, keep in your weapon.

SHALLOW   So do you, good Master Doctor.

HOST   Disarm them, and let them question.   *Shallow and*
70 Let them keep their limbs whole and hack   *Page take their*
our English.   *swords*

CAIUS   I pray you, let-a me speak a word with your ear. Vherefore vill you not meet-a me?

EVANS   Pray you, use your patience.— In good   *Aside to*
75 time.   *Caius/Aloud*

---

47 belike probably   **48 at most odds** at the greatest variance   **50 fourscore** eighty (literally, four times twenty)   **51 wide . . . respect** indifferent to his own reputation/far from proper consideration of himself/far from his own nature   **56 as lief** just as soon/rather   **57 mess of porridge** serving of meat and vegetable stew, eaten before the main course   **59 Hibocrates** Hippocrates, famous Greek physician of the fifth century BC   **60 a cowardly** i.e. as cowardly a   **62 he's** i.e. Evans   **69 question** dispute/debate   **70 hack our English** mangle the English language instead

CAIUS   By gar, you are de coward, de Jack dog, John ape.

EVANS   Pray you, let us not be laughing-stocks   *Aside to Caius*
to other men's humours. I desire you in friendship, and I will
one way or other make you amends.— I will knog your
80   urinal about your knave's coxcomb.   *Aloud*

CAIUS   *Diable*! Jack Rugby, mine host de Jarteer, have I not
stay for him to kill him? Have I not, at de place I did appoint?

EVANS   As I am a Christians soul, now look you, this is the
place appointed, I'll be judgement by mine host of the Garter.

85   HOST   Peace, I say, Gallia and Gaul, French and Welsh,
soul-curer and body-curer!

CAIUS   Ay, dat is very good, excellent.

HOST   Peace, I say. Hear mine host of the Garter. Am I
politic? Am I subtle? Am I a Machiavel? Shall I lose my doctor?
90   No, he gives me the potions and the motions. Shall I lose my
parson? My priest? My Sir Hugh? No, he gives me the
proverbs and the no-verbs. Give me thy hand,   *To Caius/*
terrestrial, so. Give me thy hand, celestial, so.   *To Evans*
Boys of art, I have deceived you both: I have directed you
95   to wrong places. Your hearts are mighty, your skins are
whole, and let burned sack be the issue.—   *To Page and*
Come, lay their swords to pawn.— Follow me,   *Shallow/To*
lads of peace, follow, follow, follow.   *Caius and Evans*

[*Exit*]

SHALLOW   Trust me, a mad host. Follow, gentlemen, follow.

100   SLENDER   O sweet Anne Page!   *Aside?*

[*Exeunt Shallow, Slender and Page*]

CAIUS   Ha, do I perceive dat? Have you make-a de sot of us,
ha, ha?

---

80 coxcomb head (literally, cap resembling the comb of a cock, worn by a professional fool)
82 stay waited   **84 judgement by** judged by/ruled by the judgment of   **85 Gallia and Gaul**
Wales (from the French "Galles") and France   **89 politic** cunning/wily   **subtle** crafty/sly
Machiavel intriguer/unscrupulous schemer (from Niccolò Machiavelli's *The Prince*, a
sixteenth-century treatise perceived as advocating political cunning)   **90 motions** bowel
motions (i.e. laxatives or enemas)   **92 no-verbs** warnings as to what is forbidden/(Welsh)
nonsense words   **93 terrestrial** i.e. Caius, who ministers to the body   **celestial** i.e. Evans,
who deals with spiritual matters   **94 art** skill/learning   **96 issue** outcome   **97 to pawn** i.e.
as they are no longer needed   **101 sot** fool

EVANS   This is well, he has made us his vlouting-stog. I
desire you that we may be friends, and let us knog our prains
105   together to be revenge on this same scall, scurvy cogging
companion, the host of the Garter.

CAIUS   By gar, with all my heart. He promise to bring me
where is Anne Page: by gar, he deceive me too.

EVANS   Well, I will smite his noddles. Pray you, follow.

[*Exeunt*]

Act 3 Scene 2

Enter Robin [followed by] Mistress Page

MISTRESS PAGE   Nay, keep your way, little gallant. You were wont
to be a follower, but now you are a leader. Whether had you
rather lead mine eyes, or eye your master's heels?

ROBIN   I had rather, forsooth, go before you like a man than
5   follow him like a dwarf.

MISTRESS PAGE   O, you are a flattering boy. Now I see you'll be a
courtier.

[*Enter Ford*]

FORD   Well met, Mistress Page. Whither go you?

MISTRESS PAGE   Truly, sir, to see your wife. Is she at home?

10   FORD   Ay, and as idle as she may hang together, for want of
company. I think, if your husbands were dead, you two
would marry.

MISTRESS PAGE   Be sure of that — two other husbands.

FORD   Where had you this pretty weather-cock?

15   MISTRESS PAGE   I cannot tell what the dickens his name is my
husband had him of. What do you call your knight's name,
sirrah?

---

103 vlouting-stog flouting-stock (i.e. laughingstock)   **105 scall** scald (i.e. scabby/scurvy/
contemptible)   **cogging companion** cheating rascal   **109 noddles** head   **3.2   1 keep
your way** keep going   **were wont** used   **2 Whether** which   **10 as . . . together** as idle as she
can be while remaining in one piece/those who are as idle as she is may as well keep each other
company   **15 his . . . of** is the name of the person my husband got the boy from

ROBIN   Sir John Falstaff.

FORD   Sir John Falstaff?

20 MISTRESS PAGE   He, he. I can never hit on's name. There is such a league between my good man and he. Is your wife at home indeed?

FORD   Indeed she is.

MISTRESS PAGE   By your leave, sir, I am sick till I see her.

[*Exeunt Mistress Page and Robin*]

25 FORD   Has Page any brains? Hath he any eyes? Hath he any thinking? Sure they sleep, he hath no use of them. Why, this boy will carry a letter twenty mile as easy as a cannon will shoot point-blank twelvescore. He pieces out his wife's inclination, he gives her folly motion and advantage. And 30 now she's going to my wife, and Falstaff's boy with her. A man may hear this shower sing in the wind. And Falstaff's boy with her. Good plots, they are laid, and our revolted wives share damnation together. Well, I will take him, then torture my wife, pluck the borrowed veil of modesty from the 35 so-seeming Mistress Page, divulge Page himself for a secure and wilful Actaeon, and to these violent proceedings all my neighbours shall cry aim. The clock gives me   *A clock strikes* my cue, and my assurance bids me search: there I shall find Falstaff. I shall be rather praised for this than mocked, for it is 40 as positive as the earth is firm that Falstaff is there. I will go.

[*Enter Page, Shallow, Slender, Host, Evans, Caius and Rugby*]

SHALLOW, PAGE *and* OTHERS   Well met, Master Ford.

FORD   Trust me, a good knot. I have good cheer at home, and I pray you all go with me.

SHALLOW   I must excuse myself, Master Ford.

---

21 **league** i.e. of friendship   28 **twelvescore** (from a distance of) 240 paces or yards   **pieces out** increases   29 **folly** lewdness   **motion and advantage** prompting and opportunity   31 **hear . . . wind** foresee what is to come (as one may anticipate rain before it actually arrives)   32 **revolted** i.e. from virtue and fidelity   33 **take him** catch him out/encounter him   35 **divulge** reveal   36 **wilful** willing   **Actaeon** i.e. a cuckold (due to the horns he received when turned into a stag)   37 **cry aim** applaud/shout encouragement (a term from archery)   42 **knot** group/company   **cheer** entertainment/food and drink

45 SLENDER   And so must I, sir. We have appointed to dine with
           Mistress Anne, and I would not break with her for more
           money than I'll speak of.

    SHALLOW   We have lingered about a match between Anne
           Page and my cousin Slender, and this day we shall have our
50   answer.

    SLENDER   I hope I have your good will, father Page.

    PAGE   You have, Master Slender, I stand wholly for you.
           But my wife, Master Doctor, is for you altogether.

    CAIUS   Ay, be-gar, and de maid is love-a me. My nursh-a
55   Quickly tell me so mush.

    HOST   What say you to young Master Fenton?   *To Page*
           He capers, he dances, he has eyes of youth, he writes verses,
           he speaks holiday, he smells April and May. He will carry't,
           he will carry't, 'tis in his buttons, he will carry't.

60 PAGE   Not by my consent, I promise you. The gentleman is
           of no having: he kept company with the wild prince and
           Poins. He is of too high a region, he knows too much. No, he
           shall not knit a knot in his fortunes with the finger of my
           substance. If he take her, let him take her simply: the wealth I
65   have waits on my consent, and my consent goes not that way.

    FORD   I beseech you heartily, some of you go home with
           me to dinner. Besides your cheer, you shall have sport: I will
           show you a monster. Master Doctor, you shall go, so shall
           you, Master Page, and you, Sir Hugh.

70 SHALLOW   Well, fare you well.— We shall have   *Aside to Slender*
           the freer wooing at Master Page's.

                                   [*Exeunt Shallow and Slender*]

    CAIUS   Go home, John Rugby, I come anon.   [*Exit Rugby*]

---

46 break with break my word to   **57 capers** is merry and lively/dances/leaps   **58 speaks
holiday** speaks in a lively, entertaining way/uses choice language   **carry't** be successful/carry
it off   **59 'tis . . . buttons** he has the essential quality within him/he is sure to succeed
61 having wealth, means   **wild . . . Poins** i.e. Prince Henry and Poins, who appear in
Shakespeare's *Henry IV* plays   **62 region** social standing   **63 knit a knot** secure/repair
64 substance wealth   **simply** i.e. as she is, with no dowry   **68 monster** i.e. Falstaff, imaged
here as a so-called monster exhibited at a fair   **72 anon** shortly

HOST	Farewell, my hearts. I will to my honest knight Falstaff, and drink canary with him.	[*Exit*]
75 FORD	I think I shall drink in pipe wine first with him. I'll make him dance.— Will you go, gentles?	*Aside* *Aloud*
ALL	Have with you to see this monster.	*Exeunt*

Act 3 Scene 3

running scene 10

Enter Mistress Ford and Mistress Page

MISTRESS FORD	What, John? What, Robert?
MISTRESS PAGE	Quickly, quickly! Is the buck-basket—
MISTRESS FORD	I warrant. What, Robin, I say!

[Enter John and Robert with a laundry basket]

MISTRESS PAGE	Come, come, come.
5 MISTRESS FORD	Here, set it down.
MISTRESS PAGE	Give your men the charge, we must be brief.
MISTRESS FORD	Marry, as I told you before, John and Robert, be ready here hard by in the brew-house, and when I suddenly call you, come forth, and without any pause or staggering take this basket on your shoulders: that done, trudge with it in all haste, and carry it among the whitsters in Datchet Mead, and there empty it in the muddy ditch close by the Thames side.

MISTRESS PAGE	You will do it?	*To John and Robert*
15 MISTRESS FORD	I ha' told them over and over, they lack no direction. Be gone, and come when you are called.	

[Exeunt John and Robert]

MISTRESS PAGE	Here comes little Robin.

[Enter Robin]

---

73 hearts fine friends   **74 canary** sweet wine from the Canary Islands (in Ford's response, he plays on the sense of "lively dance")   **75 pipe wine** wine from the wooden cask (**pipe** puns on the sense of "musical instrument")   **76 make him dance** i.e. make him leap/beat him **gentles** gentlemen   **77 Have with** we shall come   **3.3   2 buck-basket** laundry basket (to **buck** is to wash)   **6 charge** instructions   **8 hard** close   **brew-house** outhouse for brewing beer   **11 whitsters** bleachers of clothing   **Datchet Mead** meadow between Windsor Little Park and the River Thames

MISTRESS FORD   How now, my eyas-musket? What news with
you?

20   ROBIN   My master, Sir John, is come in at your back-door,
Mistress Ford, and requests your company.

MISTRESS PAGE   You little Jack-a-Lent, have you been true to us?

ROBIN   Ay, I'll be sworn. My master knows not of your
being here and hath threatened to put me into everlasting
25   liberty if I tell you of it: for he swears he'll turn me away.

MISTRESS PAGE   Thou'rt a good boy. This secrecy of thine shall
be a tailor to thee, and shall make thee a new doublet and
hose. I'll go hide me.

MISTRESS FORD   Do so.— Go tell thy master I am alone.   *To Robin*
[*Exit Robin*]

30   Mistress Page, remember you your cue.

MISTRESS PAGE   I warrant thee: if I do not act it, hiss me.   [*Exit*]

MISTRESS FORD   Go to, then. We'll use this unwholesome
humidity, this gross watery pumpion. We'll teach him to
know turtles from jays.

[*Enter Falstaff*]

35   FALSTAFF   Have I caught thee, my heavenly jewel? Why, now
let me die, for I have lived long enough: this is the period of
my ambition. O this blessèd hour!

MISTRESS FORD   O sweet Sir John!

FALSTAFF   Mistress Ford, I cannot cog, I cannot prate, Mistress
40   Ford. Now shall I sin in my wish: I would thy husband were
dead. I'll speak it before the best lord. I would make thee my
lady.

MISTRESS FORD   I your lady, Sir John? Alas, I should be a pitiful
lady!

45   FALSTAFF   Let the court of France show me such another. I see
how thine eye would emulate the diamond: thou hast the

---

18 eyas-musket young hawk that has not been fully trained   **22 Jack-a-Lent** figure or
puppet of a man traditionally pelted during Lent   **25 liberty** i.e. unemployment   **turn me
away** sack me   **33 humidity** dampness/collection of fluids (i.e. Falstaff)   **pumpion** pumpkin
34 turtles from jays turtledoves (proverbially faithful) from brightly colored birds (i.e. loose
women)   **35 Have . . . jewel?** a slightly adapted line from Philip Sidney's sonnet sequence
Astrophil and Stella   **36 period** goal/climax   **39 cog** cheat/flatter   **prate** prattle/brag

right arched beauty of the brow that becomes the ship-tire,
the tire-valiant, or any tire of Venetian admittance.

MISTRESS FORD   A plain kerchief, Sir John: my brows become
50   nothing else, nor that well neither.

FALSTAFF   Thou art a tyrant to say so: thou wouldst make an
absolute courtier, and the firm fixture of thy foot would give
an excellent motion to thy gait in a semi-circled farthingale.
I see what thou wert if Fortune thy foe were not, Nature thy
55   friend. Come, thou canst not hide it.

MISTRESS FORD   Believe me, there's no such thing in me.

FALSTAFF   What made me love thee? Let that persuade thee
there's something extraordinary in thee. Come, I cannot cog
and say thou art this and that, like a many of these lisping
60   hawthorn-buds that come like women in men's apparel and
smell like Bucklersbury in simple time. I cannot. But I love
thee, none but thee —and thou deservest it.

MISTRESS FORD   Do not betray me, sir. I fear you love Mistress
Page.

65   FALSTAFF   Thou mightst as well say I love to walk by the
Counter-gate, which is as hateful to me as the reek of a
lime-kiln.

MISTRESS FORD   Well, heaven knows how I love you, and you
shall one day find it.

70   FALSTAFF   Keep in that mind, I'll deserve it.

MISTRESS FORD   Nay, I must tell you, so you do, or else I could not
be in that mind.

---

47 ship-tire ornamental headdress shaped like or inspired by a ship   **48 tire-valiant** elaborate
headdress   **Venetian admittance** accepted as fashionable in stylish Venice   **49 kerchief**
simple head covering   **become** suit   **52 absolute** perfect   **firm . . . foot** confident tread
53 semi-circled farthingale semicircular boned petticoat worn underneath the back of the
dress   **54 Fortune . . . friend** i.e. Nature has favored Mistress Ford with beauty but Fortune
has prevented her from being a lady (Falstaff continues to imply that he could raise her estate)
60 hawthorn-buds i.e. budding courtiers/affected young gallants   **61 Bucklersbury** street in
the City of London known for shops selling medicinal herbs   **simple time** midsummer, when
herbs (simples) were most readily available   **66 Counter-gate** gate to the Counter, a debtor's
prison in Southwark   **reek** smoke/foul smell   **67 lime-kiln** kiln for making mortar

ROBIN   Mistress Ford, Mistress Ford, here's   *Speaks within*
Mistress Page at the door, sweating and blowing   *or enters*
75 and looking wildly, and would needs speak with you presently.

FALSTAFF   She shall not see me: I will ensconce me behind the
arras.   *Falstaff hides himself*

MISTRESS FORD   Pray you, do so: she's a very tattling woman.

[*Enter Mistress Page*]   *Robin may enter here*

What's the matter? How now?

80 MISTRESS PAGE   O Mistress Ford, what have you done? You're
shamed, you're overthrown, you're undone forever!

MISTRESS FORD   What's the matter, good Mistress Page?

MISTRESS PAGE   O, well-a-day, Mistress Ford, having an honest
man to your husband, to give him such cause of suspicion!

85 MISTRESS FORD   What cause of suspicion?

MISTRESS PAGE   What cause of suspicion? Out upon you! How
am I mistook in you?

MISTRESS FORD   Why, alas, what's the matter?

MISTRESS PAGE   Your husband's coming hither, woman, with all
90 the officers in Windsor, to search for a gentleman that he
says is here now in the house by your consent, to take an ill
advantage of his absence. You are undone.

MISTRESS FORD   'Tis not so, I hope.

MISTRESS PAGE   Pray heaven it be not so, that you have such a
95 man here! But 'tis most certain your husband's coming,
with half Windsor at his heels, to search for such a one. I
come before to tell you. If you know yourself clear, why, I am
glad of it: but if you have a friend here, convey, convey him
out. Be not amazed, call all your senses to you, defend your
100 reputation, or bid farewell to your good life forever.

MISTRESS FORD   What shall I do? There is a gentleman my dear
friend — and I fear not mine own shame so much as his peril.

---

74 blowing puffing   **75 presently** immediately   **76 ensconce me** hide myself   **77 arras**
large tapestry wall-hanging   **81 undone** ruined   **83 well-a-day** expression of regret   **84 to**
as   **86 Out upon you!** expression of frustration and condemnation   **97 clear** innocent/free
from blame   **98 friend** lover   **99 amazed** stunned   **100 good life** i.e. existence as a
respectable woman/reputation

I had rather than a thousand pound he were out of the house.

105 MISTRESS PAGE For shame, never stand 'you had rather' and 'you had rather'. Your husband's here at hand! Bethink you of some conveyance— in the house you cannot hide him. O, how have you deceived me? Look, here is a basket. If he be of any reasonable stature, he may creep in here, and throw foul
110 linen upon him, as if it were going to bucking. Or — it is whiting-time— send him by your two men to Datchet Mead.

MISTRESS FORD He's too big to go in there. What shall I do?

FALSTAFF Let me see't, let me see't, O, let me see't!   *Comes out*
I'll in, I'll in. Follow your friend's counsel. I'll in.   *of hiding*

115 MISTRESS PAGE What, Sir John Falstaff? Are these   *Aside to Falstaff*
your letters, knight?

FALSTAFF I love thee. Help me away. Let me creep in here. I'll
never—   *Gets into the basket. They cover him with foul*

MISTRESS PAGE Help to cover your master, boy.—   *linen/To Robin*
120 Call your men, Mistress Ford.— You dissembling   *To Falstaff*
knight!

MISTRESS FORD What, John! Robert! John!   [*Exit Robin*]
[*Enter John and Robert*]
Go take up these clothes here quickly. Where's the cowl-staff?
Look, how you drumble! Carry them to the   *They attempt to*
125 laundress in Datchet Mead. Quickly, come.   *fit the cowl-staff*
[*Enter Ford, Page, Caius and Evans*]

FORD Pray you, come near. If I suspect without   *To Page,*
cause, why then make sport at me, then let   *Caius and Evans*
me be your jest, I deserve it. How now? Whither bear you this?

130 JOHN To the laundress, forsooth.

MISTRESS FORD Why, what have you to do whither they bear it? You were best meddle with buck-washing.

---

105 stand waste time (saying)   **107 conveyance** contrivance to get Falstaff out of the house
111 whiting-time bleaching time   **120 dissembling** deceptive   **123 cowl-staff** pole used by
two people to carry a **cowl** (tub or basket)   **124 drumble** move sluggishly   **131 what . . . do**
what business is it of yours   **132 You . . . buck-washing** a proper concern of yours is it to
interfere with washing clothes

FORD   Buck? I would I could wash myself of the buck!
Buck, buck, buck! Ay, buck! I warrant you, buck — and of
135   the season too, it shall appear.

                                  [Exeunt John and Robert with the basket]
Gentlemen, I have dreamed tonight. I'll tell you my dream.
Here, here, here be my keys: ascend my chambers, search,
seek, find out. I'll warrant we'll unkennel the fox. Let me stop
this way first. So, now uncape.   *Locks the door*

140   PAGE   Good Master Ford, be contented. You wrong yourself
too much.

FORD   True, Master Page. Up, gentlemen. You shall see
sport anon. Follow me, gentlemen.   *[Exit]*

EVANS   This is fery fantastical humours and jealousies.

145   CAIUS   By gar, 'tis no the fashion of France: it is not jealous
in France.

PAGE   Nay, follow him, gentlemen. See the issue of his
search.

                               [Exeunt Page, Caius and Evans]

MISTRESS PAGE   Is there not a double excellency in this?

150   MISTRESS FORD   I know not which pleases me better, that my
husband is deceived, or Sir John.

MISTRESS PAGE   What a taking was he in, when your husband
asked who was in the basket!

MISTRESS FORD   I am half afraid he will have need of washing, so
155   throwing him into the water will do him a benefit.

MISTRESS PAGE   Hang him, dishonest rascal! I would all of the
same strain were in the same distress.

MISTRESS FORD   I think my husband hath some special suspicion
of Falstaff's being here, for I never saw him so gross in his
160   jealousy till now.

---

133 Buck laundry, but Ford puns on the senses of "stag," whose horns represent cuckoldry,
and "lecherous man"   **134 of the season** in the rutting season   **136 tonight** i.e. last night
137 chambers inner rooms/bedrooms   **138 unkennel** drive out   **139 uncape** uncover
(or perhaps a printer's error for "escape" or "uncase")   **140 contented** calm/satisfied
152 taking agitated state   **154 need of washing** i.e. as he may have urinated or defecated in
fright   **157 strain** nature

MISTRESS PAGE   I will lay a plot to try that, and we will yet have more tricks with Falstaff: his dissolute disease will scarce obey this medicine.

MISTRESS FORD   Shall we send that foolish carrion, Mistress
165 Quickly, to him, and excuse his throwing into the water, and give him another hope, to betray him to another punishment?

MISTRESS PAGE   We will do it: let him be sent for tomorrow eight o'clock to have amends.

[*Enter Ford, Page, Caius and Evans*]

FORD   I cannot find him. Maybe the knave bragged of that
170 he could not compass.

MISTRESS PAGE   Heard you that?   *Aside to Mistress Ford*

MISTRESS FORD   You use me well, Master Ford, do you?

FORD   Ay, I do so.

MISTRESS FORD   Heaven make you better than your thoughts!

175 FORD   Amen!

MISTRESS PAGE   You do yourself mighty wrong, Master Ford.

FORD   Ay, ay, I must bear it.

EVANS   If there be any pody in the house, and in the chambers, and in the coffers, and in the presses, heaven
180 forgive my sins at the day of judgement.

CAIUS   By gar, nor I too. There is no bodies.

PAGE   Fie, fie, Master Ford, are you not ashamed? What spirit, what devil suggests this imagination? I would not ha' your distemper in this kind for the wealth of Windsor Castle.

185 FORD   'Tis my fault, Master Page. I suffer for it.

EVANS   You suffer for a pad conscience: your wife is as honest a 'omans as I will desires among five thousand, and five hundred too.

CAIUS   By gar, I see 'tis an honest woman.

190 FORD   Well, I promised you a dinner. Come, come, walk in the park, I pray you pardon me. I will hereafter make known

---

161 try test   **164 carrion** old bag/whore   **170 compass** achieve/embrace   **172 use** treat
179 presses large cupboards   **184 distemper . . . kind** bad temper/disordered mind of this
sort   **187 as . . . desires** as I could possibly wish for (unintentionally punning on the sense of
"as I could desire sexually")

to you why I have done this. Come, wife, come, Mistress Page.
I pray you pardon me. Pray heartily pardon me.

PAGE   Let's go in, gentlemen, but trust me, we'll   *To Caius*
195   mock him.— I do invite you tomorrow morning   *and Evans*
to my house to breakfast. After, we'll a-birding   *To Ford,*
together, I have a fine hawk for the bush.   *Caius and Evans*
Shall it be so?

FORD   Anything.

200   EVANS   If there is one, I shall make two in the company.

CAIUS   If there be one or two, I shall make-a the turd.

FORD   Pray you, go, Master Page.

[*Exeunt all but Evans and Caius?*]

EVANS   I pray you now remembrance tomorrow on the
lousy knave, mine host.

205   CAIUS   Dat is good, by gar, with all my heart.

EVANS   A lousy knave, to have his gibes and his mockeries.

Exeunt

Act 3 Scene 4   *running scene 11*

Enter Fenton [and] Anne

FENTON   I see I cannot get thy father's love,
Therefore no more turn me to him, sweet Nan.

ANNE   Alas, how then?

FENTON   Why, thou must be thyself.

5   He doth object I am too great of birth,
And that, my state being galled with my expense,
I seek to heal it only by his wealth.
Besides these, other bars he lays before me:
My riots past, my wild societies,

---

196 a-birding hunt small birds using a **hawk** to drive them into leafless bushes
203 remembrance . . . host i.e. let us remember the revenge we have planned on the Host
for the trick he played on us over the duel   **3.4   2 turn** refer   **4 be thyself** i.e. take matters
into your own hands   **6 state . . . expense** my estate being damaged by my spending
galled made sore through chafing   **8 bars** obstacles   **9 riots** wasteful/dissipated lifestyle
societies companionships

10   And tells me 'tis a thing impossible
        I should love thee but as a property.

ANNE   Maybe he tells you true.

FENTON   No, heaven so speed me in my time to come!
        Albeit I will confess thy father's wealth
15   Was the first motive that I wooed thee, Anne,
        Yet, wooing thee, I found thee of more value
        Than stamps in gold or sums in sealèd bags.
        And 'tis the very riches of thyself
        That now I aim at.

20 ANNE   Gentle Master Fenton,
        Yet seek my father's love, still seek it, sir.
        If opportunity and humblest suit
        Cannot attain it, why, then — hark you hither!   *They speak apart*

[*Enter Shallow, Slender and Mistress Quickly*]

SHALLOW   Break their talk, Mistress Quickly. My kinsman shall
25   speak for himself.

SLENDER   I'll make a shaft or a bolt on't. 'Slid, 'tis but venturing.

SHALLOW   Be not dismayed.

SLENDER   No, she shall not dismay me: I care not for that, but
        that I am afeard.

30 MISTRESS QUICKLY   Hark ye, Master Slender would speak a word
        with you.

ANNE   I come to him.— This is my father's   *Aside to Fenton*
        choice.
        O, what a world of vile ill-favoured faults
        Looks handsome in three hundred pounds a year!

35 MISTRESS QUICKLY   And how does good Master Fenton? Pray you,
        a word with you.   *They speak apart*

SHALLOW   She's coming. To her, coz. O boy, thou hadst a father!

---

13 speed prosper   **17 stamps** coins (stamped with an image)   **24 Break** interrupt
26 I'll . . . on't i.e. I'll do it one way or another (a **shaft** is a slender arrow used in a longbow,
while a **bolt** is the shorter, thicker one used in a crossbow)   **'Slid** by God's eyelid (a common
phrase)   **but venturing** only a matter of having a go   **27 dismayed** frightened; Slender's
reply suggests that he does not understand the word   **33 ill-favoured** ugly   **37 thou . . .**
father i.e. remember that you had a valiant father/a father who once wooed a woman; Slender
misunderstands this as a prompt for conversation with Anne

SLENDER   I had a father, Mistress Anne: my uncle can tell you
good jests of him. Pray you, uncle, tell Mistress Anne the jest
40   how my father stole two geese out of a pen, good uncle.

SHALLOW   Mistress Anne, my cousin loves you.

SLENDER   Ay, that I do, as well as I love any woman in
Gloucestershire.

SHALLOW   He will maintain you like a gentlewoman.

45   SLENDER   Ay, that I will, come cut and long-tail, under the
degree of a squire.

SHALLOW   He will make you a hundred and fifty pounds
jointure.

ANNE   Good Master Shallow, let him woo for himself.

50   SHALLOW   Marry, I thank you for it: I thank you for that good
comfort. She calls you, coz. I'll leave you.   *Stands aside*

ANNE   Now, Master Slender.

SLENDER   Now, good Mistress Anne.

ANNE   What is your will?

55   SLENDER   My will? 'Od's heartlings, that's a pretty jest indeed!
I ne'er made my will yet, I thank heaven. I am not such a
sickly creature, I give heaven praise.

ANNE   I mean, Master Slender, what would you with me?

SLENDER   Truly, for mine own part, I would little or nothing
60   with you. Your father and my uncle hath made motions. If it
be my luck, so; if not, happy man be his dole. They can tell
you how things go better than I can. You may ask your
father, here he comes.

[*Enter Page and Mistress Page*]

PAGE   Now, Master Slender — love him, daughter Anne.—
65   Why, how now? What does Master Fenton here?
You wrong me, sir, thus still to haunt my house:
I told you, sir, my daughter is disposed of.

---

45 come . . . long-tail come what may (literally, refers to a horse/dog with either a docked or a
long tail)   48 jointure marriage settlement provided for the wife by the husband in the event
of his death   54 will wish (Slender understands the legal sense of the term; there may also be
a play on the sense of "sexual desire")   55 'Od's heartlings by God's dear heart   60 motions
urgings   61 happy . . . dole i.e. may the man who gets you be happy with his lot   66 haunt
hang around

FENTON   Nay, Master Page, be not impatient.

MISTRESS PAGE   Good Master Fenton, come not to my child.

70 PAGE   She is no match for you.

FENTON   Sir, will you hear me?

PAGE   No, good Master Fenton.—
Come, Master Shallow. Come, son Slender, in.—
Knowing my mind, you wrong me, Master Fenton.

[Exeunt Page, Shallow and Slender]

75 MISTRESS QUICKLY   Speak to Mistress Page.

FENTON   Good Mistress Page, for that I love your daughter
In such a righteous fashion as I do,
Perforce, against all checks, rebukes and manners,
I must advance the colours of my love
80   And not retire. Let me have your good will.

ANNE   Good mother, do not marry me to yond fool.

MISTRESS PAGE   I mean it not, I seek you a better husband.

MISTRESS QUICKLY   That's my master, Master Doctor.

ANNE   Alas, I had rather be set quick i'th'earth,
85   And bowled to death with turnips!

MISTRESS PAGE   Come, trouble not yourself. Good Master Fenton,
I will not be your friend nor enemy:
My daughter will I question how she loves you,
And as I find her, so am I affected.
90   Till then, farewell, sir. She must needs go in,
Her father will be angry.

FENTON   Farewell, gentle mistress.— Farewell, Nan.

[Exeunt Mistress Page and Anne]

MISTRESS QUICKLY   This is my doing, now. 'Nay,' said I, 'will you
cast away your child on a fool, and a physician? Look on
95   Master Fenton.' This is my doing.

FENTON   I thank thee, and I pray thee once   *Gives her a ring*
tonight, Give my sweet Nan this ring. There's for   *and money*
thy pains.

---

76 for that because   **78 Perforce** of necessity   **checks** rebukes/obstacles   **manners** means
of behaving (to me)   **79 advance the colours** raise the flag (as if toward an opposing army)
81 yond yonder   **84 set quick** buried alive (up to the neck)   **89 affected** inclined   **96 once**
at some point   **97 There's** i.e. there's money

MISTRESS QUICKLY   Now heaven send thee good fortune.

[Exit Fenton]

100 A kind heart he hath. A woman would run through fire and water for such a kind heart. But yet I would my master had Mistress Anne, or I would Master Slender had her: or, in sooth, I would Master Fenton had her. I will do what I can for them all three, for so I have promised, and I'll be as good as

105 my word — but speciously for Master Fenton. Well, I must of another errand to Sir John Falstaff from my two mistresses. What a beast am I to slack it!   *Exit*

Act 3 Scene 5   *running scene 12*

Enter Falstaff

FALSTAFF   Bardolph, I say!

[Enter Bardolph]

BARDOLPH   Here, sir.

FALSTAFF   Go fetch me a quart of sack: put a toast in't.

[Exit Bardolph]

Have I lived to be carried in a basket like a barrow of butcher's

5 offal, and to be thrown in the Thames? Well, if I be served such another trick, I'll have my brains ta'en out and buttered, and give them to a dog for a new-year's gift. The rogues slighted me into the river with as little remorse as they would have drowned a blind bitch's puppies, fifteen i'th'litter. And

10 you may know by my size that I have a kind of alacrity in sinking: if the bottom were as deep as hell, I should down. I had been drowned, but that the shore was shelvy and shallow — a death that I abhor, for the water swells a man — and what a thing should I have been when I had been

15 swelled? I should have been a mountain of mummy.

[Enter Bardolph with sack]

---

103 sooth truth   **105 speciously** malapropism for "specially"   **of** be on   **3.5   3 quart** i.e. two pints   **toast** piece of hot toast sometimes added to wine   **4 barrow** barrow-load   **8 slighted me** tipped me contemptuously   **9 blind bitch's puppies** the newborn, blind puppies of a bitch   **11 down** sink   **12 shore was shelvy** banks were sloping   **15 mummy** dead flesh

BARDOLPH   Here's Mistress Quickly, sir, to speak with you.

FALSTAFF   Come. let me pour in some sack to the Thames
water, for my belly's as cold as if I had swallowed snowballs
for pills to cool the reins. Call her in.

20   BARDOLPH   Come in, woman.

[*Enter Mistress Quickly*]

MISTRESS QUICKLY   By your leave, I cry you mercy! Give your
worship good morrow.

FALSTAFF   Take away these chalices. Go, brew me   To Bardolph
a pottle of sack finely.

25   BARDOLPH   With eggs, sir?

FALSTAFF   Simple of itself. I'll no pullet-sperm in my brewage.—
How now?   [*Exit Bardolph*]

MISTRESS QUICKLY   Marry, sir, I come to your worship from
Mistress Ford.

30   FALSTAFF   Mistress Ford? I have had ford enough. I was thrown
into the ford, I have my belly full of ford.

MISTRESS QUICKLY   Alas the day, good heart, that was not her
fault. She does so take on with her men: they mistook their
erection.

35   FALSTAFF   So did I mine, to build upon a foolish woman's
promise.

MISTRESS QUICKLY   Well, she laments, sir, for it, that it would
yearn your heart to see it. Her husband goes this morning
a-birding. She desires you once more to come to her between
40   eight and nine. I must carry her word quickly. She'll make
you amends, I warrant you.

FALSTAFF   Well, I will visit her. Tell her so, and bid her think
what a man is. Let her consider his frailty, and then judge of
my merit.

---

19 reins kidneys   **21 cry you mercy** beg your pardon   **24 pottle** drinking vessel containing
half a gallon (equivalent to four pints)   **26 Simple** plain/unmixed (with eggs)   **I'll** I'll have
pullet-sperm chicken seed (i.e. eggs)   **31 ford** river water   **33 take on with** rant at, berate
34 erection malapropism for "direction" (i.e. instruction; Falstaff's response brings in the
architectural and phallic senses)   **38 yearn** move to compassion   **43 frailty** moral frailty
(contrasted here with Falstaff's supposed resolution in keeping his appointment with Mistress
Ford)

45 MISTRESS QUICKLY   I will tell her.

FALSTAFF   Do so. Between nine and ten, say'st thou?

MISTRESS QUICKLY   Eight and nine, sir.

FALSTAFF   Well, be gone. I will not miss her.

MISTRESS QUICKLY   Peace be with you, sir.   [*Exit*]

50 FALSTAFF   I marvel I hear not of Master Broom. He sent me word to stay within. I like his money well. O, here he comes.

[*Enter Ford, disguised as Broom*]

FORD   Bless you, sir!

FALSTAFF   Now, Master Broom, you come to know what hath passed between me and Ford's wife.

55 FORD   That indeed, Sir John, is my business.

FALSTAFF   Master Broom, I will not lie to you: I was at her house the hour she appointed me.

FORD   And sped you, sir?

FALSTAFF   Very ill-favouredly, Master Broom.

60 FORD   How so, sir? Did she change her determination?

FALSTAFF   No, Master Broom, but the peaking cornuto her husband, Master Broom, dwelling in a continual 'larum of jealousy, comes me in the instant of our encounter, after we had embraced, kissed, protested, and, as it were, spoke the
65 prologue of our comedy: and at his heels a rabble of his companions, thither provoked and instigated by his distemper, and, forsooth, to search his house for his wife's love.

FORD   What, while you were there?

FALSTAFF   While I was there.

70 FORD   And did he search for you, and could not find you?

FALSTAFF   You shall hear. As good luck would have it, comes in one Mistress Page, gives intelligence of Ford's approach: and, in her invention and Ford's wife's distraction, they conveyed me into a buck-basket.

75 FORD   A buck-basket?

---

48 miss fail to meet   **58 sped you** were you successful   **59 ill-favouredly** poorly
60 determination intention/decision   **61 peaking cornuto** skulking/mean-spirited cuckold
62 'larum alarm/agitation   **63 comes me** comes (**me** is an intensifier)   **64 protested** declared (love)

FALSTAFF   Yes, a buck-basket! Rammed me in with foul shirts
and smocks, socks, foul stockings, greasy napkins, that,
Master Broom, there was the rankest compound of villainous
smell that ever offended nostril.

80   FORD   And how long lay you there?

FALSTAFF   Nay, you shall hear, Master Broom, what I have
suffered to bring this woman to evil for your good. Being
thus crammed in the basket, a couple of Ford's knaves, his
hinds, were called forth by their mistress to carry me in the
85   name of foul clothes to Datchet Lane: they took me on their
shoulders, met the jealous knave their master in the door,
who asked them once or twice what they had in their basket.
I quaked for fear, lest the lunatic knave would have searched
it, but fate, ordaining he should be a cuckold, held his hand.
90   Well, on went he for a search, and away went I for foul
clothes. But mark the sequel, Master Broom. I suffered the
pangs of three several deaths: first, an intolerable fright, to
be detected with a jealous rotten bell-wether: next, to be
compassed, like a good bilbo in the circumference of a peck,
95   hilt to point, heel to head, and then, to be stopped in like a
strong distillation with stinking clothes that fretted in their
own grease. Think of that, a man of my kidney, think of
that — that am as subject to heat as butter — a man of
continual dissolution and thaw: it was a miracle to scape
100   suffocation. And in the height of this bath, when I was
more than half stewed in grease like a Dutch dish, to be

---

76 Rammed perhaps, coming after **buck**, with a play on "ram" (male sheep, horned like
the buck, and also associated with lust)   **77 that** so that   **83 knaves, his hinds** servants
(both terms may also be derogatory)   **89 held** withheld   **91 mark** note   **92 several**
separate   **93 detected with** discovered by   **rotten** diseased   **bell-wether** ram (sometimes
castrated) wearing a bell around his neck as a means of leading the flock   **94 compassed**
surrounded/bent over like a strong sword   **bilbo** sword from Bilbao, town in Spain noted for
excellent sword manufacture   **peck** two-gallon container used to store dry goods
95 stopped shut, stoppered   **96 distillation** concentrated substance   **fretted** became
corroded/fermented   **97 kidney** constitution/nature   **99 dissolution** melting/dissolving
(puns on the sense of "loose living")   **101 Dutch dish** the Dutch were supposedly very fond of
butter

thrown into the Thames, and cooled, glowing hot, in that
surge, like a horse-shoe. Think of that — hissing hot —
think of that, Master Broom.

105 FORD   In good sadness, sir, I am sorry that for my sake you
have suffered all this. My suit then is desperate. You'll
undertake her no more?

FALSTAFF   Master Broom, I will be thrown into Etna, as I have
been into Thames, ere I will leave her thus. Her husband is
110 this morning gone a-birding. I have received from her
another embassy of meeting: 'twixt eight and nine is the
hour, Master Broom.

FORD   'Tis past eight already, sir.

FALSTAFF   Is it? I will then address me to my appointment.
115 Come to me at your convenient leisure, and you shall know
how I speed. And the conclusion shall be crowned with your
enjoying her. Adieu. You shall have her, Master Broom.
Master Broom, you shall cuckold Ford.   [*Exit*]

FORD   Hum! Ha! Is this a vision? Is this a dream? Do I
120 sleep? Master Ford awake, awake, Master Ford! There's a hole
made in your best coat, Master Ford. This 'tis to be married,
this 'tis to have linen and buck-baskets. Well, I will proclaim
myself what I am. I will now take the lecher. He is at my
house. He cannot scape me, 'tis impossible he should. He
125 cannot creep into a halfpenny purse, nor into a pepper-box.
But, lest the devil that guides him should aid him, I will
search impossible places. Though what I am I cannot avoid,
yet to be what I would not shall not make me tame. If I have
horns to make one mad, let the proverb go with me: I'll be
130 horn-mad.   *Exit*

---

105 good sadness all seriousness   **108 Etna** volcano in Sicily   **111 embassy** message
120 hole . . . coat i.e. even I have a fault (proverbial; possibly with sexual connotations)
125 halfpenny purse small purse for small coins   **127 what I am** i.e. a cuckold   **130 horn-mad** wildly enraged, like a horned beast/madly jealous like a cuckold

Act 4 Scene 1

Enter Mistress Page, Mistress Quickly [and] William

MISTRESS PAGE   Is he at Master Ford's already, think'st thou?

MISTRESS QUICKLY   Sure he is by this, or will be presently. But truly he is very courageous mad about his throwing into the water. Mistress Ford desires you to come suddenly.

5   **MISTRESS PAGE**   I'll be with her by and by. I'll but bring my young man here to school. Look where his master comes. 'Tis a playing-day, I see.

[Enter Evans]

How now, Sir Hugh, no school today?

EVANS   No, Master Slender is let the boys leave to play.

10   **MISTRESS QUICKLY**   Blessing of his heart!

MISTRESS PAGE   Sir Hugh, my husband says my son profits nothing in the world at his book. I pray you, ask him some questions in his accidence.

EVANS   Come hither, William. Hold up your head. Come.

15   **MISTRESS PAGE**   Come on, sirrah, hold up your head. Answer your master, be not afraid.

EVANS   William, how many numbers is in nouns?

WILLIAM PAGE   Two.

MISTRESS QUICKLY   Truly, I thought there had been one number
20   more, because they say, 'Od's nouns'.

EVANS   Peace your tattlings! What is 'fair', William?

WILLIAM PAGE   *Pulcher*.

MISTRESS QUICKLY   Polecats? There are fairer things than polecats, sure.

4.1   2 by this by this time   **3 courageous** vigorously/extremely, or possibly a malapropism for "outrageous(ly)"   **4 suddenly** immediately   **7 playing-day** holiday   **9 is . . . play** i.e. has asked that the boys be given a holiday, the privilege of a visitor to the school   **13 accidence** principles of Latin grammar; the following examples are drawn from William Lilly and John Colet's *A Short Introduction of Grammer*, the official prescribed text for schools   **18 Two** i.e. single and plural   **20 'Od's nouns'** Quickly is confusing the abbreviated phrase "by God's (i.e. Christ's) wounds" with the idea of odd numbers   **21 Peace your tattlings!** Leave off your prattling!   **23 Polecats** weasel-like animals/whores (pronounced in a more similar manner than today, Quickly is confusing the word with the Latin *pulcher*)

25   EVANS   You are a very simplicity 'oman. I pray you peace.
      What is *lapis*, William?

      WILLIAM PAGE   A stone.

      EVANS   And what is 'a stone', William?

      WILLIAM PAGE   A pebble.

30   EVANS   No, it is *lapis*. I pray you, remember in your prain.

      WILLIAM PAGE   *Lapis.*

      EVANS   That is a good William. What is he, William, that
      does lend articles?

      WILLIAM PAGE   Articles are borrowed of the pronoun, and be
35   thus declined:
      Singulariter, nominativo, hic, haec, hoc.

      EVANS   *Nominativo, hig, hag, hog*, pray you mark: *genitivo,
      huius.* Well, what is your accusative case?

      WILLIAM PAGE   *Accusativo, hinc—*   *Faltering*

40   EVANS   I pray you, have your remembrance, child, *accusativo,
      hing, hang, hog.*

      MISTRESS QUICKLY   'Hang-hog' is Latin for bacon, I warrant you.

      EVANS   Leave your prabbles, 'oman. What is the focative
      case, William?

45   WILLIAM PAGE   O, — *vocativo*, O.

      EVANS   Remember, William, focative is *caret*.

      MISTRESS QUICKLY   And that's a good root.

      EVANS   'Oman, forbear.

      MISTRESS PAGE   Peace!

50   EVANS   What is your genitive case plural, William?

      WILLIAM PAGE   Genitive case?

      EVANS   Ay.

---

33 articles i.e. the (definite article) or a/an (indefinite article)   **34 Articles . . . hoc** a direct
quotation from Lilly's *Grammer*   **pronoun** part of speech used to designate an object without
naming it directly; e.g. "this/that"   **36 *Singulariter*** in the singular   ***nominativo*** in the
nominative case   ***hic, haec, hoc*** common Latin pronouns   **37 *genitivo*** the genitive case (is)
39 *hinc* the correct form is in fact *hunc*, though Evans fails to spot this (unless his subsequent
hing is a printer's error for *hung*)   **41 *hing, hang, hog*** i.e. *hunc, hanc, hoc*   **42 "Hang-hog"**
hanging up a pig is necessary to produce bacon   **43 prabbles** silly chatter/irritating
interruptions   **focative** i.e. vocative; Evans's pronunciation inadvertently plays on "fuck"
44 case plays on the sense of "vagina"   **45 O** suggestive of the vagina   **46 *caret*** Latin for "is
missing"; Quickly's response shows that she hears the word as "carrot," which, along with
root, is slang for "penis"

WILLIAM PAGE   Genitive: *horum, harum, horum*.

MISTRESS QUICKLY   Vengeance of Ginny's case, fie on her! Never
55   name her, child, if she be a whore.

EVANS   For shame, 'oman.

MISTRESS QUICKLY   You do ill to teach the child such words: he
teaches him to hick and to hack, which they'll do fast enough
of themselves, and to call 'horum' — fie upon you!

60   **EVANS**   'Oman, art thou lunatics? Hast thou no
understandings for thy cases and the numbers of the
genders? Thou art as foolish Christian creatures as I would
desires.

MISTRESS PAGE   Prithee, hold thy peace.   *To Mistress Quickly*

65   **EVANS**   Show me now, William, some declensions of your
pronouns.

WILLIAM PAGE   Forsooth, I have forgot.

EVANS   It is *qui, quae, quod*. If you forget your *quies*, your
quaes, and your *quods*, you must be preeches. Go your ways,
70   and play, go.

MISTRESS PAGE   He is a better scholar than I thought he was.

EVANS   He is a good sprag memory. Farewell, Mistress Page.

MISTRESS PAGE   Adieu, good Sir Hugh.   [*Exit Evans*]
Get you home, boy. Come, we stay too long.   *Exeunt*

Act 4 Scene 2   *running scene 14*

Enter Falstaff [*and*] *Mistress Ford*   *The basket is brought out*

FALSTAFF   Mistress Ford, your sorrow hath eaten up my
sufferance. I see you are obsequious in your love, and I
profess requital to a hair's breadth, not only, Mistress Ford,
in the simple office of love, but in all the accoutrement,

---

53 *horum* plays on "whore"   ***harum*** plays on "hare" (another slang term for a prostitute)
54 Vengeance of a plague upon   **Ginny's case** Quickly misunderstands "genitive case" as
"this woman Ginny's case (vagina)"   **58 hick . . . hack** drink (hiccup) and to go whoring/to
have sex (with whores)   **65 declension** the variation of a pronoun etc. through its different
cases   **69 preeches** breeched (i.e. whipped on the buttocks)   **72 sprag** i.e. sprack (smart/
alert)   **4.2   2 sufferance** suffering   **obsequious** compliant/dutiful   **4 office** role/(sexual)
performance   **4 accoutrement** adornments, apparel

5   complement and ceremony of it. But are you sure of your
       husband now?

MISTRESS FORD   He's a-birding, sweet Sir John.

MISTRESS PAGE   What, ho, gossip Ford! What, ho!   *Within*

MISTRESS FORD   Step into th'chamber, Sir John.   [*Exit Falstaff*]
[*Enter Mistress Page*]

10   **MISTRESS PAGE**   How now, sweetheart, who's at home besides
       yourself?

MISTRESS FORD   Why, none but mine own people.

MISTRESS PAGE   Indeed?

MISTRESS FORD   No, certainly.— Speak louder.   *Whispers to her*

15   **MISTRESS PAGE**   Truly, I am so glad you have nobody here.

MISTRESS FORD   Why?

MISTRESS PAGE   Why, woman, your husband is in his old lines
       again: he so takes on yonder with my husband, so rails
       against all married mankind, so curses all Eve's daughters
20   of what complexion soever, and so buffets himself on the
       forehead, crying, 'Peer out, peer out!', that any madness I
       ever yet beheld seemed but tameness, civility and patience
       to this his distemper he is in now. I am glad the fat knight is
       not here.

25   **MISTRESS FORD**   Why, does he talk of him?

MISTRESS PAGE   Of none but him, and swears he was carried
       out, the last time he searched for him, in a basket: protests to
       my husband he is now here, and hath drawn him and the
       rest of their company from their sport to make another
30   experiment of his suspicion. But I am glad the knight is not
       here: now he shall see his own foolery.

MISTRESS FORD   How near is he, Mistress Page?

MISTRESS PAGE   Hard by, at street end. He will be here anon.

MISTRESS FORD   I am undone. The knight is here.

---

5 complement accompanying etiquette   **sure of** secure from   **8 gossip** friend   **12 people**
i.e. servants   **17 lines** tricks   **18 takes on** rants   **20 complexion** appearance/coloring
21 Peer out i.e. show yourselves (addressed to his cuckold's horns)   **23 to** compared to
30 experiment trial

35   MISTRESS PAGE   Why then you are utterly shamed, and he's but
      a dead man. What a woman are you? Away with him, away
      with him! Better shame than murder.

    MISTRESS FORD   Which way should he go? How should I bestow
      him? Shall I put him into the basket again?

    [*Enter Falstaff*]

40   FALSTAFF   No, I'll come no more i'th'basket. May I not go out
      ere he come?

    MISTRESS PAGE   Alas, three of Master Ford's brothers watch the
      door with pistols, that none shall issue out: otherwise you
      might slip away ere he came. But what make you here?

45   FALSTAFF   What shall I do? I'll creep up into the chimney.

    MISTRESS FORD   There they always use to discharge their birding-
      pieces. Creep into the kiln-hole.

    FALSTAFF   Where is it?

    MISTRESS FORD   He will seek there, on my word. Neither press,
50   coffer, chest, trunk, well, vault, but he hath an abstract for
      the remembrance of such places, and goes to them by his
      note: there is no hiding you in the house.

    FALSTAFF   I'll go out then.

    MISTRESS PAGE   If you go out in your own semblance, you die,
55   Sir John — unless you go out disguised.

    MISTRESS FORD   How might we disguise him?

    MISTRESS PAGE   Alas the day, I know not. There is no woman's
      gown big enough for him: otherwise he might put on a hat, a
      muffler and a kerchief, and so escape.

60   FALSTAFF   Good hearts, devise something: any extremity rather
      than a mischief.

    MISTRESS FORD   My maid's aunt, the fat woman of Brentford,
      has a gown above.

---

38 bestow dispose of/stow (him) away   **44 what make you** what are you doing   **46 use . . .
birding-pieces** make it a custom to fire their guns   **47 kiln-hole** opening to the oven
50 abstract list   **54 semblance** appearance   **59 muffler** scarf covering part of the face and
the neck   **61 mischief** injury, misfortune   **62 Brentford** originally "Brainford," a village
between Windsor and London, known for amorous assignations   **63 above** upstairs

MISTRESS PAGE   On my word, it will serve him: she's as big as he
65   is — and there's her thrummed hat and her muffler too. Run
up, Sir John.

MISTRESS FORD   Go, go, sweet Sir John. Mistress Page and I will
look some linen for your head.

MISTRESS PAGE   Quick, quick! We'll come dress you straight: put
70   on the gown the while.   [*Exit Falstaff*]

MISTRESS FORD   I would my husband would meet him in this
shape. He cannot abide the old woman of Brentford; he swears
she's a witch, forbade her my house and hath threatened to
beat her.

75 **MISTRESS PAGE**   Heaven guide him to thy husband's cudgel, and
the devil guide his cudgel afterwards!

MISTRESS FORD   But is my husband coming?

MISTRESS PAGE   Ay, in good sadness is he, and talks of the basket
too, howsoever he hath had intelligence.

80 **MISTRESS FORD**   We'll try that, for I'll appoint my men to carry
the basket again, to meet him at the door with it, as they did
last time.

MISTRESS PAGE   Nay, but he'll be here presently. Let's go dress
him like the witch of Brentford.

85 **MISTRESS FORD**   I'll first direct my men what they shall do with
the basket. Go up, I'll bring linen for him straight.   [*Exit*]

MISTRESS PAGE   Hang him, dishonest varlet! We cannot misuse
him enough.

We'll leave a proof, by that which we will do,
Wives may be merry, and yet honest too.
90   We do not act that often jest and laugh,
'Tis old but true: still swine eat all the draff.   [*Exit*]

[*Enter Mistress Ford with John and Robert*]

---

65 thrummed fringed/with a shaggy surface   **68 look** look for   **69 straight** straight away
70 the while in the meantime   **72 shape** outward appearance/disguise   **78 good sadness**
all seriousness   **79 intelligence** information   **80 try** test   **87 dishonest** deceitful, lecherous
89 honest chaste, virtuous   **90 act** actually commit misdeeds/have sex   **91 still** quiet
draff swill, leftovers given to pigs

MISTRESS FORD   Go, sirs, take the basket again on your shoulders. Your master is hard at door. If he bid you set it down, obey him. Quickly, dispatch.   [*Exit*]

95 JOHN   Come, come, take it up.

ROBERT   Pray heaven it be not full of knight again.

JOHN   I hope not, I had as lief bear so much   *John and Robert* lead.   *lift the basket*

[*Enter Ford, Page, Shallow, Caius and Evans*]

FORD   Ay, but if it prove true, Master Page, have you any
100 way then to unfool me again?— Set down the   *John and Robert* basket, villain.   *set down the*

Somebody call my wife. Youth in a basket! O, you   *basket* panderly rascals, there's a knot, a gin, a pack, a conspiracy against me. Now shall the devil be shamed. What, wife, I say!
105 Come, come forth. Behold what honest clothes you send forth to bleaching.

PAGE   Why, this passes, Master Ford. You are not to go loose any longer, you must be pinioned.

EVANS   Why, this is lunatics, this is mad as a mad dog!

110 SHALLOW   Indeed, Master Ford, this is not well indeed.

FORD   So say I too, sir.

[*Enter Mistress Ford*]

Come hither, Mistress Ford — Mistress Ford the honest woman, the modest wife, the virtuous creature, that hath the jealous fool to her husband. I suspect without cause,
115 mistress, do I?

MISTRESS FORD   Heaven be my witness you do, if you suspect me in any dishonesty.

FORD   Well said, brazen-face, hold it out! Come forth, sirrah!   *Pulls clothes out of the basket*

120 PAGE   This passes.

---

93 hard at close by/right at the   **94 dispatch** hurry   **97 as lief** rather   **99 Ay . . . again?** Ford's reply to whatever Page has just said—presumably something to the effect of "if it prove false that Falstaff is there, you will look like a fool"   **103 panderly** pimping/go-between **gin** gang   **104 Now . . . shamed** i.e. now the truth will out (proverbial: "speak the truth and shame the devil")   **107 passes** surpasses/is excessive   **108 be pinioned** have your wings clipped   **118 hold it out** keep up your deception

MISTRESS FORD	Are you not ashamed? Let the clothes alone.
FORD	I shall find you anon.
EVANS	'Tis unreasonable. Will you take up your wife's clothes? Come away.
125 **FORD**	Empty the basket, I say! *To John and Robert*
PAGE	Why, man, why?
FORD	Master Page, as I am a man, there was one conveyed out of my house yesterday in this basket. Why may not he be there again? In my house I am sure he is. My intelligence is
130	true, my jealousy is reasonable. Pluck me *To John and Robert* out all the linen.
MISTRESS FORD	If you find a man there, he shall die a flea's death. *John and Robert empty the basket*
PAGE	Here's no man.
135 **SHALLOW**	By my fidelity, this is not well, Master Ford. This wrongs you.
EVANS	Master Ford, you must pray, and not follow the imaginations of your own heart. This is jealousies.
FORD	Well, he's not here I seek for.
140 **PAGE**	No, nor nowhere else but in your brain.
FORD	Help to search my house this one time. If I find not what I seek, show no colour for my extremity, let me forever be your table-sport. Let them say of me, 'As jealous as Ford, that searched a hollow walnut for his wife's leman.' Satisfy
145	me once more, once more search *John and Robert refill the basket* with me. *and exeunt with it*
MISTRESS FORD	What, ho, Mistress Page, come you and the old woman down. My husband will come into the chamber.
FORD	Old woman? What old woman's that?
150 **MISTRESS FORD**	Why, it is my maid's aunt of Brentford.
FORD	A witch, a quean, an old cozening quean! Have I not forbid her my house? She comes of errands, does she? We are

---

132 flea's death i.e. a miserable death/he shall be crushed like a parasitic insect   **135 fidelity** faith   **142 show . . . extremity** offer no excuse for my extreme behavior   **143 table-sport** joke among company   **144 leman** lover   **151 quean** hussy/whore   **cozening** cheating   **152 of** on

simple men, we do not know what's brought to pass under
the profession of fortune-telling. She works by charms, by
155   spells, by th'figure, and such daubery as this is, beyond our
element. We know nothing. Come down, you   *Takes a cudgel*
witch, you hag, you! Come down, I say!

MISTRESS FORD   Nay, good sweet husband.— Good gentlemen,
let him not strike the old woman.

[*Enter Mistress Page leading Falstaff in woman's clothes*]

160   MISTRESS PAGE   Come, Mother Prat, come, give me your hand.

FORD   I'll prat her. Out of my door, you witch,   *Beats Falstaff*
you rag, you baggage, you polecat, you runnion! Out, out! I'll
conjure you, I'll fortune-tell you.   [*Exit Falstaff*]

MISTRESS PAGE   Are you not ashamed? I think you have killed
165   the poor woman.

MISTRESS FORD   Nay, he will do it. 'Tis a goodly credit for you.

FORD   Hang her, witch!

EVANS   By yea and no, I think the 'oman is a witch indeed. I
like not when a 'oman has a great peard. I spy a great peard
170   under his muffler.

FORD   Will you follow, gentlemen? I beseech you, follow.
See but the issue of my jealousy. If I cry out thus upon no
trail, never trust me when I open again.

PAGE   Let's obey his humour a little further. Come,
175   gentlemen.

[*Exeunt Ford, Page, Shallow, Caius and Evans*]

MISTRESS PAGE   Trust me, he beat him most pitifully.

MISTRESS FORD   Nay, by th'mass, that he did not: he beat him
most unpitifully, methought.

---

153 **under the profession** in the name   155 **by th'figure** by drawing up horoscopes
daubery trickery   156 **element** understanding (literally, the element in which one rightfully
belongs)   160 **Mother Prat** prat means "a trick" though it was also slang for the buttocks
161 **prat** practice tricks on/beat (or simply a nonce-word derived from the name)   162 **rag**
worthless wretch   **runnion** abusive term for a woman, perhaps "mangy old bag"
166 **'Tis . . . you** i.e. that will reflect well on you (said in irony)   168 **By . . . no** a very mild
oath (moderated from the Quarto text's stronger "By Jesu")   172 **cry . . . trail** bark like a
hunting dog when there is in fact no scent   173 **open** bark loudly at a scent   174 **obey his
humour** humor him

MISTRESS PAGE   I'll have the cudgel hallowed and hung o'er the
180   altar. It hath done meritorious service.

MISTRESS FORD   What think you? May we, with the warrant of
womanhood and the witness of a good conscience, pursue
him with any further revenge?

MISTRESS PAGE   The spirit of wantonness is, sure, scared out of
185   him. If the devil have him not in fee-simple, with fine and
recovery, he will never, I think, in the way of waste, attempt
us again.

MISTRESS FORD   Shall we tell our husbands how we have served
him?

190 MISTRESS PAGE   Yes, by all means, if it be but to scrape the
figures out of your husband's brains. If they can find in their
hearts the poor unvirtuous fat knight shall be any further
afflicted, we two will still be the ministers.

MISTRESS FORD   I'll warrant they'll have him publicly shamed,
195   and methinks there would be no period to the jest, should he
not be publicly shamed.

MISTRESS PAGE   Come, to the forge with it, then shape it. I would
not have things cool.   *Exeunt*

Act 4 Scene 3   *running scene 15*

Enter Host and Bardolph

BARDOLPH   Sir, the German desires to have three of your horses.
The duke himself will be tomorrow at court, and they are
going to meet him.

HOST   What duke should that be comes so secretly? I hear
5   not of him in the court. Let me speak with the gentlemen.
They speak English?

---

179 hallowed blessed/dedicated to God   **180 meritorious** deserving of reward   **181 warrant**
assurance/authorization (with play on the legal sense: "document authorizing a judicial
sentence")   **184 wantonness** lust   **185 fee-simple** absolute possession (legal term used of
land or property)   **fine and recovery** legal procedures employed to transfer the ownership of
land   **186 waste** legal term referring to the damage or alteration of land or property by a
tenant (puns on "waist")   **188 served** treated (with a play on the sense of "had sex with")
191 figures fantasies   **193 ministers** agents   **195 period** conclusion   **197 shape it** i.e. as
one would mold hot iron in the **forge**

BARDOLPH   Ay, sir. I'll call them to you.

HOST   They shall have my horses, but I'll make them pay,
I'll sauce them. They have had my house a week at command.
10   I have turned away my other guests. They must come off, I'll
sauce them. Come.   *Exeunt*

Act 4 Scene 4   *running scene 16*

Enter Page, Ford, Mistress Page, Mistress Ford and Evans

EVANS   'Tis one of the best discretions of a 'oman as ever I
did look upon.

PAGE   And did he send you both these letters at an instant?

MISTRESS PAGE   Within a quarter of an hour.

5   FORD   Pardon me, wife. Henceforth do what thou wilt.
I rather will suspect the sun with cold
Than thee with wantonness. Now doth thy honour stand,
In him that was of late an heretic,
As firm as faith.

10   PAGE   'Tis well, 'tis well, no more.
Be not as extreme in submission as in offence.
But let our plot go forward. Let our wives
Yet once again, to make us public sport,
Appoint a meeting with this old fat fellow,
15   Where we may take him and disgrace him for it.

FORD   There is no better way than that they spoke of.

PAGE   How? To send him word they'll meet him in the park
at midnight? Fie, fie, he'll never come.

EVANS   You say he has been thrown in the rivers and has
20   been grievously peaten as an old 'oman. Methinks there
should be terrors in him, that he should not come. Methinks
his flesh is punished, he shall have no desires.

PAGE   So think I too.

4.3   9 sauce them make them pay overly high prices   **at command** at their disposal
10 come off pay up   **4.4   1 'Tis . . . 'oman** she is one of the most prudent/sensible women
3 an instant the same time   **8 heretic** unbeliever/holder of unorthodox religious beliefs

MISTRESS FORD   Devise but how you'll use him when he comes,
25   And let us two devise to bring him thither.

MISTRESS PAGE   There is an old tale goes that Herne the hunter,
Sometime a keeper here in Windsor Forest,
Doth all the winter-time, at still midnight,
Walk round about an oak, with great ragged horns,
30   And there he blasts the tree, and takes the cattle,
And makes milch-kine yield blood, and shakes a chain
In a most hideous and dreadful manner.
You have heard of such a spirit, and well you know
The superstitious idle-headed eld
35   Received and did deliver to our age
This tale of Herne the hunter for a truth.

PAGE   Why, yet there want not many that do fear
In deep of night to walk by this Herne's Oak.
But what of this?

40 MISTRESS FORD   Marry, this is our device:
That Falstaff at that oak shall meet with us.

PAGE   Well, let it not be doubted but he'll come,
And in this shape. When you have brought him thither,
What shall be done with him? What is your plot?

45 MISTRESS PAGE   That likewise have we thought upon, and thus:
Nan Page my daughter, and my little son,
And three or four more of their growth, we'll dress
Like urchins, oafs and fairies, green and white,
With rounds of waxen tapers on their heads,
50   And rattles in their hands. Upon a sudden,
As Falstaff, she and I are newly met,
Let them from forth a sawpit rush at once

---

24 use treat/behave toward   **26 Herne the hunter** huntsman of great skill who was wounded
after saving the king from a vicious stag; his own life was saved when the dead beast's antlers
were tied to his head, but he was later framed for or caught poaching and hanged himself from
an oak in Windsor Great Park, which he is said to haunt   **27 Sometime** at one point/formerly
29 ragged rough, jagged   **30 blasts** withers   **takes** bewitches   **31 milch-kine** dairy cows
34 eld people from the past   **37 want** lack   **43 shape** disguise/appearance   **47 growth** size
48 urchins goblins/elves   **oafs** goblin or elf children/changelings   **49 tapers** candles
52 sawpit pit over which wood was laid to be sawn

With some diffusèd song. Upon their sight,
We two in great amazèdness will fly:
55   Then let them all encircle him about,
And fairy-like to pinch the unclean knight,
And ask him why, that hour of fairy revel,
In their so sacred paths he dares to tread
In shape profane.
60   MISTRESS FORD   And till he tell the truth,
Let the supposèd fairies pinch him sound,
And burn him with their tapers.
MISTRESS PAGE   The truth being known,
We'll all present ourselves, dis-horn the spirit,
65   And mock him home to Windsor.
FORD   The children must
Be practised well to this, or they'll ne'er do't.
EVANS   I will teach the children their behaviours, and I will
be like a jack-an-apes also, to burn the knight with my taber.
70   FORD   That will be excellent. I'll go buy them vizards.
MISTRESS PAGE   My Nan shall be the queen of all the fairies,
Finely attirèd in a robe of white.
PAGE   That silk will I go buy.— And in that time   *Aside*
Shall Master Slender steal my Nan away,
75   And marry her at Eton.—
Go, send to Falstaff straight.   *To Mrs Page and Mrs Ford*
FORD   Nay, I'll to him again in name of Broom:
He'll tell me all his purpose. Sure, he'll come.
MISTRESS PAGE   Fear not you that.— Go get us properties and
80   tricking for our fairies.   *To Page, Ford and Evans*
EVANS   Let us about it. It is admirable pleasures and fery
honest knaveries.   [*Exeunt Page, Ford and Evans*]
MISTRESS PAGE   Go, Mistress Ford,
Send quickly to Sir John, to know his mind.
                            [*Exit Mistress Ford*]

---

53 **diffusèd** confused, disordered   61 **sound** soundly   70 **vizards** masks   75 **Eton** village
over the river from Windsor   79 **properties** theatrical props   80 **tricking** adornments

85   I'll to the Doctor. He hath my good will,
     And none but he, to marry with Nan Page.
     That Slender, though well landed, is an idiot,
     And he my husband best of all affects.
     The Doctor is well moneyed, and his friends
90   Potent at court. He, none but he, shall have her,
     Though twenty thousand worthier come to crave her.   [*Exit*]

Act 4 Scene 5   *running scene 17*

Enter Host [and] Simple

HOST   What wouldst thou have, boor? What, thick-skin?
            Speak, breathe, discuss: brief, short, quick, snap.

SIMPLE   Marry, sir, I come to speak with Sir John Falstaff
            from Master Slender.

5 HOST   There's his chamber, his house, his castle, his
            standing-bed and truckle-bed. 'Tis painted about with the
            story of the Prodigal, fresh and new. Go, knock and call. He'll
            speak like an Anthropophaginian unto thee. Knock, I say.

SIMPLE   There's an old woman, a fat woman, gone up into
10   his chamber. I'll be so bold as stay, sir, till she come down. I
            come to speak with her indeed.

HOST   Ha? A fat woman? The knight may be robbed. I'll
            call.— Bully knight, bully Sir John! Speak from thy lungs
            military. Art thou there? It is thine host, thine Ephesian, calls.

15 FALSTAFF How now, mine host?   *Above or within*

HOST   Here's a Bohemian-Tartar tarries the coming down
            of thy fat woman. Let her descend, bully, let her descend. My
            chambers are honourable. Fie! Privacy? Fie!

---

87 well landed in possession of a good amount of land   **88 he . . . affects** my husband favors
him most   **4.5   1 boor** peasant, ill-bred fellow   **thick-skin** idiot   **2 discuss** declare
6 standing-bed and truckle-bed the **truckle-bed** was a smaller bed on casters kept beneath the
main (**standing**) bed   **7 Prodigal** the Prodigal (extravagant) Son, who appears in the biblical
parable (Luke 15)   **8 Anthropophaginian** cannibal   **13 lungs military** military lungs
14 Ephesian boon companion/fellow degenerate   **16 Bohemian-Tartar** i.e. savage, dissolute
person   **18 Privacy** seclusion, concealment (implying that Falstaff has been having sex with
the "woman")

[Enter Falstaff]

FALSTAFF   There was, mine host, an old fat woman even now
20   with me, but she's gone.

SIMPLE   Pray you, sir, was't not the wise woman of Brentford?

FALSTAFF   Ay, marry, was it, mussel-shell. What would you
with her?

SIMPLE   My master, sir, my Master Slender, sent to her, seeing
25   her go through the streets, to know, sir, whether one Nim, sir,
that beguiled him of a chain, had the chain or no.

FALSTAFF   I spake with the old woman about it.

SIMPLE   And what says she, I pray, sir?

FALSTAFF   Marry, she says that the very same man that beguiled
30   Master Slender of his chain, cozened him of it.

SIMPLE   I would I could have spoken with the woman herself:
I had other things to have spoken with her too, from him.

FALSTAFF   What are they? Let us know.

HOST   Ay, come. Quick.

35 **SIMPLE**   I may not conceal them, sir.

HOST   Conceal them, or thou diest.

SIMPLE   Why, sir, they were nothing but about Mistress Anne
Page, to know if it were my master's fortune to have her or no.

FALSTAFF   'Tis, 'tis his fortune.

40 **SIMPLE**   What, sir?

FALSTAFF   To have her or no. Go, say the woman told me so.

SIMPLE   May I be bold to say so, sir?

FALSTAFF   Ay, sir, like who more bold.

SIMPLE   I thank your worship. I shall make my master glad
45   with these tidings.   *[Exit]*

HOST   Thou art clerkly, thou art clerkly, Sir John. Was
there a wise woman with thee?

FALSTAFF   Ay, that there was, mine host, one that hath taught
me more wit than ever I learned before in my life. And I paid
50   nothing for it neither, but was paid for my learning.

---

21 wise woman woman skilled in magic   **22 mussel-shell** perhaps Simple is gaping open-
mouthed or is being imaged as something worthless and insignificant   **26 beguiled** deceived
35 conceal malapropism for "reveal"   **43 like . . . bold** as bold as the boldest   **46 clerkly**
learned

[*Enter Bardolph*]

BARDOLPH   Out, alas, sir. Cozenage, mere cozenage!

HOST   Where be my horses? Speak well of them, varletto.

BARDOLPH   Run away with the cozeners, for so soon as I came
beyond Eton, they threw me off from behind one of them, in
55   a slough of mire, and set spurs and away, like three German
devils, three Doctor Faustuses.

HOST   They are gone but to meet the duke, villain. Do not
say they be fled. Germans are honest men.

[*Enter Evans*]

EVANS   Where is mine host?

60   HOST   What is the matter, sir?

EVANS   Have a care of your entertainments. There is a friend
of mine come to town tells me there is three cozen-germans
that has cozened all the hosts of Readings, of Maidenhead, of
Colebrook, of horses and money. I tell you for good will, look
65   you. You are wise and full of gibes and vlouting-stocks, and
'tis not convenient you should be cozened. Fare you well.

[*Exit*]

[*Enter Caius*]

CAIUS   Vere is mine host de Jarteer?

HOST   Here, Master Doctor, in perplexity and doubtful
dilemma.

70   CAIUS   I cannot tell vat is dat. But it is tell-a me dat you
make grand preparation for a duke de Jamany. By my trot,
dere is no duke that the court is know to come. I tell you for
good will. Adieu.   [*Exit*]

---

51 mere absolute   **52 varletto** i.e. varlet, loosely Italianized by the Host   **55 slough of mire**
muddy bog   **56 Doctor Faustuses** In Christopher Marlowe's play of the same name, Doctor
Faustus, a German, sold his soul to the devil; this passage seems to allude to a scene in which
three characters are thrown in a mire   **61 entertainments** the hospitality you provide for
your guests   **62 cozen-germans** cheating Germans/men pretending to be Germans (plays
on "cousin german"—i.e. first cousin)   **63 Readings . . . Colebrook** small towns not far
from Windsor (**Readings** is Caius' Welsh plural for Reading; **Colebrook** is now Colnbrook)
65 vlouting-stocks flouts (i.e. mockery); literally flouting-stocks (i.e. laughingstocks)
66 convenient appropriate   **71 Jamany** i.e. Germany   **72 that . . . come** i.e. who is known
to have arrived or is due to arrive at court

HOST   Hue and cry, villain, go!— Assist me,   *To Bardolph/To*
75   knight, I am undone!—   *Falstaff/To Bardolph*
        Fly, run, hue and cry, villain! I am undone!

                                  [*Exeunt Host and Bardolph*]

FALSTAFF   I would all the world might be cozened, for I have
        been cozened and beaten too. If it should come to the ear of
        the court, how I have been transformed and how my
80   transformation hath been washed and cudgelled, they would
        melt me out of my fat drop by drop, and liquor fishermen's
        boots with me. I warrant they would whip me with their fine
        wits till I were as crestfallen as a dried pear. I never prospered
        since I forswore myself at primero. Well, if my wind were but
85   long enough, I would repent.

[*Enter Mistress Quickly*]

        Now, whence come you?

MISTRESS QUICKLY   From the two parties, forsooth.

FALSTAFF   The devil take one party and his dam the other,
        and so they shall be both bestowed. I have suffered more for
90   their sakes, more than the villainous inconstancy of man's
        disposition is able to bear.

MISTRESS QUICKLY   And have not they suffered? Yes, I warrant,
        speciously one of them. Mistress Ford, good heart, is beaten
        black and blue, that you cannot see a white spot about her.

95 FALSTAFF   What tell'st thou me of black and blue? I was beaten
        myself into all the colours of the rainbow, and I was like to
        be apprehended for the witch of Brentford. But that my
        admirable dexterity of wit, my counterfeiting the action of
        an old woman, delivered me, the knave constable had set me
100   i'th'stocks, i'th'common stocks, for a witch.

MISTRESS QUICKLY   Sir, let me speak with you in your chamber.
        You shall hear how things go, and, I warrant, to your content.
        Here is a letter will say somewhat — good hearts, what ado

---

74 Hue . . . villain a cry used to call for the pursuit of a criminal (addressed to Bardolph)
81 liquor smear with oil or grease (to render waterproof)   **84 forswore . . . primero** cheated in
a card game but swore that I had not   **wind** breath   **88 dam** mother   **89 bestowed** got rid
of   **93 speciously** malapropism for "specially"   **96 like** likely/about   **97 But** were it not for
the fact that

here is to bring you together! Sure, one of you does not serve
105   heaven well, that you are so crossed.

FALSTAFF   Come up into my chamber.   *Exeunt*

Act 4 Scene 6   *running scene 17 continues*

Enter Fenton [and] Host

HOST   Master Fenton, talk not to me. My mind is heavy. I
will give over all.

FENTON   Yet hear me speak. Assist me in my purpose,
And, as I am a gentleman, I'll give thee
5   A hundred pound in gold more than your loss.

HOST   I will hear you, Master Fenton, and I will, at the
least, keep your counsel.

FENTON   From time to time I have acquainted you
With the dear love I bear to fair Anne Page,
10   Who mutually hath answered my affection —
So far forth as herself might be her chooser —
Even to my wish. I have a letter from her
Of such contents as you will wonder at;
The mirth whereof so larded with my matter,
15   That neither singly can be manifested
Without the show of both. Fat Falstaff
Hath a great scene. The image of the jest
I'll show you here at large. Hark, good mine host:
Tonight at Herne's Oak, just 'twixt twelve and one,
20   Must my sweet Nan present the Fairy Queen —
The purpose why is here — in which disguise,
While other jests are something rank on foot,
Her father hath commanded her to slip
Away with Slender, and with him at Eton

---

105 **crossed** thwarted   **4.6**   2 **over** up (my efforts in support of your pursuit of Anne Page)
7 **counsel** secret   11 **So far forth** insofar   12 **to** in accordance with   14 **mirth** i.e. the
humorous account of the humiliation of Falstaff   **larded . . . matter** intermingled with my
current concerns   17 **scene** i.e. role in the drama   **image** idea   18 **at large** in full (Fenton
may be showing the Host Anne's letter)   22 **rank on foot** abundantly afoot

25   Immediately to marry. She hath consented. Now, sir,
        Her mother — ever strong against that match
        And firm for Doctor Caius — hath appointed
        That he shall likewise shuffle her away,
        While other sports are tasking of their minds,
30   And at the dean'ry, where a priest attends,
        Straight marry her. To this her mother's plot
        She, seemingly obedient, likewise hath
        Made promise to the doctor. Now, thus it rests:
        Her father means she shall be all in white,
35   And in that habit, when Slender sees his time
        To take her by the hand and bid her go,
        She shall go with him. Her mother hath intended,
        The better to denote her to the doctor —
        For they must all be masked and vizarded —
40   That quaint in green she shall be loose enrobed,
        With ribbons pendent flaring 'bout her head;
        And when the doctor spies his vantage ripe,
        To pinch her by the hand, and on that token,
        The maid hath given consent to go with him.

45   **HOST**   Which means she to deceive, father or mother?

     FENTON   Both, my good host, to go along with me.
        And here it rests, that you'll procure the vicar
        To stay for me at church, 'twixt twelve and one,
        And, in the lawful name of marrying,
50   To give our hearts united ceremony.

     HOST   Well, husband your device. I'll to the vicar.
        Bring you the maid, you shall not lack a priest.

     FENTON   So shall I evermore be bound to thee:
        Besides, I'll make a present recompense.   *Exeunt*

---

28 shuffle smuggle   **29 tasking of** occupying   **30 dean'ry** house belonging to the dean of a
church   **33 it rests** the matter stands   **35 habit** clothing   **38 denote** mark out   **40 quaint**
prettily/fashionably   **loose enrobed** loosely dressed/gowned with an outer garment
41 pendent hanging   **flaring** spread out/waving in the wind   **42 vantage** opportunity
43 token sign   **48 stay** wait   **51 husband** manage (with an obvious pun)   **device** plan
54 present immediate

Act 5 Scene 1   *running scene 17 continues*

Enter Falstaff [and] Mistress Quickly

FALSTAFF   Prithee, no more prattling. Go, I'll hold. This is the
third time. I hope good luck lies in odd numbers. Away, go.
They say there is divinity in odd numbers, either in nativity,
chance, or death. Away.

5   MISTRESS QUICKLY   I'll provide you a chain, and I'll do what I can
to get you a pair of horns.

FALSTAFF   Away, I say. Time wears. Hold up your head, and
mince.   [*Exit Mistress Quickly*]

[*Enter Ford, disguised as Broom*]

How now, Master Broom? Master Broom, the matter will be
10   known tonight, or never. Be you in the park about midnight,
at Herne's Oak, and you shall see wonders.

FORD   Went you not to her yesterday, sir, as you told me
you had appointed?

FALSTAFF   I went to her, Master Broom, as you see, like a poor
15   old man, but I came from her, Master Broom, like a poor old
woman. That same knave Ford, her husband, hath the finest
mad devil of jealousy in him, Master Broom, that ever
governed frenzy. I will tell you, he beat me grievously, in the
shape of a woman, for in the shape of man, Master Broom, I
20   fear not Goliath with a weaver's beam, because I know also
life is a shuttle. I am in haste. Go along with me, I'll tell you
all, Master Broom. Since I plucked geese, played truant and
whipped top, I knew not what 'twas to be beaten till lately.
Follow me, I'll tell you strange things of this knave Ford, on
25   whom tonight I will be revenged, and I will deliver his wife
into your hand. Follow. Strange things in hand, Master
Broom. Follow.   *Exeunt*

5.1   **1 hold** keep the appointment   **3 divinity** divine power   **7 wears** wears away/is running
out   **8 mince** i.e. get moving (literally, walk daintily/trippingly)   **20 Goliath . . . beam**
according to the Bible, the giant Goliath had a spear like a weaver's beam (i.e. wooden roller in
a loom)   **21 shuttle** another quotation adapted from the Bible; a **shuttle** was an instrument
used in weaving for passing thread to and fro   **23 whipped top** made a top (child's toy) spin
by lashing it   **26 in hand** are happening

Act 5 Scene 2

Enter Page, Shallow [and] Slender

PAGE   Come, come. We'll couch i'th'castle-ditch till we see the light of our fairies. Remember, son Slender, my daughter—

SLENDER   Ay, forsooth, I have spoke with her and we have a
5   nay-word how to know one another: I come to her in white, and cry 'mum', she cries 'budget', and by that we know one another.

SHALLOW   That's good too. But what needs either your 'mum' or her 'budget'? The white will decipher her well enough. It
10   hath struck ten o'clock.

PAGE   The night is dark: light and spirits will become it well. Heaven prosper our sport! No man means evil but the devil, and we shall know him by his horns. Let's away. Follow me.   *Exeunt*

Act 5 Scene 3

Enter Mistress Page, Mistress Ford [and] Caius

MISTRESS PAGE   Master Doctor, my daughter is in green. When you see your time, take her by the hand, away with her to the deanery, and dispatch it quickly. Go before into the park. We two must go together.

5 CAIUS   I know vat I have to do. Adieu.

MISTRESS PAGE   Fare you well, sir.   [*Exit Caius*]
My husband will not rejoice so much at the abuse of Falstaff as he will chafe at the Doctor's marrying my daughter. But 'tis no matter. Better a little chiding than a great deal of
10   heartbreak.

MISTRESS FORD   Where is Nan now, and her troop of fairies? And the Welsh devil Hugh?

5.2 **1 couch** lie/hide **5 nay-word** code word **6 "mum" . . . "budget"** "mumbudget" was a phrase meaning "keep silent" **9 decipher** reveal **11 become** suit **5.3** **3 dispatch** get on with it/conclude it **8 chafe** be vexed/inflamed

MISTRESS PAGE   They are all couched in a pit hard by Herne's
Oak, with obscured lights, which, at the very instant of
15   Falstaff's and our meeting, they will at once display to the
night.

MISTRESS FORD   That cannot choose but amaze him.

MISTRESS PAGE   If he be not amazed, he will be mocked. If he be
amazed, he will every way be mocked.

20   MISTRESS FORD   We'll betray him finely.

MISTRESS PAGE   Against such lewdsters and their lechery.
Those that betray them do no treachery.

MISTRESS FORD   The hour draws on. To the Oak, to the Oak!

Exeunt

Act 5 Scene 4   *running scene 18 continues*

Enter Evans [disguised, with others as] Fairies

EVANS   Trib, trib, fairies. Come, and remember your parts.
Be pold, I pray you. Follow me into the pit, and when I give
the watch-'ords, do as I pid you. Come, come, trib, trib.

Exeunt

Act 5 Scene 5   *running scene 18 continues*

Enter Falstaff [disguised as Herne]

FALSTAFF   The Windsor bell hath struck twelve, the minute
draws on. Now, the hot-blooded gods assist me! Remember,
Jove, thou wast a bull for thy Europa. Love set on thy horns.
O powerful Love, that in some respects makes a beast a man,
5   in some other a man a beast. You were also, Jupiter, a swan
for the love of Leda. O omnipotent Love, how near the god

---

14 obscured concealed   **17 choose but amaze** fail to terrify/astound   **5.4   1 Trib** trip
(i.e. come on/move nimbly)   **3 watch-'ords** watchwords (i.e. password/signal)
5.5   3 Jove . . . Europa Europa, daughter of the king of Phoenicia, was carried away by Jove,
king of the gods; disguised as a bull, he swam to Crete with her on his back   **6 Leda** in the
guise of a swan, **Jupiter** (or **Jove**) seduced Leda, wife of the king of Sparta

drew to the complexion of a goose. A fault done first in the
form of a beast. O Jove, a beastly fault! And then another
fault in the semblance of a fowl. Think on't, Jove, a foul fault!
10   When gods have hot backs, what shall poor men do? For me,
I am here a Windsor stag, and the fattest, I think, i'th'forest.
Send me a cool rut-time, Jove, or who can blame me to piss
my tallow? Who comes here? My doe?

[*Enter Mistress Ford and Mistress Page*]

MISTRESS FORD   Sir John? Art thou there, my deer? My male deer?
15   **FALSTAFF**   My doe with the black scut! Let the sky rain potatoes,
let it thunder to the tune of Greensleeves, hail kissing-comfits
and snow eryngoes. Let there come a tempest of provocation,
I will shelter me here.   *Embraces her*

MISTRESS FORD   Mistress Page is come with me, sweetheart.
20   **FALSTAFF**   Divide me like a bribed buck, each a haunch: I will
keep my sides to myself, my shoulders for the fellow of this
walk, and my horns I bequeath your husbands. Am I a
woodman, ha? Speak I like Herne the hunter? Why, now is
Cupid a child of conscience: he makes restitution. As I am a
25   true spirit, welcome.   *Horns within*

MISTRESS PAGE   Alas, what noise?

MISTRESS FORD   Heaven forgive our sins.

FALSTAFF   What should this be?

MISTRESS FORD *and* **MISTRESS PAGE**   Away, away!   *They run off*
30   **FALSTAFF**   I think the devil will not have me damned, lest the
oil that's in me should set hell on fire. He would never else
cross me thus.

---

8 fault sin, with particular application to fornication and possible play on "vagina"   **10 backs**
loins   **12 rut-time** mating season   **piss my tallow** piss away my fat; stags were thought to
urinate more frequently during the mating season, by the end of which their energetic
behavior had caused them to lose weight   **13 doe** female deer/mate/whore   **14 deer** puns
on "dear"   **15 scut** tail/vulva   **potatoes** sweet or Spanish potatoes were considered
aphrodisiacs   **16 kissing-comfits** confectionary for sweetening the breath   **17 eryngoes**
candied roots of the sea holly; a type of sweetmeat viewed as an aphrodisiac   **provocation**
sexual stimulation   **19 sweetheart** puns on "sweet hart" (i.e. male deer)   **20 Divide . . . buck**
in order to conceal the theft, stolen (**bribed**) deer were cut up and divided rapidly among the
poachers   **21 fellow . . . walk** gamekeeper of this part of the wood   **23 woodman** hunter/
womanizer/lunatic   **24 Cupid . . . restitution** i.e. Cupid is conscientiously making amends to
me   **31 oil** i.e. grease/fat   **32 cross** thwart

Enter [Evans, disguised as before; Pistol, as Hobgoblin; Mistress
Quickly, Anne and others, as] Fairies [with tapers]

MISTRESS QUICKLY   Fairies black, grey, green and white,
   You moonshine revellers and shades of night,
35   You orphan heirs of fixèd destiny,
   Attend your office and your quality.
   Crier Hobgoblin, make the fairy oyez.

PISTOL   Elves, list your names. Silence, you airy toys.
   Cricket, to Windsor chimneys shalt thou leap.
40   Where fires thou find'st unraked and hearths unswept,
   There pinch the maids as blue as bilberry,
   Our radiant queen hates sluts and sluttery.

FALSTAFF   They are fairies, he that speaks to them shall
   die.   *Aside*
   I'll wink and couch: no man their works must eye.   *Lies down*
45   EVANS   Where's Bede? Go you, and where you   *upon his face*
   find a maid
   That ere she sleep has thrice her prayers said,
   Raise up the organs of her fantasy:
   Sleep she as sound as careless infancy.
   But those as sleep and think not on their sins,
50   Pinch them, arms, legs, backs, shoulders, sides and shins.

MISTRESS QUICKLY   About, about.
   Search Windsor Castle, elves, within and out.
   Strew good luck, oafs, on every sacred room,
   That it may stand till the perpetual doom,
55   In state as wholesome as in state 'tis fit,
   Worthy the owner and the owner it.

Hobgoblin another name for Puck or Robin Goodfellow   **34 shades** spirits   **35 orphan**
parentless/neglected/friendless   **heirs . . . destiny** offspring who have set roles to carry
out/inheritors of destiny (perhaps with the power to influence it)   **36 Attend . . . quality**
attend to your duties and particular occupations   **37 Crier** town crier, maker of public
announcements   **oyez** i.e. "hear ye"   **38 list** listen for   **toys** insubstantial creatures
40 unraked without coals and ashes heaped together to maintain burning through the night
41 bilberry small blue-black fruit   **44 wink** shut my eyes   **eye** observe   **47 Raise . . .**
fantasy stimulate her imagination, give her delightful dreams   **48 Sleep she** may she sleep
careless free from anxiety   **49 as** who   **51 About** about it/to action   **53 oafs** elves
54 perpetual doom judgment day   **55 as . . . fit** as sound in condition as it is deserving of
dignity   **56 Worthy** worthy of

The several chairs of order look you scour
With juice of balm and every precious flower.
Each fair instalment, coat, and sev'ral crest,
60   With loyal blazon evermore be blest.
And nightly meadow-fairies, look you sing,
Like to the Garter's compass, in a ring.
Th'expressure that it bears, green let it be,
More fertile-fresh than all the field to see.
65   And *Honi soit qui mal y pense* write
In em'rald tufts, flowers purple, blue and white,
Like sapphire, pearl and rich embroidery,
Buckled below fair knighthood's bending knee.
Fairies use flowers for their character.
70   Away, disperse. But till 'tis one o'clock,
Our dance of custom round about the oak
Of Herne the hunter, let us not forget.

EVANS   Pray you, lock hand in hand, yourselves in order set.
And twenty glow-worms shall our lanterns be,
75   To guide our measure round about the tree.
But stay, I smell a man of middle-earth.

FALSTAFF   Heavens defend me from that Welsh fairy,   *Aside*
lest he transform me to a piece of cheese!

PISTOL   Vile worm, thou wast o'erlooked even in   *To Falstaff*
80   thy birth.

MISTRESS QUICKLY   With trial-fire touch me his finger-end.
If he be chaste, the flame will back descend
And turn him to no pain. But if he start,
It is the flesh of a corrupted heart.

---

57 **several . . . order** individual seats assigned to the Knights of the Garter (in the castle chapel)   58 **balm** fragrant herbs   59 **instalment** stall (i.e. place or seat assigned to a knight) **coat** coat of arms   **crest** heraldic device originally worn on a helmet   60 **blazon** banner bearing the coat of arms   62 **compass** circle (i.e. the Garter ribbon, worn below the knee) 63 **Th'expressure** picture, expression (i.e. fairy ring or circle of darker green grass) 65 *Honi . . . pense* "shamed be he who thinks evil (of it)" (the French motto that appeared on the Garter ribbons)   68 **Buckled** tied   69 **character** writing   71 **dance of custom** customary dance   75 **measure** stately dance   76 **man of middle-earth** i.e. a mortal, dwelling on the earth (midway between heaven and hell)   78 **cheese** supposedly the favorite food of the Welsh   79 **o'erlooked** looked on with the evil eye, bewitched   81 **trial-fire** testing fire   **touch me** touch (me is emphatic)   83 **turn** expose   **start** recoil, flinch

85 PISTOL   A trial, come.

    EVANS   Come, will this wood take   *They burn him with their tapers*
        fire?

    FALSTAFF   O, O, O!

    MISTRESS QUICKLY   Corrupt, corrupt, and tainted in desire.

90   About him, fairies, sing a scornful rhyme,
        And, as you trip, still pinch him to your time.

    FAIRIES   [*sing*] *The Song*
        Fie on sinful fantasy,
        Fie on lust and luxury!   *During this song they pinch Falstaff.*

95   Lust is but a bloody fire,   *Caius comes one way and steals away*
        Kindled with unchaste desire,   *a boy in green; Slender another way and*
        Fed in heart, whose flames aspire,   *takes off a boy in white; and Fenton*
        As thoughts do blow them, higher   *comes and steals away Anne.*
            and higher.
        Pinch him, fairies, mutually,   *A noise of hunting is heard within.*

100   Pinch him for his villainy.   *All the Fairies run away.*
        Pinch him and burn him and turn him about,   *Falstaff pulls off his*
        Till candles and starlight and moonshine be out.   *buck's head*
    [*Enter Page, Ford, Mistress Page and Mistress Ford*]   *and rises*

    PAGE   Nay, do not fly, I think we have watched you now.
        Will none but Herne the hunter serve your turn?

105 MISTRESS PAGE   I pray you, come, hold up the jest no higher.
        Now, good Sir John, how like you Windsor wives?
        See you these, husband? Do not these fair yokes   *Points to horns*
        Become the forest better than the town?

    FORD   Now, sir, who's a cuckold now? Master Broom,
110   Falstaff's a knave, a cuckoldly knave: here are his horns,
        Master Broom. And, Master Broom, he hath enjoyed nothing
        of Ford's but his buck-basket, his cudgel, and twenty pounds

---

86 wood i.e. Falstaff's finger   **90 About** surround   **91 trip** dance/skip   **still** continually
93 fantasy imaginings/amorous desire   **94 luxury** lechery   **green . . . Anne** the original
Quarto stage direction has Caius taking a boy *in red*, Slender one *in green*, and Anne *in white*;
see "Text" in Key Facts   **95 bloody fire** fire in the blood/lustful fire   **99 mutually** all together
103 watched spied and caught   **104 serve your turn** do for you   **105 hold . . . higher**
maintain the joke no more   **107 yokes** Falstaff's antlers are shaped like the oxen's yoke

of money, which must be paid to Master Broom. His horses are arrested for it, Master Broom.

115 **MISTRESS FORD**   Sir John, we have had ill luck, we could never meet. I will never take you for my love again, but I will always count you my deer.

FALSTAFF   I do begin to perceive that I am made an ass.

FORD   Ay, and an ox too. Both the proofs are extant.

120 **FALSTAFF**   And these are not fairies. I was three or four times in the thought they were not fairies, and yet the guiltiness of my mind, the sudden surprise of my powers, drove the grossness of the foppery into a received belief, in despite of the teeth of all rhyme and reason, that they were fairies. See

125 now how 'Wit may be made a Jack-a-Lent, when 'tis upon ill employment!'

EVANS   Sir John Falstaff, serve Got, and leave   *Unmasks* your desires, and fairies will not pinse you.

FORD   Well said, fairy Hugh.

130 **EVANS**   And leave you your jealousies too, I pray you.

FORD   I will never mistrust my wife again till thou art able to woo her in good English.

FALSTAFF   Have I laid my brain in the sun and dried it, that it wants matter to prevent so gross o'erreaching as this? Am I

135 ridden with a Welsh goat too? Shall I have a coxcomb of frieze? 'Tis time I were choked with a piece of toasted cheese.

EVANS   Seese is not good to give putter. Your belly is all putter.

FALSTAFF   'Seese' and 'putter'? Have I lived to stand at the taunt

140 of one that makes fritters of English? This is enough to be the decay of lust and late-walking through the realm.

---

114 **arrested** seized by legal warrant (until the debt is paid)   116 **meet** encounter one another amorously   117 **deer** puns on "dear"   119 **proofs** i.e. his horns   **extant** apparent/ protruding   122 **surprise . . . powers** ambush of my faculties/understanding   123 **foppery** trickery, foolery   **in . . . of** in spite of, the face of   125 **Wit** intelligence   **Jack-a-Lent** figure of a man traditionally pelted during Lent, butt of jokes   134 **wants matter** lacks the means **o'erreaching** deception   135 **with** by   **coxcomb** fool's cap (with a crest like a cock's comb) 136 **frieze** coarse woolen cloth   140 **fritters** fried scraps of battered meat   141 **late-walking** going out with whores late at night

MISTRESS PAGE   Why Sir John, do you think, though we would
   have thrust virtue out of our hearts by the head and
   shoulders, and have given ourselves without scruple to hell,
145   that ever the devil could have made you our delight?

FORD   What, a hodge-pudding? A bag of flax?

MISTRESS PAGE   A puffed man?

PAGE   Old, cold, withered and of intolerable entrails?

FORD   And one that is as slanderous as Satan?

150 PAGE   And as poor as Job?

FORD   And as wicked as his wife?

EVANS   And given to fornications, and to taverns, and sack,
   and wine, and metheglins, and to drinkings, and swearings,
   and starings, pribbles and prabbles?

155 FALSTAFF   Well, I am your theme. You have the start of me. I
   am dejected. I am not able to answer the Welsh flannel.
   Ignorance itself is a plummet o'er me. Use me as you will.

FORD   Marry, sir, we'll bring you to Windsor, to one Master
   Broom, that you have cozened of money, to whom you should
160   have been a pander. Over and above that you have suffered, I
   think to repay that money will be a biting affliction.

PAGE   Yet be cheerful, knight. Thou shalt eat a posset
   tonight at my house, where I will desire thee to laugh at my
   wife, that now laughs at thee. Tell her Master Slender hath
165   married her daughter.

MISTRESS PAGE   Doctors doubt that. If Anne Page be my   *Aside*
   daughter, she is, by this, Doctor Caius' wife.

[*Enter Slender*]

SLENDER   Whoa ho, ho, father Page!

---

146 **hodge-pudding** pudding made from a random assortment of ingredients   **bag of flax**
sack of flax (plant fibers used for cloth)   147 **puffed** swollen   148 **intolerable** insufferable/
excessively large/impossible to carry   150 **Job** in the Bible, Job suffered great poverty; his **wife**
advised him to curse God for it   153 **metheglins** spiced liquor of Welsh origin   154 **starings**
glares   155 **theme** subject (of your mockery)   **start of** advantage over   156 **dejected** cast
down, humbled, humiliated   **flannel** coarse woolen cloth   157 **Ignorance . . . me** I am
searched to the very depths by ignorance itself (i.e. Evans); may pun on "plumbet" (woolen
fabric)   **plummet** device for measuring the depth of the sea   159 **should . . . pander** were to
have been a pimp   162 **posset** hot drink made with milk, liquor, and spices   167 **this** this
time, now

PAGE   Son, how now? How now, son, have you dispatched?

170 SLENDER   Dispatched? I'll make the best in Gloucestershire know on't. Would I were hanged, la, else.

PAGE   Of what, son?

SLENDER   I came yonder at Eton to marry Mistress Anne Page, and she's a great lubberly boy. If it had not been i'th'church,

175 I would have swinged him, or he should have swinged me. If I did not think it had been Anne Page, would I might never stir — and 'tis a postmaster's boy.

PAGE   Upon my life, then, you took the wrong.

SLENDER   What need you tell me that? I think so, when I took

180 a boy for a girl. If I had been married to him, for all he was in woman's apparel, I would not have had him.

PAGE   Why, this is your own folly. Did not I tell you how you should know my daughter by her garments?

SLENDER   I went to her in green, and cried 'mum', and she

185 cried 'budget', as Anne and I had appointed, and yet it was not Anne, but a postmaster's boy.   [*Exit*]

MISTRESS PAGE   Good George, be not angry. I knew of your purpose, turned my daughter into white, and indeed, she is now with the Doctor at the deanery, and there married.

[*Enter Caius*]

190 CAIUS   Vere is Mistress Page? By gar, I am cozened. I ha' married *un garçon*, a boy, *un paysan*, by gar, a boy. It is not Anne Page. By gar, I am cozened.

MISTRESS PAGE   Why, did you take her in white?

CAIUS   Ay, by gar, and 'tis a boy. By gar, I'll raise all Windsor.
                    [*Exit*]

195 FORD   This is strange. Who hath got the right Anne?

---

169 dispatched managed things   **172 Of what** i.e. **know** of what   **174 lubberly** loutish
175 swinged beaten   **177 postmaster** keeper of post horses (which were hired out for the
swift conveyance of messages)   **178 took the wrong** went wrong (in following instructions);
Slender responds to the sense of "made a mistake (in thinking the boy was Anne)"   **181 had
him** accepted him as my wife/had sex with him   **184 green** most editors emend to "white" for
consistency with the setup in 5.2   **188 white** most editors emend to "green" for consistency
with the setup in 4.6   **191 *paysan*** peasant   **193 white** most editors emend to "green" for
consistency with the setup in 5.3   **194 raise** rouse

PAGE   My heart misgives me. Here comes Master Fenton.
[*Enter Fenton and Anne*]
    How now, Master Fenton?

ANNE   Pardon, good father. Good my mother, pardon.

PAGE   Now, mistress, how chance you went not with
200 Master Slender?

MISTRESS PAGE   Why went you not with Master Doctor, maid?

FENTON   You do amaze her. Hear the truth of it:
    You would have married her most shamefully,
    Where there was no proportion held in love.
205 The truth is, she and I, long since contracted,
    Are now so sure that nothing can dissolve us.
    Th'offence is holy that she hath committed,
    And this deceit loses the name of craft,
    Of disobedience, or unduteous title,
210 Since therein she doth evitate and shun
    A thousand irreligious cursèd hours
    Which forcèd marriage would have brought upon her.

FORD   Stand not amazed, here is no   *To Page and Mistress Page*
    remedy.
    In love the heavens themselves do guide the state.
215 Money buys lands, and wives are sold by fate.

FALSTAFF   I am glad, though you have ta'en a   *To Page and*
    special stand to strike at me, that your arrow   *Mistress Page*
    hath glanced.

PAGE   Well, what remedy? Fenton, heaven give thee joy!
220 What cannot be eschewed must be embraced.

FALSTAFF   When night-dogs run, all sorts of deer are chased.

MISTRESS PAGE   Well, I will muse no further. Master Fenton,
    Heaven give you many, many merry days.
    Good husband, let us every one go home,

---

202 amaze bewilder   **204 proportion . . . love** balanced, mutual loving relationship
205 contracted engaged (secretly)   **206 sure** firmly bound   **209 unduteous title**
undutifulness   **title** name   **210 evitate** avoid   **214 guide the state** rule matters
217 stand advantageous position from which a hunter may shoot   **218 glanced** struck
superficially   **222 muse** wonder/grumble

225   And laugh this sport o'er by a country fire,
        Sir John and all.
FORD   Let it be so. Sir John,
        To Master Broom you yet shall hold your word,
        For he tonight shall lie with Mistress Ford.   *Exeunt*

TEXTUAL NOTES

Q = First Quarto text of 1602
F = First Folio text of 1623
Q3 = a correction introduced in the Third Quarto text of 1630
F2 = a correction introduced in the Second Folio text of 1632
Ed = a correction introduced by a later editor
SD = stage direction
SH = speech heading (i.e. speaker's name)

List of parts = Ed

All entrances mid-scene = Ed. F *groups names of all characters in each scene at beginning of scene*
1.1.24 py'r lady *spelled* per-lady *in* F   **136–39** *set as verse* = Q. F = *set as prose*   **137 latten** = Q *(spelled* laten*).* F = Latine   **152 careers** *spelled* Car-eires *in* F   **215 contempt** = Ed. F = content
1.3.0 SD *and Robin* = Ed. F = *Page (pageboy)*   **14 lime** = Q. F = Liue   **46 legion** = Ed. Q = legions. F = legend   **52 oeillades** *spelled* illiads *in* F   **73 o'th'hoof** = F2. F = ith'hoofe   **74 humour** = Q. F = honor
1.4.39 *une boîtie en vert* = Ed. F = vnboyteene verd   **44–45 chaud. Je m'en vais voir à le Court la grande affaire** = Ed. F = *chando, Ie man voi a le Court la grand affaires*   **79 baillez** = Ed. F = ballow   **109 good-year** = Ed. F = good-ier
2.1.1 I = Q3. *Not in* F   **51 praised** = Ed. F = praise   **190 cavalier** *spelled* Caualeire *in* F   **191 SH FORD** = Q. F = *Shal*   **193 Broom** = F *(spelled* Broome). *Ford's disguised name is* Brooke *throughout* Q
2.2.33 That I am = Q. *Not in* F   **207 exchange** = Q3. F = enchange
2.3.50 A word = Q. F = a
3.1.4 Petty = Ed. F = pittie   **92 Give . . . terrestrial, so** = Q. *Not in* F   **98 lads** = Q. F = Lad
3.3.30 cue *spelled* Qu *in* F   **54 Fortune thy foe were not, Nature thy friend** = F2 *punctuation. Comma after* foe *in* F   **67 kiln** = Ed. F = kill   **130 SH JOHN** = Ed. F = *Ser*   **164 foolish** = F2. F = foolishion
3.4.13 SH FENTON = Q3. *Not in* F   **65 Fenton** = Ed. F = *Fenter*
3.5.26 sperm *spelled* Spersme *in* F
4.1.60 lunatics = Ed. F = Lunaties
4.2.47 kiln = Ed. F = Kill   **85 direct** = Q3. F = direct direct   **87 misuse him** = F2. F = misuse   **95, 97 SH JOHN** = Ed. F = *1. Ser*   **96 SH ROBERT** = Ed.

F = *2. Ser*   **97 as lief** = F2. F = liefe as   **126 SH PAGE** = Ed. F = *M. Ford.*
159 not strike = Q3. F = strike

4.3.9 house = Q. F = houses

4.4.6 cold = Ed. F = gold   **31 makes** = F2. F = make   **60 SH MISTRESS
FORD** = Ed. F = *Ford*

4.5.35 SH SIMPLE = Ed. F = *Fal.*   **46 art** = Q. F = are

4.6.38 denote = Ed. F = deuote

5.2.3 daughter = F2. *Omitted in* F

5.3.12 Hugh = Ed. F = Herne

5.5.53 oafs *spelled* Ouphes *in* F   **64 More** = F2. F = Mote   **92 SH FAIRIES** =
Ed. *Not in* F   **94–102** *Stage direction based on* Q, *but with colors of costumes
altered to conform to* F—*see "Text" in Key Facts*   **191 *un paysan*** = Ed. F =
oon pesant

SCENE-BY-SCENE ANALYSIS

ACT 1 SCENE 1

Lines 1–91: Justice Shallow, accompanied by Slender, complains to Parson Evans about Falstaff. Comedy is generated by Shallow's self-importance, Slender's misuse of language, and Parson Evans's Welsh accent. This presentation of the Justice and the Parson, significant figures in their community, establishes the play's focus on "Middle England" and its inhabitants. The conversation turns to Anne Page, and Evans's idea that she should marry Slender. Any potential romance is quickly undermined by Slender's description of Anne: she "has brown hair, and speaks small like a woman." Evans's repeated references to Anne's future inheritance of "seven hundred pound" draws attention to the link between love and money. They arrive at Page's house, where Falstaff is visiting.

Lines 92–270: Shallow claims that Falstaff has "beaten [his] men, killed [his] deer, and broke open [his] lodge." Falstaff's mocking and ready confession highlights both his amorality and wit, contrasting with the slower intellect of Shallow and his companions. Slender accuses Pistol of picking his purse, which Pistol denies, leading Slender to accuse Nim and Bardolph in turn. They also deny it and accuse Slender of being drunk and unable to remember. As they argue, Anne brings wine and the Mistresses Ford and Page arrive. Page encourages everyone to go in and "drink down all unkindness." Shallow, Slender, and Evans remain and are joined by Slender's servant, Simple. As Slender asks Simple for his "Book of Riddles," Shallow impatiently points out that they are waiting for him, and that Evans has made a tentative proposal of marriage to Anne on his behalf. They ask Slender if he would like to marry Anne; he says that he will do as his cousin wishes. When asked whether he loves Anne, he responds that "if there be no great love in the beginning, yet heaven may decrease it upon better acquaintance." Anne calls them to dinner. Shallow and Evans leave the couple alone. Anne tries to persuade Slender to come in to dinner. He refuses, giving a series of excuses and making awkward conversation until a page comes out and summons them.

ACT 1 SCENE 2

Evans sends Simple with a message to Mistress Quickly asking for her support in Slender's courtship of Anne.

ACT 1 SCENE 3

At the Garter Inn, Falstaff tells the Host that he cannot afford to keep all of his followers and the Host offers Bardolph a job as tapster. Falstaff announces that he is glad to be rid of him, as "His thefts were too open." He tells Pistol and Nim that he has no money and needs a new scam. He reveals his intention to "make love to Ford's wife," believing that she is attracted to him, and, more important, that "she has all the rule of her husband's purse." He shows them a letter he has written to Mistress Ford, and another he has written to Page's wife, who he claims also gave him "good eyes" and "bears the purse" in the Page household. Pistol and Nim refuse to deliver the letters, and after Falstaff has gone they decide to tell Ford and Page about Falstaff's intention to seduce their wives.

ACT 1 SCENE 4

Mistress Quickly sends John Rugby to watch for their master while she talks to Simple, knowing that Caius does not like strangers in his house. She agrees to help Evans further the match between Slender and Anne. Rugby announces that Caius is coming, and Mistress Quickly hides Simple. Caius, whose confused speech and exaggerated French accent render him a figure of fun, sends Mistress Quickly to fetch "a green-a box" from the closet. He then remembers some herbs that he needs from the closet and finds Simple. Mistress Quickly claims that Simple has merely brought her a message from Evans and tries to stop him from revealing the content of the letter. Simple tells Caius the truth, however, and the doctor sends Rugby for some paper.

As he writes a letter, Mistress Quickly reveals that Caius is in love with Anne Page himself. Caius sends Simple off with a letter for Evans, revealing that it contains a challenge and threatens to cut the priest's throat. Mistress Quickly argues that Evans is only speaking on behalf of his friend, but Caius is unmoved. Mistress Quickly reassures him that Anne is in love with him and he leaves for the court. When he has gone, Mistress Quickly reveals her contempt for Caius and her knowledge that Anne is not interested in him. She is interrupted by Fenton, yet another suitor to Anne. Mistress Quickly now assures Fenton that Anne loves him, and Fenton gives her money to forward his suit, revealing Mistress Quickly's motives: she will benefit by acting as go-between for all of the suitors. Once he has gone, she doubts his chances of success, claiming that Anne does not love him either.

ACT 2 SCENE 1

Lines 1–96: Mistress Page is reading her love letter from Falstaff. Any notions of romance are undermined by the letter's prosaic approach and faint praise: Falstaff points out that, like him, she is "not young" and they both enjoy drinking. She is indignant that Falstaff, a "drunkard," has addressed her in this way, and exclaims that she has given him no encouragement. She declares she will "be revenged on him . . . as sure as his guts are made of puddings." Mistress Ford enters, and after some prevarication, she shows Mistress Page her letter from Falstaff, angrily asking how she can be "revenged." The women quickly realize that Falstaff has sent them identical messages. Mistress Page suggests that they lead Falstaff on. Mistress Ford agrees but is worried about her husband's jealousy. Ford and Page arrive, accompanied by Pistol and Nim. The women move aside to discuss their revenge on the "greasy knight," Falstaff.

Lines 97–150: Pistol tells Ford that Falstaff "affects" his wife. Ford is disbelieving at first, making the unflattering comment that his wife is "not young," but Pistol continues to warn him, making humorous references to cuckoldry. Nim warns Page that Falstaff loves his wife and they leave. Ford reveals his jealousy: he seems inclined to believe Pistol "a good sensible fellow." Page, however, describes Nim as "a drawling, affecting rogue" and says that he "will not believe" him. Their wives approach and Page and his wife greet each other cheerfully, but Mistress Ford is concerned that Ford is "melancholy." He orders her home, and she realizes that he has "some crotchets in [his] head." Mistress Quickly arrives to see Anne, and the women agree in an aside that she can be their messenger to the "paltry knight," Falstaff.

Lines 151–213: Ford and Page discuss what they have been told by Pistol and Nim. Page dismisses their claims, adding that all Falstaff is likely to get from his wife is "sharp words," but Ford is unsure. The Host of the Garter arrives, followed by Shallow, who tells them that there is to be "a fray" between Evans and Caius. Ford asks the Host for "a word" and they draw aside, and then Page and Shallow also speak aside. Ford bribes the Host to introduce him to Falstaff, but asks him to say his name is "Broom." The Host, Shallow, and Page go to watch the duel, leaving Ford alone. He considers that Page is a fool to trust his wife and decides to investigate further, using his disguise as Broom to tackle Falstaff.

ACT 2 SCENE 2

Lines 1–122: Falstaff refuses to lend money to Pistol, complaining about the number of times he has had to "pawn" his reputation by lying for Pistol and Nim. Pistol points out that Falstaff had a cut of whatever they stole, and Falstaff argues that he would not "endanger [his] soul" for free. Robin announces the arrival of Mistress Quickly. She draws Falstaff aside with a message from Mistress Ford. Comedy is generated through her verbosity and Falstaff's impatience but she finally tells him that Mistress Ford thanks him "a thousand times" for his letter and wishes him to know that her husband will be out of their house "between ten and eleven." Falstaff promises to be there and Mistress Quickly tells him that Mistress Page also sends "hearty commendations" and has said to tell him that although her husband is "seldom from home," she "hopes there will come a time" when she can see Falstaff. Falstaff is convinced and asks if the two women have discussed him with each other. Mistress Quickly reassures him and says that he must use Robin as a go-between with Mistress Page. He agrees and sends him off with Mistress Quickly. Pistol follows in pursuit of Quickly, who he characterizes as a "punk" (prostitute), claiming that she will be his "prize."

Lines 123–275: Bardolph brings Falstaff a drink, telling him it's from "one Master Broom" who wishes to speak with him. Falstaff sends him to fetch Broom, while gloating to himself over having won over both Mistress Page and Mistress Ford. Ford arrives, disguised as Broom. He shows Falstaff a bag of money and offers it to him in exchange for a favor. He pretends that he (Broom) is in love with Mistress Ford and has "pursued" her without success. He flatters Falstaff and offers him the money to use his superior "art of wooing" to "lay an amiable siege to the honesty of this Ford's wife." Falstaff is willing, but puzzled, and "Broom" explains that if he can destroy Mistress Ford's reputation of "honour" and "purity," she will have no defense against him. Falstaff takes the money and promises that Broom will "enjoy Ford's wife," explaining that the lady has already arranged for him to visit her in her husband's absence. He explains that he intends to use Mistress Ford as "the key of the cuckoldly rogue's coffer," unaware that he is talking to the man he intends to cuckold. He leaves, continuing to insult Ford. Alone, Ford is furious that his wife has apparently made an assignation with Falstaff and intends to have his revenge.

ACT 2 SCENE 3

Caius boasts that he will kill Evans in the duel. The Host arrives with Shallow, Slender, and Page to watch the fight. Caius explains that Evans has not come because he is "de coward." In an aside, the Host sends the others to Frogmore where Evans is, promising to bring Caius along. He then tells Caius that Anne Page is at a feast in Frogmore, and offers to take him there.

ACT 3 SCENE 1

Evans searches for Caius, expressing his intention to "knog his urinals about his knave's costard." Like Caius, his language renders him
comic and undermines the potentially serious nature of the forth-
coming "duel." Page, Shallow, and Slender arrive. They pretend to
wonder why Evans has his sword and is dressed only in his "doublet
and hose." Slender says nothing throughout the scene except "O
sweet Anne Page!" This is comically at odds with his previous
approach to Anne, and ironic that Slender, a genuine rival to Caius,
should be a spectator to the duel rather than a participant. Caius and
the Host arrive, and everyone urges him and Evans to debate rather
than fight. They exchange insults, but Evans suggests they make
friends, realizing that they are only making "laughing-stocks" of
themselves. When the others have left, Caius and Evans realize that
the Host has made fools of them and unite in order to get even, creating an unlikely alliance and another "revenge plot" in the confused machinations of the play.

ACT 3 SCENE 2

Ford meets Mistress Page and Robin on their way to Mistress Ford.
When they leave, Ford comments that Page is a fool: his wife is
clearly cuckolding him with Falstaff, and Robin is their go-between.
He decides that his wife and Mistress Page are both involved with Falstaff and are in league with each other (which they are). He decides
to reveal their deception. He meets Page, Shallow, Slender, the Host,
Evans, Caius, and Rugby and invites them to accompany him to his
house, knowing Falstaff is there. Shallow and Slender decline: they
are due to dine with Anne Page. Page favors Slender's suit to Anne,
but adds that his wife is in favor of Caius. Caius insists that Mistress
Quickly has told him that Anne loves him. The Host suggests that Fenton "will carry't," as "he writes verses, he speaks holiday, he smells
April and May," but Page says that he will not consent to the match,
and that there will be no dowry if Anne marries Fenton. Ford urges
that some of them go home to dine with him, suggesting that they

shall "have sport" if they do. Slender and Simple go to see Anne and the Host goes to find Falstaff but the others accompany Ford home.

ACT 3 SCENE 3

Lines 1–135: Mistress Ford and Mistress Page order the servants to bring a laundry basket and give them hurried instructions: they are to wait until called and then take it "without any pause or staggering," and "empty it in the muddy ditch close by the Thames side." Mistress Page goes to hide and Mistress Ford sends Robin to fetch Falstaff. Falstaff begins his seduction by paying her extravagant compliments when Robin announces that Mistress Page is on her way, and Falstaff hides "behind the arras." Mistress Page arrives and the two women stage a conversation for Falstaff's benefit. Mistress Page tells Mistress Ford she is "undone": her husband is on his way "with all the officers in Windsor" to search for the man she has with her. The dramatic irony is compounded by the audience's knowledge that Ford is genuinely about to arrive, as Mistress Ford "confesses" to her friend that she has a man concealed. Mistress Page pretends to notice the linen basket and suggests that Mistress Ford's gentleman-friend hide in it to be carried out by her servants. Falstaff, entirely deceived by the women's performance, emerges from hiding and climbs into the laundry basket. In an aside, he tells Mistress Page that he loves her before they cover him with clothes. Ford arrives with the others as the servants are carrying the basket out.

Lines 136–206: Ford urges his companions to search the house for "the fox," Falstaff. Unconvinced, they comment on his jealous nature before following him. The two women discuss the success of their plan. Mistress Ford says that she has never seen her husband so jealous and suspects that he knew Falstaff was there. Mistress Page says she'll "lay a plot to try that," and adds that they can "yet have more tricks with Falstaff." They decide to send Mistress Quickly with another message: Falstaff is to come again to Mistress Ford at eight o'clock the next day. Ford and the others return having found no evidence of Falstaff, and Ford is criticized for his jealous behavior. Page arranges for the men to meet at his house the next morning for breakfast before going hawking. Evans and Caius agree that they will get their revenge on the Host the next day.

ACT 3 SCENE 4

Fenton complains to Anne that her father will never sanction their marriage: despite his high status, Fenton has spent most of his fortune during his dissipated youth. He confesses to Anne that initially he wooed her for her father's fortune, but that he found that she had "more value / Than stamps in gold or sums in sealèd bags." Anne repeats that he must continue to seek her father's approval, implying that she is not as indifferent to Fenton as Mistress Quickly has suggested. They are joined by Mistress Quickly, Shallow, and Slender. Shallow orders Mistress Quickly to interrupt Anne and Fenton so that Slender may court Anne. Anne tells Fenton, in an aside, that "ill-favoured" Slender is her father's choice. Slender makes inept attempts to woo Anne, assisted by Shallow, who points out the financial benefits of marrying his cousin. As Slender continues his courtship, Anne's parents arrive. Page encourages Slender and tells Fenton not to "haunt" his house. He refuses to listen to Fenton, and invites Shallow and Slender in, leaving Anne and Fenton with Mistress Page and Mistress Quickly. Mistress Page assures Anne that she does not want her to marry Slender, saying that Caius would be a "better husband." She says she will be neither "friend nor enemy" to Fenton, but agrees that she will support Anne if she loves him. She takes Anne indoors, and Mistress Quickly tells Fenton that Anne's encouragement is her doing and he thanks her, before giving her a ring to give to Anne. Alone, Mistress Quickly declares her preference for all three suitors, before going to deliver the message from Mistresses Page and Ford to Falstaff.

ACT 3 SCENE 5

Falstaff sends Bardolph to fetch him a drink and muses on recent events. He is indignant at having been "carried in a basket like a barrow of butcher's offal." Bardolph shows in Mistress Quickly. When Falstaff learns that she has come from Mistress Ford he refuses to listen but she persuades him that Mistress Ford is sorry and wishes to make amends. He agrees that he will visit her between eight and nine, and Mistress Quickly goes to tell Mistress Ford. Falstaff wonders why he has not heard from Broom, just as Ford appears in disguise. Falstaff tells Broom that he was at Ford's house at the appointed time, but that Ford came home and interrupted him, so he was forced to hide in a laundry basket. His indignation mounts as he describes the scene to the disguised Ford, ironically insulting the man he is speaking to as a "lunatic knave" and a "jealous rotten bell-wether." He announces that he has not given up: he will call on Mistress Ford again while her husband is out "a-birding." Broom informs him that it is "past eight" and Falstaff hurries off to Ford's house, promising that Broom "shall cuckold Ford." Alone, Ford vents his fury and pursues Falstaff to his house.

ACT 4 SCENE 1

Mistress Quickly tells Mistress Page that Falstaff is at Ford's house and Mistress Page says that she will go there after she has taken her son, William, to school. Evans arrives and tests William on his Latin. Mistress Quickly comically misinterprets the Latin words.

ACT 4 SCENE 2

Lines 1–98: Mistress Ford has succeeded in convincing Falstaff that she is sorry and he assures her that he loves her. Mistress Page arrives and calls out, and Mistress Ford urges Falstaff to hide in "th'chamber" next door. Once again they act out a conversation for the listening Falstaff: Mistress Page pretends to be glad that "the fat knight" is not there, as Ford is approaching the house with the other men, adding that he will be there "anon." Mistress Ford again "confesses" that Falstaff is there and Mistress Page tells her that he is a "dead man" if Ford catches him. Falstaff emerges, and Mistress Page tells him that Ford's brothers are guarding the house doors "with pistols." The two women suggest that he disguise himself in clothes belonging to Mistress Ford's maid's aunt, "the fat woman of Brentford." Falstaff runs to put on the gown, and Mistress Ford hopes that

Ford meets with the disguised Falstaff as he "cannot abide the old woman of Brentford . . . and hath threatened to beat her." Mistress Page says that somehow Ford knows about the laundry basket, and the women decide to use this as a decoy. Mistress Page delivers a little rhyme that neatly sums up the play to the effect that "Wives may be merry, and yet honest too." Mistress Page goes to dress Falstaff, and Mistress Ford instructs her servants to take up the laundry basket again, but to "set it down" if Ford asks them to.

Lines 99–198: Ford arrives and orders his servants to set down the laundry basket. He calls angrily for his wife. Mistress Ford enters, and he accuses her of "brazen-face" dishonesty before starting to pull clothes from the basket. He orders his servants to "Empty the basket," but finds only clothes. Page, Shallow, and Evans suggest that it is all his jealous imagination. Mistress Ford calls Mistress Page to come down with "the old woman." On learning that his maid's aunt is in the house, Ford flies into another fury and takes up his cudgel. Mistress Ford begs the other men not to let him "strike the old woman." Mistress Page then leads the disguised Falstaff through, and Ford beats him out of the house before inviting the others to search for Falstaff. They agree to "humour" him "a little further," and follow. Alone, Mistress Ford and Mistress Page delight in the beating Falstaff has received. They agree that they have had their revenge and decide to tell their husbands everything in the hope that Falstaff will be "publicly shamed."

ACT 4 SCENE 3

Bardolph informs the Host that some German noblemen wish to hire three of his horses. The Host agrees, intending to overcharge the Germans, but it seems likely that this is part of Caius and Evans's plan for revenge.

ACT 4 SCENE 4

Mistress Ford and Mistress Page have told their husbands about Falstaff. Ford begs his wife's pardon, promising that he will "suspect the sun with cold" rather than suspect her of "wantonness" in the future.

Page says that they must publicly disgrace Falstaff. The women have suggested that they lure him to "the park at midnight," and Mistress Page now reveals her plan. There is an oak in Windsor Forest, supposedly haunted by the spirit of Herne the Hunter. She proposes that they meet Falstaff there, asking him to come disguised as Herne. Then her children and several others, dressed "Like urchins, oafs and fairies," with candles on their heads and "rattles in their hands," will appear. Mistress Page and Mistress Ford will pretend to run away with fright, and the children, "fairy-like," will encircle Falstaff, asking why "their so sacred paths he dares to tread." They will then pinch him and burn him with their candles until he tells the truth, at which point the adults will appear and "mock him home to Windsor." As they make plans for this, Page adds in an aside that this will be the ideal opportunity for Slender to steal Anne away and marry her. In a brief soliloquy, however, Mistress Page reveals that she is going to find Caius, determined that he shall marry Anne.

ACT 4 SCENE 5

Simple is looking for Falstaff, and the Host directs him to Falstaff's chamber, but Simple says that he has seen "a fat woman" go up there. Falstaff emerges, and Simple inquires whether the woman in his chamber was "the wise woman of Brentford," as he wishes to consult her on behalf of his master. Slender wants to know whether Nim has stolen a chain from him and whether he will marry Anne Page. Falstaff pretends that he has consulted the wise woman, and gives Simple ambiguous answers to both questions. Once Simple has gone, the Host questions Falstaff about the wise woman, also receiving ambiguous answers. They are interrupted by Bardolph, who reports that the Germans have stolen the Host's horses. As the Host argues that "Germans are honest men," Evans arrives. He warns the Host that "three cozen-germans" have been robbing hosts in other towns of their horses and money. Caius then comes to tell the Host that there is no "duke de Jamany" at court. The Host realizes that he is "undone" before rushing off, accompanied by Bardolph, and the audience understands that Evans and Caius have had their revenge. Falstaff reflects that he, too, has been "cozened": by Mistress Page and

Mistress Ford. Mistress Quickly arrives, but Falstaff says that he has "suffered" enough for the sake of the two women. Mistress Quickly promises that she has news that will "content" him, and they go to his chamber.

ACT 4 SCENE 6

The Host is miserable and refuses to help Fenton any more in his pursuit of Anne. Fenton offers him "a hundred pound in gold" and tells him of a letter from Anne, detailing the plan against Falstaff. Both of Anne's parents have suggested she use the occasion to elope with their preferred suitor: Page has told Slender that Anne will be masked and dressed in white, and Mistress Page has told Caius that she will be dressed in green. Fenton explains that Anne means to deceive both parents and leave with him. He asks the Host to arrange for the vicar to wait for them in the church so that they can be married, and the Host agrees.

ACT 5 SCENE 1

Falstaff tells Mistress Quickly that he will keep the appointment at the oak tree, and she offers to help him disguise himself as Herne. As she leaves, Ford arrives disguised as Broom. Falstaff tells him to be at Herne's oak at midnight, where he "shall see wonders." He describes the beating he received the day before, and ironically adds that he will be revenged on the "knave Ford" by delivering his wife into Broom's hands.

ACT 5 SCENE 2

Page, Slender, and Shallow watch for the lights of the disguised children. Page reminds Slender that Anne will be in white.

ACT 5 SCENE 3

Mistress Page reminds Caius that Anne will be in green. She and Mistress Ford head off to the oak.

ACT 5 SCENE 4

Evans leads the "fairies" to the oak.

ACT 5 SCENE 5

At midnight Falstaff arrives, disguised as Herne, contemplating the "rut-time" he is about to have. He meets Mistress Ford and Mistress Page and says they may "divide" him between them "like a bribed buck." The sound of horns is heard and the women run away. The "fairies" and "hobgoblins" come in with their candles, singing. Frightened, Falstaff lies down. Evans pretends to smell "a man of middle-earth," and the fairies burn and pinch Falstaff while singing of his "sinful fantasy" and "unchaste desire." As they dance, an unwitting Slender runs away with a boy dressed in white, and Caius leaves with a boy dressed in green. Meanwhile, Fenton steals away with Anne. Hunting horns are heard again and the fairies run away as Falstaff removes his disguise. Ford and Page arrive with their wives and mock and insult Falstaff, who realizes he has been deceived. He delivers another of the play's lighthearted "morals": "Wit may be made a Jack-a-lent, when 'tis upon ill employment!" Slender arrives and tells Page that he ran away with "a postmaster's boy" by mistake. Mistress Page reveals that Anne has run away with Caius, but Caius himself arrives and reveals that he, too, has "married *un garçon.*" Finally, Fenton arrives with Anne to announce their marriage. He chastises those who would have married her "Where there was no proportion held in love," purely for social or financial gain. Page relents over the marriage and, with the various enmities resolved and forgiven, they all "go home" to "laugh this sport o'er by a country fire."

THE MERRY WIVES OF WINDSOR IN PERFORMANCE: THE RSC AND BEYOND

The best way to understand a Shakespeare play is to see it or ideally to participate in it. By examining a range of productions, we may gain a sense of the extraordinary variety of approaches and interpretations that are possible—a variety that gives Shakespeare his unique capacity to be reinvented and made "our contemporary" four centuries after his death.

We begin with a brief overview of the play's theatrical and cinematic life, offering historical perspectives on how it has been performed. We then analyze in more detail a series of productions staged over the last half century by the Royal Shakespeare Company. The sense of dialogue between productions that can only occur when a company is dedicated to the revival and investigation of the Shakespeare canon over a long period, together with the uniquely comprehensive archival resource of promptbooks, program notes, reviews, and interviews held on behalf of the RSC at the Shakespeare Birthplace Trust in Stratford-upon-Avon, allows an "RSC stage history" to become a crucible in which the chemistry of the play can be explored.

Modern theater is dominated by the figure of the director, who must hold together the whole play, whereas the actor must concentrate on his or her part. The director's viewpoint is therefore especially valuable. Shakespeare's plasticity is wonderfully revealed when we hear directors of highly successful productions answering the same questions in very different ways. In addition, we have the perspective of a major actor who has played Falstaff in versions not only of *The Merry Wives* but also of the *Henry IV* plays.

FOUR CENTURIES OF *MERRY WIVES*: AN OVERVIEW

Apocryphal anecdotes circulating since the early eighteenth century tell us that *The Merry Wives of Windsor* was composed in only fourteen days at the command of Queen Elizabeth, who wished to see Falstaff in love.[1] True or not, this story has had an important effect on the play: originally associated with the highest reaches of English society, the play's apparent weaknesses were blamed by later critics on its being written quickly and to order. The performance history of the play has persistently cast it as a lightweight, though crowd-pleasing, entertainment.

The play's known stage life begins at court in 1601 (fittingly, at Windsor[2]), though some critics have suggested it was originally written for the 1597 Garter Feast, at which Lord Hunsdon (patron of Shakespeare's company) was elected to the order. The Quarto title (*Sir John Falstaff and the Merry Wives of Windsor*) confirms that Falstaff was the main attraction, and the part may have been originated by the company clown Will Kempe. The play is a uniquely ensemble-driven piece, however, and leading actors have excelled as the Wives, Ford, Evans, Caius, and others.

The play remained popular throughout the seventeenth century, with two court revivals under James I, and it was one of the first plays revived after the Interregnum. Unusually for the Restoration, Shakespeare's text was left largely intact, though it was not to everyone's taste. Samuel Pepys reluctantly saw it three times and, despite being initially impressed by the presentation of Caius and "the country gentleman" (perhaps Ford or Slender), found the play consistently "ill done," and a 1667 performance "did not please me at all—in no part."[3]

In 1702 John Dennis's adaptation *The Comical Gallant* premiered at Drury Lane. Dennis drew on French neoclassic notions of bourgeois comedy, restructured it into five scenes, and used it to assert conservative patriarchal values, notably in Page's closing lines:

Let all men learn from Fenton's generous proceeding to avoid the curse that attends a clandestine Marriage, and the dreadful consequence of a Parents just displeasure.

But Heav'n will Crown this Marriage with success,
Which Love and Duty thus conspire to bless.[4]

The adaptation was deservedly unsuccessful. In the 1704–05 season, however, Shakespeare's text was performed at court with Thomas Betterton as Falstaff and Mrs. Barry and Mrs. Bracegirdle as the wives. At Lincoln's Inn Fields in 1720, the twenty-seven-year-old James Quin first played Falstaff, and he dominated the play across London for the next thirty years. However, "this comedy was so perfectly played in all its parts, that the critics in acting universally celebrated the merit of the performers."[5] Already, and unusually, critics valued *Merry Wives* for its ensemble opportunities rather than as a star showcase. Delane and Stephens were among the other eighteenth-century actors to play Falstaff, although Quin's jovial knight cast a long shadow.

The play's American fortunes began at Philadelphia's Southwark Theater in 1770. Interestingly, one of the earliest American performances featured one of the few women to play Falstaff, Mrs. Webb (1786), though William Winter remarked: "Mrs. Webb's obesity appears to have been her sole qualification for the part."[6] Mrs. Glover was a more successful Falstaff at London's Haymarket in 1833, "one of the best stage 'old women' ever seen."[7] The play reached New York in 1789.

Many of the great nineteenth-century actors appeared in *Merry Wives* (although J. P. Kemble [1840] and Charles Kean [1851] preferred Ford for themselves), and even Charles Dickens mounted an amateur performance in 1848 as a benefit for Shakespeare's Birthplace. George Bartley's 1815 performance was praised for its lack of buffoonery, and his "bursting exultation of gratified vanity"[8] upon reading Mistress Ford's final letter was singled out as exemplary of his neatly characterized performance, while the 1824 Drury Lane production starring William Dowton betrayed an operatic influence, with spectacular scenery depicting Windsor and the forest, musical interludes, and a Fenton who "happily had nothing to do but sing."[9] The greatest Falstaff of the century, though, was Samuel Phelps, and one account of an 1857 Sadler's Wells performance suggests why:

[Falstaff is] a respectable scoundrel . . . a gentleman, who does everything—even mean tricks—with decorum and equanimity, partly because such affairs are nothing new to him, and partly because he really believes in the honour that he intends to do the citizens' wives . . . Phelps gives a fine representation of the unshakable complacency of a shameless cynicism that has long abandoned any sense of right and wrong and exchanged them for the security and dignity of a white-bearded rogue. This Falstaff is no mere comic figure, but a character portrait, thoroughly true to life.[10]

In an 1872 New York adaptation by William Winter, Augustin Daly reclaimed the play as a refined modern comedy, and he played Falstaff until the end of the century.

Where later American productions struggled to capture the peculiar "Englishness" of the play, Daly's success stemmed from being bold enough to make it a play about the *American* middle classes: its decorum was praised, with characters "in satins and silks and velvets of graceful shape and agreeably harmonized tints . . . The text is shorn of all its vulgarity."[11]

The play debuted at Stratford-upon-Avon under Frank Benson, whose productions were revived regularly between 1887 and 1919. Benson played Caius, though neither role nor production was among his most celebrated: "The Duelling scene was an unmitigated travesty. Shakespeare shows his wit in playing on words and not in stupid horseplay."[12] Benson's succession of Falstaffs included George Weir, Oscar Asche, and William Calvert. Benson established another popular feature: "Nothing could have been prettier than the little army of fairies and sprites, who disported themselves before Herne's Oak."[13] Benson's run at Stratford was interrupted briefly by Patrick Kirwan's 1914 version, praised for an absence of pantomime business but not for its lead. One critic drily noted: "Kirwan had two qualifications for Sir John Falstaff: the ability to look the part and a passing knowledge of the lines."[14]

During this period, Herbert Beerbohm Tree played Falstaff in London and New York. He was criticized for a heavily made-up performance "more remarkable as an exhibition of the resources of

1. Augustin Daly's 1886 New York production "reclaimed the play as a refined modern comedy." His "success stemmed from being bold enough to make it a play about the American middle classes."

theatrical disguise than as an original or inspired interpretation of the fat knight. [Falstaff's character is] not only concealed, it is annihilated."[15] Beerbohm Tree closed his 1916 New York celebrations of Shakespeare's tercentenary with the play, whose Keystone Kops–style knockabout comedy was disliked, though G. W. Anson's Bardolph surprisingly stood out. Unfortunately for Beerbohm Tree, James K. Hackett's production at New York's Criterion earlier in 1916 had been surprisingly successful. At ten days' notice, the comedian Tom Wise learned Falstaff's lines and bowled over critics: "he rolled from scene to scene quivering like a mountain of jelly, as he boozed and guzzled and boasted, and entangled himself in the snares set by those zestful wives."[16] Wise's fresh performance reenergized a play that too often merely reprised former glories.

Oscar Asche presented a winter-set version at London's Her Majesty's Theatre in 1911, significantly breaking from the usual midsummer atmosphere. In 1919, following Benson's retirement, William Bridges-Adams took over at Stratford with William Calvert as Falstaff. This Falstaff "was a nimble-witted and light-hearted old rogue, who has the good humour to laugh at his own misfortunes,"[17] but again it was the ensemble playing that impressed. Character moments succeeded better than farce, particularly the meetings of Falstaff and "Brook." Bridges-Adams successfully revived the play for several London and Stratford seasons, with Falstaffs including Baliol Holloway and Roy Byford.

Theodore Komisarjevsky deliberately defied tradition at Stratford in 1935, turning the play into a musical farce with a bustling stage. Ford was an Edwardian melodrama villain, while Neil Porter's "vitriolic French doctor livens up the whole production, though in doing so he utters some vulgarities which would not be allowed in any other modern show."[18] The deliberately artificial setting of colored houses and layered entrances divided critics: some found it self-consciously arty, others enjoyed a "brilliant, colourful, musical piece of theatricality."[19] The Strand Theatre offered a more straightforward version in 1942, with Donald Wolfit playing an attractively comic Falstaff.

The text itself was once more the subject of criticism at Stratford in 1940. Despite prejudices, however, Ben Iden Payne's strong company prevailed: "Thea Holme and Clare Harris, as the Wives, see to it that for once 'merry' is the operative word,"[20] while Baliol Holloway's bitter Ford was a standout. Holloway triumphantly returned to Stratford as Falstaff in 1943, directing himself in a production noted for the details amid the chaos: "After the undignified dive into the basket, . . . the small suspicious eye that Falstaff turns on the second invitation to dalliance" rendered audiences helpless, while Abraham Sofaer's Ford "set the jealous husband on the rampage early on . . . at times, the character grew to proportions of authentic tragedy."[21] Critics of *Merry Wives* by now needed no innovation from productions, just solid traditional performances. This was not satisfied by Robert Atkins, directing and playing Falstaff two years later at the Shakespeare Memorial Theatre. Atkins was a noted Falstaff in *Henry IV*, but here

He refuses to let Falstaff expand. The ripe fulsome manner is narrowed down, the old man is tetchy where he should be indignant, and annoyed where he should flash with royal rage . . . Falstaff's demands are so heavy that an actor may meet them valiantly and still not encompass all of the swell, the unction and the fat humour that make up his mental and physical enormity.[22]

Memories of past Falstaffs thus served as standards against which modern actors were judged. Glen Byam Shaw directed Anthony Quayle in the last pre-RSC production at Stratford in 1955. In a wintry landscape (paying tribute to Asche), Quayle "waddled and straddled and lurched, and blew, and gurgled, and wheezed and roared his way through Falstaff's indignities,"[23] but critics felt it was still "a performance by a serious actor who integrally lacks a naturally comic personality as he lacks Falstaff's stomach."[24]

Mel Shapiro's 1965 San Diego production projected Hogarthian prints and turned Falstaff's cronies into eighteenth-century high-

2. Glen Byam Shaw's 1955 production at the Shakespeare Memorial Theatre with Anthony Quayle, who "waddled and straddled and lurched, and blew, and gurgled, and wheezed and roared his way through Falstaff's indignities," with Joyce Redman as Mistress Ford.

waymen, while Josephine Wilson's 1975 production at London's Mermaid theater "seems to be set not in Windsor but in some Breughelian limbo where everyone is afflicted either by missing teeth, curlicued noses or mirthful convulsions."[25] Attempts to make this gentle comedy more ugly or complex were still resisted on both sides of the proscenium arch. By contrast, Donald Moffat's 1963 Ohio production was "beautifully articulated and surprisingly chaste."[26]

Several American and Canadian productions, rather than following Daly's lead in breaking away from the play's Englishness, tried to capture it with mixed results. Michael Kahn's 1971 Connecticut Shakespeare Festival version evoked the bustle of Elizabethan life, but missed the play's domestic interest in the process. The 1978 Restoration-set production at Stratford, Ontario, was more successful:

> In approaching *Merry Wives* as an essentially middle-class play—perhaps the only genuine middle-class play Shakespeare ever wrote—[director Peter] Moss attempted to create something more than a one-joke entertainment about the tricks played on an aging knight.[27]

As the century progressed, attempts were made to link *Merry Wives* to the history plays. Jon Jory's 1976 American Conservatory Theater production opened and closed with "a 'sadly fallen' Falstaff (Ray Reinhardt) sitting on a darkened stage listening to himself in *Henry IV, Part I* pleading with Prince Hal not to banish him."[28] Jory imagined the play as a comic interlude in a broken life, Falstaff's comic humiliation a pathetic reflection of his earlier disfavor. The BBC's links were lighter, foreshadowing Quickly and Pistol's affair as the camera caught a secret tryst behind a shed.

Another strong ensemble elevated Michael Rudman's 1990 Chichester production. Penelope Keith and Phyllida Law's wives ran rings around Bill Maynard's Falstaff: "one moment he is submitting to massage and pounding away on a sort of Elizabethan exercise bike, bare stomach bulging; the next, Keith's love-tricks have reduced him to arthritic exhaustion."[29] Northern Broadsides produced the play in 1993 and 2001, both times with Barrie Rutter directing and playing Falstaff. The conviviality and accessibility of Broadsides' style worked in the play's favor, whether in Conrad Nelson's Host taking over the interval bar or through the songs that interspersed the evening. Rutter's Falstaff was relatively unlikeable, "a beer-bellied bully sporting, at one point, an MCC tie," while Mistress Page was "a vehement social climber, straight out of Alan Ayckbourn."[30] Comedy was generated through the recognizability of these English stereotypes.

Terry Hands's 1995 National production was tinted by nostalgia. The set was a country haven evoking England's rural past, which one critic commented "looked disconcertingly like a living museum, part of a Shakespeare theme-park."[31] Richard McCabe's darkly comic Ford stood out:

> He is particularly hilarious at the moment when the character is confronted for the second time with the suspect laundry basket. He gives the receptacle such an insanely thorough search that he ends up covered by it and crawling about the stage like some demented tortoise.[32]

Ford, in the hands of a strong actor, continued to reap rewards. At Regent's Park in 1999, "Paul Raffield [was] a treat, eyes popping and face distorting with the effort of concealing his ludicrous jealousy."[33] In the twenty-first century, Falstaff's prominence diminished in favor of a group dynamic. Both Michael Bodganov's 2002 Ludlow Festival production and the celebrated 2008 version at Shakespeare's Globe used their outdoor settings to create a participatory and convivial air, companies and audiences sharing a festival atmosphere. California Shakespeare Theater, meanwhile, opened its 2006 season with an imaginative puppet version.

Merry Wives has enjoyed most international success in operatic adaptations, of which Verdi's *Falstaff* (1893) is the most famous. Arrigo Boito's plot omits several characters and makes Nanetta Ford (Anne Page) and Fenton more central. Doctor Cajus (the sole rival for

Nanetta's love) is married to Bardolfo in the final scene's comic climax, while Falstaff is bolstered by the insertion of material including the catechism of honor from *Henry IV Part I*. A favorite with audiences and musicians, the opera remains in the repertory of major companies worldwide.

While the opera has been filmed several times, Shakespeare's play has received only one important screen adaptation, that for the BBC/Time Life series in 1982. Director David Jones saw the play as documentary as well as comedy, and the naturalistic set drew on Shakespeare's Birthplace for architectural details. The all-star cast included Richard Griffiths as Falstaff, Prunella Scales and Judy Davis as a lively pair of wives, and Ben Kingsley's Ford, whose "bustling brow-beating little man [gave] the theatrical voltage an increasing boost on every one of his increasingly welcome appearances."[34] The production intelligently realized that the closely observed class politics of small-town life was the stuff of modern British sitcoms, and was pitched accordingly.

The play's transference to the non-English-speaking world has been relatively limited, although it premiered in Vienna as early as 1771. Hans Rothe burlesqued it as *Falstaff in Windsor* in the early 1930s, but the most interesting German production was that of Gustaf Gründgens in Berlin, 1941: "Anything crude was studiously avoided . . . Gründgens directed Will Dohm as Sir John to portray the memory and indication of a better self beneath that mountain of fat."[35] Overturning the received impression of the play as outright farce, the play succeeded as a comedy of character.

While its European fortunes have not been illustrious, in 1950s Japan the play was a core part of Koreya Senda's early work for the Haiuyze (Actor's Theatre). More recently, Yasunari Takahashi adapted the play as *The Braggart Samurai* in the Kyogen tradition, aiming "to transform the fertility of a Shakespearean forest into the simplicity of a Japanese garden."[36] Brought to London in 1991, this adaptation was praised for its intelligent reimagining within traditional Japanese class systems, demonstrating a broader cultural applicability than is often realized.

Merry Wives' success may be qualified, but Falstaff himself remains an internationally recognizable icon, even outgrowing his own play in translation and adaptation. The parting shots of Taka-hashi's braggart samurai are perhaps the best testament to the dura-bility of both character and play:

> I for one will go on laughing until the very end. I shall be the one to laugh last and best. And I swear by this gigantic belly that my philosophy shall never change. (*He laughs . . . a thun-dering, Gargantuan-scale laugh.*)[37]

AT THE RSC

Onstage Popularity

Underrated in the study as lowbrow entertainment because of its predominantly farcical elements, *The Merry Wives of Windsor* has nevertheless always been popular on the stage for exactly those rea-sons: the practical stagecraft of the comic set pieces is superb. During Shakespeare's lifetime *Merry Wives* was performed repeatedly both at court and on the commercial stage; the play has remained in the the-atrical repertoire ever since.

The RSC have staged *Merry Wives* about every five years, fre-quently scheduling it either as Christmas entertainment (1964, 1995, 1996, 2003, 2006) or to kick-start their summer season (1968, 1979, 1985); apart from the 2002 touring version, which opened in the Swan, the play's size and energy have always secured it a mainstage home.

It has only once been staged alongside the *Henry IV* plays, in 1975. This might seem at first surprising, given the RSC's penchant for themed seasons, but playing Falstaff in all three plays is a tremen-dous burden on any actor, and the juxtaposition of the plays perhaps underlines too much the discontinuities in characterization and backstory.

Tone—Farce or Comedy?

Among a director's first decisions in staging *Merry Wives* are where on the comedic spectrum to pitch it and how realistic to make it. The farcical cartoon approach has proved tempting. However, it is significant that, over this half century at least, those RSC productions that have chosen to ground the play very firmly in a detailed social context have been the most successful, both at the box office and with the critics; those that have emphasized the farcical clowning at the expense of this context have had a more mixed response.

Within this framework, the decision how far to make Ford's jealousy real and painful to watch, how far enjoyably ludicrous, is often key. From 1985 onward, productions have tended to take Ford's sufferings increasingly seriously, giving added depth to the marital relationships though at the expense of some comic momentum. The choice for the actor of Falstaff is whether to stress the character's repeated failures or his irrepressibility in these defeats; the latter always seems to produce more rewarding results.

Although *Merry Wives* may seem to be a surefire winner, it is surprising how difficult it has proved to pull off totally successfully; reviewers are quick to grumble about a Falstaff or Ford that is insufficiently frenetic, while also demanding a convincingly realistic framework and a heartwarming ending.

Period Setting

Merry Wives is Shakespeare's only English comedy and although theoretically set in the fifteenth century, in the reign of Henry V, it clearly portrays the emerging small-town bourgeoisie of the Elizabethan world. As such, it has traditionally been played in an at least nominally Elizabethan setting, the main question being the degree of accuracy or realism to employ and how far any comic anachronisms or stylization could be pushed. Director Bill Alexander, actively seeking a contrast with previous productions, concluded the 1950s was the only other era that offered suitable social parallels; Rachel Kavanaugh came to a very similar conclusion for her late 1940s version. Otherwise RSC productions have remained resolutely Tudor.

They have also remained predominantly autumnal, in keeping with the "raw, rheumatic day" of the duel, the promised "posset" and "sea-coal fire" of the final reconciliation, and, perhaps most important, the age of the protagonists. Despite two influential wintry productions in 1911 and 1955, a snowy setting seems to work against the warmth of the comedy and has not been an option seen at the RSC. In line with this favored autumnal setting, the masque at Herne's oak has since 1979 frequently had a Halloween flavor.

Repeat Techniques

There is much that these RSC productions have in common. From 1975 onward, all have opened with a pre-show sequence, showing the daily life of the town and establishing the characters and their relationships. Occasionally productions have underlined the irruption of outsiders into this, whether Shallow and Slender in their Morris (1985) or Falstaff and his lads by motorbike (2006). Repeatedly directors have capitalized on the children needed for the masque, using these in the opening and as a linking device between scenes, and also to pad out and lighten the Latin lesson.

Mistress Page, the organizer and family woman, and the more frivolous childless Mistress Ford are regularly distinguished as brunette and blonde respectively; dark green outfits for Mistress Page and a lighter, brighter color, often orange or red, for Mistress Ford consistently recur, with Mistress Ford also marked out by lower necklines or more extravagant trimmings.

The play's performance template is exceptionally strong: business inherent but not specified in the text occurs repeatedly in very similar patterns. Every Ford seems to end up in the buck-basket; a false mustache for Broom is an obvious form of disguise, leading to the inevitable moment of delayed agony when it is ripped off; Simple regularly passes Quickly and Caius the articles from the closet, and Caius equally regularly delays the moment of realization in a double take. Dartboards identify both the modernized pubs, and decorative antlers are common at the Garter in any period. Dry ice sets the scene for the duel, and Dr. Caius frequently sports a full fencing outfit plus mask; his surgery is characterized by a skeleton or skull. Falstaff is discovered in a bath after his ducking, or changing behind a settle. The only black character is the outsider, Fenton. One fairy is comically late throughout Act 5, and/or unable to see through a mask. Shallow is included in the final revenge sequence, while Slender brings on his "wife" still veiled, to allow a dramatic reveal. Most of the productions close with an interpolated song or dance number, though many undercut this afterward with an image of isolation. Even the blocking and the positioning of furniture and doorways are surprisingly consistent, and an upper-level walkway seems de rigueur.

Finally, it is noteworthy that, although it is the wives who have the upper hand both morally and intellectually and who drive the main plot, it is the men who have the majority of the comic business and who dominate the reviews. The critics are unfailingly surprised to discover the role of Dr. Caius a star turn.

Directorial Reshaping

The text of *Merry Wives* is notoriously unreliable, with the Folio version twice the length of the "bad" Quarto, and the Garter speech an only partially relevant insert. Terry Hands produced a successful composite script in 1968, much copied later.

The "Germans" subplot is usually either removed or rearranged wholly within Act 4 Scene 5. As a result, the third plotting scene (Act 4 Scene 4) follows immediately after the witch of Brentford scene (Act 4 Scene 2), necessitating some directorial sleight of hand to cover the time lapse. The Latin lesson has gradually shrunk and finally vanished; the Garter speech is frequently cut in whole or part; other speaking parts in the masque are regularly reallocated, often excluding Pistol and even, on occasion, Quickly. Ad-libs for Dr. Caius seem repeatedly condoned.

The culmination of this process is, obviously, Greg Doran's adaptation of the play as *Merry Wives, The Musical,* of which more below . . .

1964: Christmas at the Aldwych

The RSC's first *Merry Wives* opened at the Aldwych in December 1964. Directed by John Blatchely, this was a "pantomime version,"[38] "conceived as a farcical knockabout."[39] It garnered the mixed reviews common to such interpretations and did not transfer to Stratford.

André François's design was highly stylized, the Tudor half-timbering clearly two-dimensional; even the painted canvas buck-basket had a fake bottom, enabling Falstaff to "march away"[40] in full view of the audience. The bright cartoon costumes in whites, yellows, "acid greens and pinks"[41] were controversial: many found them charming and elegant, reminded pleasurably of Tenniel's *Alice* drawings; to others, Falstaff's "series of yellow rings, expanding from chin to stomach,"[42] suggested a more contemporary image, "a parody of the Michelin tyre man."[43]

Clive Swift as Falstaff "emphasise[d] his cold, cynical, mercenary egotism";[44] the *Times* reviewer saw him as "a worried, slow-speaking, and half-defeated character who provided his antagonists with little to deflate." Brenda Bruce and Patsy Byrne as the wives struck "a credibly human compromise between intrigue and virtue";[45] Timothy West won repeated praise in the usually thank-less part of Page, giving "a self-effacingly intelligent portrait of mid-dle-class sobriety which [lent] conviction to every scene in which he appear[ed]."[46] However, Ian Richardson's "brilliant" Ford was an acknowledged triumph, to be reprised repeatedly for the next ten years: "consumed with greedy groundless jealousy . . . his fanatical grey face and precise jerky gait . . . spitting frenzy and baffled mad-ness were unforgettable."[47]

1968–70: Hands's Sparkling RSC Debut in a Context of Social Realism

Any disappointments in 1964 were more than made up for by the next production. Directed for the RST by a young Terry Hands mak-ing his Stratford debut, the 1968 production was an unqualified success with both critics and audiences. It was to transfer to the Aldwych, go out on a national tour, and return again for a second Stratford season before being sent out on a further tour, this time to Japan. It was revived again in 1975, followed by yet another London transfer.

The key to the production's success was twofold. Hands grounded the play in a detailed, sharply observed social context, giving it what Philip French writing in the *New Statesman* described as "solidity, a rooted quality."[48] He continued:

3. Terry Hands's 1968 RSC production: Brenda Bruce as Mistress Page and Elizabeth Spriggs as Mistress Ford were "pretty well flawless."

The burghers, Ford and Page and their wives, are presented as extraordinarily pleased with their way of life, self-congratulatory in their finery, proud of their well-ordered homes, and looking happily on as their children play in the clean streets and get a veneer of improving culture from Sir Hugh Evans.[49]

Similarly, Michael Billington commented on the 1976 revival:

The virtue of Hands's production is that it realises money rather than sex is the mainspring of the plot . . . getting and spending is the theme; and Hands places this against a fully-realised country town . . . where the children run through the streets playing football, conkers and Opiesque* games and where the bourgeoisie close ranks against the threat of knightly invasion.[50]

Within this context, however, Hands pushed everything to extremes: "Bursting with high spirits and parading its priapic jokes . . . on the surface the evening looks one of exaggeration: the Welsh are so Welsh, the French are so French, and isn't it going to be so smelly in the Thames tonight";[51] "The formula is to play everything for all it's worth."[52] It proved a winning combination: Hands had "performed . . . a miracle . . . A truly funny play."[53]

The interpretation was, of course, highly dependent on its actors. Richardson (Ford) and Bruce (Mistress Page) were recast in their 1964 roles, winning praise as before, though this time as members of an outstanding ensemble. They were joined by Jeffrey Dench as Page, and Elizabeth Spriggs as a Mistress Ford who for once "hover[ed] on the brink of giving [Falstaff] credence,"[54] "waking to the joys of intrigue with endearingly innocent delight."[55] D. A. N. Jones commented in *The Listener*:

The wives are pretty well flawless. Ford would necessarily be jealous about a wife like Elizabeth Spriggs. There are secrets and mysteries in this marriage . . . It is equally understandable that Page should not be worried . . . Independent and boyish, his wife is quite familiar and comprehensible to him; their marriage is more easy-going, less exciting.[56]

---

* Iona and Peter Opie collected and documented children's literature, toys, and games.

Young considered Brewster Mason an "admirable" Falstaff, with an "almost leonine head above a vast pear-shaped body, and a knightly dignity that never [forsook] him," adding: "The contrast of Falstaff's courtly pretensions with his frivolous behaviour . . . [had never been] better nor more consistently suggested."[57] The production's powerful closing image showed Falstaff, alone on stage after the townsfolk had left, exiting with his "podgy" page Robin in his arms, "quell[ing] the laughter" with "a sudden serious moment" which suggested that Falstaff was "more generous than any of them."[58]

Timothy O'Brien's design was Elizabethan in tone, with realistic costumes against a stylized set. The palette was subtle and warmly autumnal, oranges, greens, and browns predominating with occasional blues and reds. The attractive and substantial costumes displayed period detail while appearing with their floral designs to be made of tapestry; a flooring of patchwork carpet squares echoed the checkered motif of the settings, "Toytown building blocks" which formed "skeletal scenes through and about which the company [could] move, generally at an indignant run."[59]

1975: Revival as Part of Falstaff Season

In 1975 Terry Hands revived the production again, this time as the culmination of a Stratford season that opened with *Henry V* and then added both parts of *Henry IV*; Mason returned to play Falstaff throughout. Richardson, Dench, and Bruce reprised Ford, Page, and Mistress Page once more, though Barbara Leigh-Hunt replaced Spriggs as Mistress Ford. The production itself remained essentially the same, and resulted in the same favorable reviews.

On the subsequent London transfer, special notice went to two newcomers: Irving Wardle praised the "maladroit precision" of Ben Kingsley as Slender and commented: "Ann Hasson converts Anne Page from the usual insipid virgin into a downright tough girl, characteristically seen charging downstage to snarl at us that rather than marry Slender she would be 'sat in the earth and bowled to death with turnips.' "[60]

1979: Revenge Comedy Ends in Reconciliation

Trevor Nunn's similarly realistic production four years later was another success, emphasizing "such themes as the pursuit of money, revenge, and underhanded sexual intrigue."[61] Michael Billington in the *Guardian* concluded:

> The Terry Hands production was . . . funnier but Mr Nunn uncovers more in the text. I had never, for instance, noticed before how everyone is obsessed with revenge . . . Nunn offers us not rampant farce but a revenge comedy that ends . . . in reconciliatory handshakes as everyone drifts back to their safe cosy world.[62]

Analyzing the play's financial transactions, Benedict Nightingale suggested:

> By fixing the play so firmly in its tiny grasping world, Nunn is able to bring out what perhaps it subliminally is, Shakespeare's protest at a materialism, greed and indifference to people that infects the newly-prosperous bourgeoisie as much as . . . the crook or near-crook classes.[63]

Nunn was the first to characterize the Herne's Oak sequence as Halloween festivities, transforming the mood and introducing an eerie tone. Thomas Laroque considered that he successfully made the audience's "flesh creep," but complained this made "the return to light hearted comedy or farce . . . all the more difficult."[64]

John Napier's lavish Elizabethan settings were universally admired, providing a supportively detailed context of "half-timbered houses, mullioned windows, rows of washing, leaf-shedding branches and a Windsor signpost" signaling "a play built round a specific bourgeois society . . . of birding, hare coursing and hot venison pasties."[65] Both set and costumes were in sepia, brown, black, white, with touches of red for Falstaff and Robin.

However, despite the play's overall success, John Woodvine was regarded as a disappointing Falstaff. Nightingale saw him as:

> a Santa on the skids, dowdy and grouchy, his old arrogance reduced to a sort of seedy vanity and his one-time ebullience to

4. Trevor Nunn's 1979 RSC production with John Woodvine and Ben Kingsley as Ford: "With his pencil-thin moustache and squeezed vowels he is the Elizabethan equivalent of a used-car salesman . . . particularly brilliant at playing his disguised scenes with Falstaff on a note of wheezy jollity and then releasing manic screams of rage."

no more than a shrivelled nostalgia for the sack and the sex he now seems scarcely capable of enjoying . . . his nose is as sharp as a pen, and he always looks likely to begin babbling of green fields.[66]

So yet again, the comic honors went to Ford, here played by Ben Kingsley:

With his pencil-thin moustache and squeezed vowels he is the Elizabethan equivalent of a used-car salesman . . . particularly brilliant at playing his disguised scenes with Falstaff on a note of wheezy jollity and then releasing manic screams of rage the

second the fat knight has left the room . . . [he] builds to a marvellous pitch of cuckolded rage and is the only Ford I have seen
to fling the dirty washing out of the buck-basket not once but
twice.[67]

Susan Tracy as "a lascivious-eyed Mrs Ford"[68] and Jane Downs as
Mrs. Page were "merry enough but perhaps a little too wise and
self-confident," though this was "more than offset by a randy and
truculent Mrs. Quickly (Lila Kaye) who . . . seem[ed] to enjoy herself as much as the audience . . . eye-winking, glib-tongued [and]
salacious."[69]

1985: "The New Elizabethans" — 1590s Give Way to 1950s

Bill Alexander continued the tradition of detailed social realism, but
made the radical choice to update the play sharply, setting it not in
the 1590s but in the "You've never had it so good" 1959 world of the
"New Elizabethans." The decision proved a triumphant success: "a
terrific show";[70] "merry from start to finish . . . another hit";[71]
"Bard in the Supermac age . . . The joke is carried off with thorough-
ness and wit."[72] William Dudley's clever symbolic set with its "witty
and striking series of period interiors"[73] made the most of the RST's
technical resources: exploiting the revolve with "virtuosity . . . sets
waltzing in and out of sight as though at the behest of some master
choreographer,"[74] as isolated self-propelled items of scenery rotated
on to suggest a 1950s suburban semi "complete with bay window,
cocktail cabinet, and radiogram,"[75] or a "roadhouse Tudor" Garter
Inn[76] with mahogany paneling, dartboard, and "Diana Dors-type
barmaid."[77] Shallow and Slender arrived in an open-top Morris,
chauffeured by Simple; the wives exchanged letters under paired
hair dryers, in what became the show's iconic image; as for Herne's
Oak, "the tree, in one of the show's most brilliant jokes, [was] a vic-
tim of Corporation bureaucracy. Peter Jeffrey's discomfited knight
[had] a mere stump on which to relax his haunches and receive the
jocund wives."[78]

The cast played their roles with gusto: "The excellent Peter Jeffrey
as Falstaff, a florid party with shifty eyes, a handlebar moustache,

breeches and yellow waistcoat, suggesting a minor public school and a murky war record [was] fruity and raucously funny,"[79] though perhaps younger and with less embonpoint than most Falstaffs. Nicky Henson's Ford, full of "sheer fury" and "humorous invention" in all the expected ways, also threw interesting "fresh light" on the character by revealing genuine though insecure love for his wife, playing Ford as "passionate rather than [just] farcical."[80]

"The Merry Wives themselves were played with marvellous panache by Janet Dale and Lindsay Duncan. Gossiping under the hairdryer . . . giggling over gins on the sofa . . . or acting out their 'overheard' dialogue . . . they were sharp, subtle and inventive."[81] But despite this praise, Nicholas Shrimpton had reservations: "They suffered nonetheless from a deep-rooted uncertainty. Were they wise and sympathetic heroines . . . or were they satirical portraits of grossly vulgar, bourgeois housewives? The actresses were not sure, as a consequence, neither was the audience." Vulgar they certainly were, Bill Alexander himself admits: "In 1600 you could portray [the wives] as jolly and warm-hearted, whereas I've portrayed them as spiky and rather tasteless, quite cruel in their judgement."[82]

In the smaller roles, there was "a superb Doctor Caius from David Bradley [playing] consistently against the stereotype of the inflammable Frenchman"[83] and an excellent performance from "Bruce Alexander as a pulpit-hungry Welsh cleric,"[84] but for Stanley Wells "the abiding delight of the production [was] Sheila Steafel's Mistress Quickly, a down-at-heel little figure of faded and bibulous gentility, incorrigibly helpful, touchingly delighted with any rewards that [might] come her way, succoured through life's trickier passages by a hip-flask, bemused by the antics of the stage furnishings, and finally, a squiffy Fairy Queen who [had] lost her way to the party."[85] Her eventual arrival at Herne's Oak as the others departed was this production's parting tragicomic moment.

1992: Return to Farce

David Thacker's 1992 production marked a return to the purely farcical approach of 1964. Once again, stylized costumes in "queasy shades of violet, green and pink"[86] stood out boldly against a cartoon set, here a cream-colored fantasy of curling staircases and

5. David Thacker's 1992 production: Ron Cook's Dr. Caius was a "preening . . . black and yellow wasp . . . twirling in a flat spin of specious rage, his codpiece bulging, his goatee beard erect," here pinioning Simple (Nick Holder) to the floor.

paper-cut-out bridges, "an origamist's delight,"[87] and the action seemed to many over-frenetic and desperate.

The critic Charles Spencer[88] complained that the production lacked the "world of carefully observed normality [necessary to provide] a solid base for the spiralling lunacy of the action," while Michael Billington lamented that the production "forfeit[ed] the two things that make the play work: a concrete sense of reality and a predatory, desperate Falstaff."[89]

As that implied, the excellent but needle-thin Benjamin Whitrow proved miscast as Falstaff, unable to "camouflage his thin man's nose, thin man's cheeks and worse, thin man's tenor voice and quick light movements";[90] "redolent of the cathedral cloister," he seemed "a minor Trollopian cleric"[91] or "game old scholarly vicar."[92] The wives (Cheryl Campbell and Gemma Jones) won limited praise in difficult circumstances—"mettlesome heroines"[93] was typical. Anton Lesser's hyperactive Ford, "a thin-lipped suburbanite within whom the obsessed Othello [was] turning somersaults of rage,"[94] was both loved and loathed. The one undisputed triumph was Ron Cook's

Caius, a "preening . . . black and yellow wasp,"[95] "twirling in a flat spin of specious rage, his codpiece bulging and his goatee beard erect, selecting his rapiers from a yellow golf bag with no idea of their size or weight until they either [belied] their sheaths or [sent] him crashing to the floor."[96]

1996: A Chekhovian Comedy—with Leslie Phillips as Falstaff

Ian Judge's production in 1996 moved the play back from farce to comedy, with a Ford (Edward Petherbridge) whose escalating jealousy was sincere and painful to watch, only gradually building to the usual manic heights. Falstaff was also younger and lighter than usual, as in 1985. The production had an almost Chekhovian feel. Critics were uncertain how to react to this new approach, many complaining that the production was "not funny enough"[97] or lacked "the degree of physical delirium required."[98] They took comfort in the traditionally farcical playing of the smaller roles—an excellent Caius and Slender stole the majority of the notices: "Guy Henry's impulsive, dolorous, weightless, elongated Dr Caius is blissfully funny . . . Christopher Luscombe's Slender is a paragon of embarrassed, apprehensive, high-bourgeois silliness."[99] This was a Slender who flounced off *with* his new "wife" at the end. Shaun Usher was more analytic:

> The latest version is quaint, pretty, intelligent and uncommonly sweet-natured for something dealing in so much brutal humiliation . . . It is gently amusing rather than hilarious . . . Perhaps there are too many styles of laughter-raising in the same place. At times, if not jarring, the mixture doesn't gel. Merry is the word, really. What's missing is true, anarchic intoxication.[100]

In keeping with the comedic rather than farcical feel was a beautiful and naturalistic set by Tim Goodchild "that effortlessly change[d] from courtyard to house to pub,"[101] a "picturesque . . . treat . . . in limed-oak, complete with staircases and raised walkway, golden autumnal trees and a prospect of the Berkshire countryside and

Windsor Castle."[102] The "agreeably exotic" costumes (Nightingale) were "an ingenious mixture of the Elizabethan and the Edwardian."[103]

Joanna Macallum as Meg Page with gardening apron and shears, "the very image of a comfortable, confident, suburban woman bent on getting as much innocent fun as she can,"[104] was well matched with "a smiley sparky Susannah York, enjoying herself and giving 'the leer of invitation' . . . as the well-off Mrs Ford."[105]

However, the "surprise casting stroke of the season and among the most marvellous" was "Leslie Phillips, that suave old comic smoothy with no Shakespearean experience":

> He has Falstaff's irrepressible swagger of spirit, and also his private sense of defeat . . . he handles the language with such relish . . . rich impishness . . . [his] nonchalance . . . is cherishable. And the more he is dumped by the good folk of Windsor, the riper his delivery of the language grows . . . he has the life-enhancing essence of Falstaff because he catches the contradictions behind so many lines.[106]

2002: 1940s Comedy at the Swan

Rachel Kavanaugh, the only woman to direct *Merry Wives* for the RSC, "discovered an emotional charge in the play that eludes most directors,"[107] exploring both psychological depths and societal tensions, without sacrificing either the play's humor or humanity, "a production . . . simply flawless in both conception and execution."[108]

The play was updated, with much loving period detail, to the immediate postwar years, "restor[ing] the recognizability which has been eroded by the passage of four centuries"[109] but also "most successfully" giving the plot "ballast" by

> present[ing] the wives as women readjusting to a world in which the independence they briefly enjoyed during the war [had been] curtailed . . . The veneer of quiet suburban order [wore] thin as the women's rebellious streak show[ed] itself and they demonstrate[d] that they like[d] and rel[ied] on each other rather more than . . . their husbands.[110]

Even Anne, "a schoolgirl in uniform," had "a mind of her own";[111] the subtle closing image showed the newly married wife exiting arms linked with her mother and Mistress Ford, as her husband went ahead with Page.

However, Lucy Tregear and Claire Carrie were "as genuinely merry a pair of wives as I can remember."[112] This successful balance was maintained throughout. The production was "a tremendously entertaining evening,"[113] and yet

> at the same time . . . reache[d] into the dark heart of the play by refusing to treat Ford as a figure of fun, the stock character of ludicrously jealous husband . . . When Tom Mannion frenziedly search[ed] the laundry-basket at its second appearance and at last topple[d] into it himself this [was] the proper climax to his obsession, but hitherto his Ford [had] taken us towards the nastier follies of suspicion.[114]

Kavanaugh also touched briefly on wider issues:

> Chuk Iwuji's American accent and flying jacket impl[ied] discreetly that Anne's beloved Fenton [was] a Yank air ace stationed somewhere in the area. Iwuji's casting [was] largely, but not entirely, colour-blind: in another astute touch, father Page's deliberate line: "She is no match for you" [was] followed by an awkward silence as all realise[d] but none address[ed] the issue of race.[115]

The casting was uniformly powerful. Richard Cordery was a "superbly mountainous Falstaff . . . with a fine relish for the sound of the words and a suggestion that they were being hauled up from some ruined treasury of a mind, as stuffed with language as his body [was] packed with fat."[116] He found "depth in the role as well as great comedy . . . accept[ing] his punishment with rare grace and dignity. It [was] unexpectedly touching."[117]

John Gross concluded: "It's a production that goes mainly for laughs, but which reminds us that the play is more than the made-to-order farce it is often assumed to be. There are constant humanising touches, and a true Shakespearean warmth at the end": "Intelligent and fun."[118]

2006: *Merry Wives, The Musical*

In 1986 Sheridan Morley described *Merry Wives* as "a play in desperate need of maybe a full orchestra and fifteen full numbers as well";[119] twenty years later the RSC obliged, with a Christmas production by Greg Doran. This was an adaptation that embraced Elizabethan dramaturgical principles in deliberately playing to the strengths of its cast and references to past successes: romantic love songs were incorporated for musical theater stars drafted in to play Anne and Fenton; Act 2 opened with a dance routine built around Simon Trinder's comic Slender; the accompaniment of pots, pans, and washboards for the title number paid tribute to the similarly feminist musical sequence in Doran's *Tamer Tamed*; Quickly's masque disguise reminded audiences of Judi Dench's Oscar-winning role as Elizabeth I. Most significantly, the role of Dench's Mistress Quickly was enormously expanded, incorporating back-history and sizable extracts from *Henry IV Part II*, to give a more substantial relationship with Falstaff. Doran also built on a frequently cut aside from Pistol (2.2.120–22), together with his unexpected reappearance at the masque, and the marriage in *Henry V*; the combined rewrites, with some additions, give us a yearning Quickly finally propositioned by Falstaff but choosing instead to go off with a swaggering leather-clad punk-Goth Pistol "young enough to be her son and old enough to know better."[120]

This "brilliantly confident production"[121] was set firmly "in a musical fantasy-land,"[122] "where Fifties New Look meets olde worlde Jacobean."[123] Paul Englishby's score was equally eclectic, offering tributes to everyone from Verdi to Lloyd Webber, Elizabethan madrigals to Gilbert and Sullivan, even a show-stopping country and western hoedown.

Simon Callow as Falstaff was "glutton dressed as ram,"[124] "with billowing silver hair . . . a tum that seem[ed] to conceal a wheelbarrow, and a fruity gurgle of an accent";[125] "Haydn Gwynne and Alexandra Gilbreath [made] eloquent, elegant wives,"[126] "manag[ing] that tricky double act of the truly touching and the randomly comic";[127] tall, gangling, mustachioed Alistair McGowan was "a Ford of Basil Fawlty fatuity and rages."[128]

There was especial praise for "Paul Chahidi as the ludicrous Frenchman . . . and Ian Hughes as the ludicrous Welshman . . . [both reveling] in producing the weirdest body language and most strangulated accents, making 'fritters of English' indeed," adding: "The reconciliation jig between these two would-be duellists is perhaps the funniest example of some really top-drawer comic choreography from Michael Ashcroft."[129] To others, Simon Trinder gave a "star performance as a fey, young yellow-bearded Slender: feckless, forlorn, artless, heart-catching, riveting in every movement, every utterance."[130]

However, it was Dench's Mistress Quickly, combining comedy, pathos, determination, and self-deprecation, who, predictably, stole the show.

THE DIRECTOR'S CUT: INTERVIEWS WITH BILL ALEXANDER AND RACHEL KAVANAUGH

Bill Alexander was born in Norfolk in 1948 and trained as a theater director at the Bristol Old Vic. His award-winning productions range from new plays to the classics. He joined the RSC as an assistant director in 1977 and became a resident director in 1980. His many RSC productions have included Howard Barker's *The Hang of the Gaol* (1978) and *Country Dancing* (1986), *Tartuffe* and a play about its author Molière, *Richard III* (1984), *Volpone* (1984), *The Merry Wives of Windsor* (1985), *A Midsummer Night's Dream* (1987), *The Merchant of Venice* (1988), *Twelfth Night* (1988), and *Cymbeline* (1988). From 1992 to 2000 Bill Alexander was artistic director of the Birmingham Repertory Theatre. He also directed the perennially popular adaptation of Raymond Briggs's *The Snowman*.

Rachel Kavanaugh has been the artistic director of the Birmingham Repertory Theatre since 2006 where her directorial credits have included *The Wizard of Oz* (2006), *Uncle Vanya* (2007), *Peter Pan: A Musical Adventure* (2007), *Hapgood* (2008), *His Dark Materials* (2009), and *Arthur and George* (2010). Her experience as a director

of Shakespeare is extensive, mostly at Regent's Park Open Air Theatre, where she has helmed productions of *A Midsummer Night's
Dream* (1997/8), *Twelfth Night* (1999), *Much Ado About Nothing*
(2000), *Love's Labour's Lost* (2001), *As You Like It* (2002), *The Two
Gentlemen of Verona* (2003), *Cymbeline* (2005), and *The Taming of
the Shrew* (2006). She first worked for the RSC directing *Alice in
Wonderland* over the 2001–02 winter season, returning a year
later to work on the production of *The Merry Wives of Windsor* that
she discusses here.

**The Merry Wives of Windsor has been called Shakespeare's most
middle class and suburban play. Do you agree, and did the design
of your production reflect this?**

BA: It is his most middle class and suburban play. The only other play
that I can think of that has such an absence of the upper and aristo-
cratic and ruling class is the *Shrew*. Falstaff is of course arguably an
aristocrat fallen amongst shopkeepers, which situation provides the
meat of the humor. However the provenance of his knighthood
remains obscure. We take from the *Henry IV* plays a sense of his
exclusion from courtly life, although no element in the plot specifi-
cally links him to those events. Is the story somehow meant to take
place after the end of *Part II* and before his death in *Henry V*? Or perhaps before the sagas, or somewhere in the middle? We don't know
and actually don't care. The play is self-contained and floats in some
parallel universe. This was one of the reasons I felt happy relocating
the play in history (which I did not do with the *Henry IV*s), looking
for the trans-historical meanings without the burden of actual historical events impinging.

It seemed to me that in social history the spirit of a new Elizabethan age in England following the coronation of the young queen
in the mid-1950s was a perfect reflection of the stress and strain
caused by class mobility at the time of the first Elizabeth; especially in
the mid-1590s when *Merry Wives* was written. The aristocracy was
becoming impoverished and turning to trade for finance and the
emerging wealthy middle class for marriage. Really it wasn't such a
mad idea of Malvolio's that he could dream of the hand of the Lady

Olivia. After all, consider the situation in *The Duchess of Malfi*. One of the really funny ideas in the play is how panic-stricken Page is at the idea of his daughter, Anne, marrying the feckless Fenton, who is undoubtedly her social superior. A couple of generations earlier he would have been delighted. The world of a fallen Falstaff came together in my mind with the world of the hero of *I'm Alright Jack*. Falstaff misunderstands his time. He believes his breeding gives him automatic access to the beds of the bourgeoisie. He reckons without their newfound self-confidence and pride, their moral strength built on financial security. At the start of the production television aerials slowly emerged from the roofs of the faux-Tudor houses of Windsor.

RK: I understand what you mean by the question, but I resist it because "middle class" and "suburban" have a slight pejorative sense about them, especially the word "suburban," which suggests that in some way it's a lesser play. It is one of the few Shakespeare plays which are almost entirely concerned with people who aren't of rank, some of whom have money and others who want money. They are people who are very conscious of their place in society, but apart from Falstaff they are not lords, ladies, or gentlemen. We are not dealing with kings and queens so I agree in the general sense of the question, but I resist it because I think it risks putting the play into a box of being not a great play. The production played in the Swan, went on a regional tour, and then went into the Old Vic. The design did reflect it insomuch as a design for a regional tour in a mobile theater can, because it was essentially the same design for each theater. The design was incredibly simple and was basically a continuation of the Swan, but the costumes were very English 1940s and so quite conservative for that group of people. They were very particular, very specific because I wanted to make a real world that the audience could recognize.

Do you see this as a play in which the women come out on top in every respect? Mistresses Page and Ford are certainly a very rewarding pair of roles.

BA: The women think Falstaff is just absolutely ridiculous, a complete and utter joke. It's really quite easy for them to come out on top given the depth of the fat knight's self-delusion. They never have a moment's doubt about what he deserves and how to deliver that humiliation. It is the fact that they are not in any way conflicted or tempted by the situation that allows the play to be a simple farce rather than a darkly tortured comedy like, say, *Troilus and Cressida* or *All's Well*. And they certainly are rewarding parts, as Lindsay Duncan and Janet Dale proved.

RK: I think that is the case, yes. They come out on top in terms of the fact that they put a plan into action and the plan succeeds. Mistress Ford and Mistress Page are the driving brains behind the play, they are the cleverest people in the play, and together they are more than the sum of their parts. What's brilliant is that the two of them together are an unstoppable force. They combat with Falstaff for our affection, but in terms of the mechanism of the play and the plot and intelligence within the play they absolutely come out on top. Even Anne Page gets what she wants in the end.

Does it matter that Shakespeare's original audience would already have met Falstaff, Justice Shallow, and others in *Henry IV,* but that many members of a modern audience will not have done so?

BA: No. See answer to question one. The play is completely stand-alone from the *Henry*s. Some would say that Falstaff and the others are not even really the same characters. Or you could say that he is just a pale shadow. In some ways it's a bit of a mystery why he wrote it. Elizabeth demanding a play about Falstaff in love is possible I suppose, but then she must have missed the point about his relationship to Hal in *Henry IV Part I.* I think he wanted to experiment with pure farce along the lines of *The Comedy of Errors* but in a contemporary English situation. I suppose it's his most Jonsonian play in that respect.

RK: No, I don't think it matters at all. I think it's my responsibility as a director to make sure that the characters are understandable and that you don't need to have seen *Henry IV* in order to enjoy the play. There are layers of resonance that you get if you have seen those other plays, but I don't think it matters at all if you don't know them.

Tell us what you and your Falstaff found through your exploration of the character and the language of the fat knight.

BA: The language of Falstaff is rich and garrulous but without the edge, wit, and irony of the character in *Henry IV*. So Peter Jeffries and I worked on the idea of the pub bore, the soaked anecdote-spewer with a touch of Terry Thomas to provide grit and a whiff of danger.

RK: He is a man whose language is like his appetite in that it's varied, fulsome, excessive, beautiful, and gross. He is a kind of mighty contradiction, in that he is both incredibly attractive and repulsive, and we love him although what he is doing is outrageous. We went through a lot of versions of the end of the play in terms of how Falstaff was left, and we realized in the end that we didn't need to try to make the audience love him or feel sorry for him because they already did all that. If you embrace the language with which he speaks, both to us and also the other characters, that is in itself so delicious that we are incredibly attracted to him as a theatrical character.

Does it make a difference that this is almost entirely a prose play, in which you don't have to spend time working with actors on the notorious iambic pentameter?

BA: Well, no, it doesn't matter; it just gives you more time to explore other things—like how to get the laughs. Nicky Henson spent far more time practicing how to somersault over the sofa than refining his speech rhythms.

RK: It doesn't mean that the language is any easier; in fact in many cases it means it's more complicated. The prose is constructed antithetically just as a lot of Shakespeare's verse is and so it requires as much careful attention as verse does.

In practical terms, how do you deal with the sheer bulk and weight of Falstaff in the laundry basket?

BA: You send the guys who have to carry it down to the gym every day.

RK: We cast two very, very strong people as John and Robert! Because it was in the Swan and then touring he had to get in the bas-

6. Rachel Kavanaugh's 2002 RSC touring production with Richard Cordery as Falstaff and Claire Carrie as Mistress Ford.

ket and they had to carry him off, we couldn't have trapdoors or any-thing so, seriously, we had to get actors who were able to do that.

Shakespeare often focuses on the destructive power of jealousy within his plays—given that *Merry Wives* is a comedy, how seriously did you take Ford's jealousy?

BA: A very good question. You have to take it very seriously for the comedy to work. His jealousy is the absolute center of the plot mechanism. If the audience don't believe in it they won't believe in the story and so won't find it funny. The essence of a sexually jealous man is that everything he sees seems to confirm his suspicions. Hence, at one point when Nicky was tearing the house apart looking for Falstaff he ripped down the curtains to find the Tory election slogan "You've never had it so good" staring him in the face. (The Fords and the Pages were obviously Tory voters, by the way.) Ford is quite literally being driven mad by jealousy, just like Leontes and Othello and Troilus and Posthumus. Us knowing that he has no cause allows

7. Bill Alexander's 1985 RSC production. Ford's jealousy was "the absolute center of the plot mechanism," with Nicky Henson as Ford, Janet Dale as Mistress Page, Lindsay Duncan as Mistress Ford, David Bradley as Dr. Caius, Bruce Alexander as Hugh Evans, Paul Webster as Page.

us to laugh in a farce-structured play. In a tragically structured play like *Othello* it makes us weep.

RK: We played it completely seriously, because for Ford that jealousy is no less than that experienced by Othello or Leontes. He is a married man just as they are, experiencing the same emotions. The context through which the audience views that may be different, but for the actor playing that role the experience is identical. Unlike *Othello* it has a happy resolution, but the experience is as intense so I think you have to take it just as seriously.

The play very much fosters stereotypes—Caius the French doctor, Sir Hugh the Welsh parson—did you adhere to these stereotypes or act against them?

BA: I made Caius a psychiatrist to stand in starker contrast to Hugh the priest. Whether this increased or diminished them as stereotypes I don't know, but it made the bitterness of their rivalry spicier. It was something the 1950s setting made possible and sharpened the humor.

RK: It's impossible to totally act against them because of the way those two particular characters are written and their very extreme modes of speech, but I didn't view them as stereotypes. I viewed them as extreme personalities who happened to be French and Welsh. I can't speak for how Shakespeare's audience would have viewed all French people or all Welsh people, but certainly within the context of our production and with a modern audience what we had was an extremely eccentric French doctor and an almost equally eccentric Welsh pastor. But it's not the fact that they are French and Welsh that makes them eccentric, it's the fact that they are particularly eccentric people who happen to be of those nationalities, and both of them, like Falstaff, enjoy speaking in their own particular way.

How did you stage the difficult "fairy scene" at the end of the play?

BA: It was pretty much all Halloween, trick or treat, headless men and zombies kind of stuff, with Sheila Steafel as the Hostess staggering around completely drunk in a full fairy outfit complete with wilting wand. Herne's Oak had been reduced to a huge stump with a notice proclaiming that The Ministry of Works had deemed it in breach of Health and Safety regulations.

RK: We set that scene on Halloween, so all the children were dressed in fancy dress costumes. Mistress Quickly was a great big fairy and the children were all little ghosts and witches and fairies. The ghost costumes worked very well for the boys who had to go off and marry, and, like everything else in the production, it had a real rationale behind it: those children could absolutely have been doing that on an evening during the period in which we set the play. And by wonderful circumstance our Press Night in Stratford was on Halloween, so it all worked out very happily.

PLAYING FALSTAFF: SIMON CALLOW

Simon Callow was born and brought up in London before going on to Queen's University, Belfast, and subsequently attending the Drama Centre London. In the early 1970s he joined the Gay Sweatshop theater company and later went on to work with the Joint Stock theater company. He played Mozart in the Royal National Theatre's original production of Peter Shaffer's *Amadeus* (1979) and starred as Tom Chance in the Channel 4 situation comedy *Chance in a Million.* Simon was nominated for a BAFTA for his role as Gareth in Mike Newell's *Four Weddings and a Funeral* (1994). Recent acting credits include Pozzo in the revival of Beckett's *Waiting for Godot* (2009). A distinguished director and writer, his directing credits include *My Fair Lady* in 1992, *Les Enfants du Paradis* for the RSC in 1995, and Stephen Oliver's *Cantabile* in 1996. His *Being an Actor* (1984) is a partly autobiographical reflection on his chosen profession, and *Love Is Where It Falls* (2007) on his relationship with the theatrical agent Peggy Ramsay. He has written biographies of Oscar Wilde, Charles Laughton, and Orson Welles and also specialized in one-man shows, including *The Mystery of Charles Dickens* by Peter Ackroyd and *Shakespeare: The Man from Stratford* by Jonathan Bate (2010). Here Simon discusses the experience of playing Falstaff in Gregory Doran's RSC 2006–07 musical version of *The Merry Wives of Windsor.*

Does it matter that Shakespeare's original audience would already have met Falstaff, Justice Shallow, and others in *Henry IV,* but that many members of a modern audience will not have done so?

Well, of course it would have been delightful for the actor playing Falstaff at the very first performance of *Merry Wives,* that wave of delighted recognition, but after that, once word had got around, it wouldn't have made much difference. By now, Falstaff is part of the collective unconscious, and whether people have seen *Henry IV* or not, they have a sense of who Falstaff is. I suspect that you're right, and that most theatergoers start by seeing *Merry Wives,* so that they have the extraordinary experience of finding when they come to the history plays that a somewhat beaten-down and marginalized character is in fact one of infinite scope.

And for you as an actor, who has also played Falstaff in a version of the *Henry IV* plays: was that helpful, or a positive hindrance? Did you think of him as the same character or did you start from scratch?

Having heard all my life that *Merry Wives* was a rather shabby spin-off, and having indeed repeated that opinion in the two little books I wrote about *Henry IV,* I was immensely excited to discover that the character is absolutely himself, simply in reduced circumstances. The history plays take place against a backdrop of war, love, life, and death; *Merry Wives* is, famously, entirely domestic and bourgeois in its world. But Falstaff himself is still Falstaff, and given half a chance, he emerges as the semi-pagan fallen monarch that we know from the other plays. Once he gets into Windsor Great Park, he is in glorious form, but already after he's been tipped into the Thames, his epic self-awareness of the absurdity of him—him!—being drowned, his emergence like an overweight Neptune, with (in our production) fishes popping out of his pants and seaweed up his nostrils, a pantheistic figure—if not actually Pan himself—is fully worthy of the other plays.

The Merry Wives of Windsor has been called Shakespeare's most middle class and suburban play. Was it important to you that he is *Sir* John Falstaff, whereas the Fords and the Pages are merely *Master* and *Mistress*?

It's important to *him*: part of the hilarity of the play is the incongruity of him finding himself among *these* people. The ongoing joke is that of a con man who complains about the quality of the people whom he is reduced to conning.

What is driving Falstaff in this play: is he really in love (the premise of the action, if we believe the old story that Queen Elizabeth asked for a play about Falstaff in love)? Or in lust? Or led primarily by the sheer pleasure of the chase and the outrageous schemes and disguises?

I think it's a ruthless commercial consideration. He notes of both Mistress Page and Mistress Ford that they control their husbands' purses; "they shall be exchequers to me," he says. The chase is an inconvenience to him; it is his poverty that drives him on.

Does it make a difference that this is almost entirely a prose role (in a prose play)? Is there something distinctive about creating a Shakespearean role without the element of iambic pentameter?

Falstaff is almost entirely a prose role in all three plays. It is the greatest prose Shakespeare ever wrote. There are more prose roles in the canon than people seem to think. When I did *As You Like It*, I was praised by a number of critics for my handling of the verse, but Orlando has virtually none, nor does Sir T. Belch [in *Twelfth Night*]. Prose gives you a certain rhythmic freedom, which gives rise to all sorts of possibilities, but with verse you have the chance of creating a kind of spell. I always feel that the underlying iambic throb is like the distant sound of a ship's engine, or, indeed, the pulse of the mother's heart as the fetus nestles inside her. Prose can be incantatory, but it also offers fantastic possibilities for building huge irregular shapes of language which create constant surprise in a way which is harder in verse.

In purely practical terms, was this an uncomfortable role? The quick changes, the confinement in a laundry basket . . .

A nightmare. Both times I've played Falstaff, I elected to play him vast in girth. Everybody in the play finds it irresistible to comment on his bulk, and it is ironic to me that now, in the early twenty-first century, when people are getting fatter and fatter, when obesity is get-

8. Simon Callow as Falstaff: "an enormity of nature," "extremely hot and itchy" in full padding, wig, beard, and mustache.

ting more and more of a problem, a tradition has grown up of play-ing Falstaff as just having a bit of a tum. I believe passionately that Falstaff has to be monumentally fat, an enormity in nature in the most literal sense. He's become a natural phenomenon, like a hillside or a whale or Orson Welles. So I wore huge padding. One of the curi-ous things about wearing huge padding is that, however light it may in reality be, one feels enormously heavy, and even the journey back to the dressing room used to take an eternity. Being chased around by fairies in Windsor Great Park was almost terminally exhausting.

As well as padding, I wore a wig, a beard, and a mustache. All of this is extremely hot, and very itchy. I'm also horribly claustrophobic, so being locked in a laundry basket is no pleasure to me whatever. Then, still spitting out bits of laundry with gallons of sweat sloshing around inside the padding, to be dressed up as Alice Ford's maid's aunt from Brainford, Mother Prat—what one does for one's art!

SHAKESPEARE'S CAREER IN THE THEATER

BEGINNINGS

William Shakespeare was an extraordinarily intelligent man who was born and died in an ordinary market town in the English Midlands. He lived an uneventful life in an eventful age. Born in April 1564, he was the eldest son of John Shakespeare, a glove maker who was prominent on the town council until he fell into financial difficulties. Young William was educated at the local grammar in Stratford-upon-Avon, Warwickshire, where he gained a thorough grounding in the Latin language, the art of rhetoric, and classical poetry. He married Ann Hathaway and had three children (Susanna, then the twins Hamnet and Judith) before his twenty-first birthday: an exceptionally young age for the period. We do not know how he supported his family in the mid-1580s.

Like many clever country boys, he moved to the city in order to make his way in the world. Like many creative people, he found a career in the entertainment business. Public playhouses and professional full-time acting companies reliant on the market for their income were born in Shakespeare's childhood. When he arrived in London as a man, sometime in the late 1580s, a new phenomenon was in the making: the actor who is so successful that he becomes a "star." The word did not exist in its modern sense, but the pattern is recognizable: audiences went to the theater not so much to see a particular show as to witness the comedian Richard Tarlton or the dramatic actor Edward Alleyn.

Shakespeare was an actor before he was a writer. It appears not to have been long before he realized that he was never going to grow into a great comedian like Tarlton or a great tragedian like Alleyn. Instead, he found a role within his company as the man who patched up old plays, breathing new life, new dramatic twists, into tired repertory pieces. He paid close attention to the work of the university-educated dramatists who were writing history plays and tragedies for the public stage in a style more ambitious, sweeping, and poetically grand than anything that had been seen before. But he may also have noted that what his friend and rival Ben Jonson would call "Marlowe's mighty line" sometimes faltered in the mode of comedy. Going to university, as Christopher Marlowe did, was all well and good for honing the arts of rhetorical elaboration and classical allusion, but it could lead to a loss of the common touch. To stay close to a large segment of the potential audience for public theater, it was necessary to write for clowns as well as kings and to intersperse the flights of poetry with the humor of the tavern, the privy, and the brothel: Shakespeare was the first to establish himself early in his career as an equal master of tragedy, comedy, and history. He realized that theater could be the medium to make the national past available to a wider audience than the elite who could afford to read large history books: his signature early works include not only the classical tragedy *Titus Andronicus* but also the sequence of English historical plays on the Wars of the Roses.

He also invented a new role for himself, that of in-house company dramatist. Where his peers and predecessors had to sell their plays to the theater managers on a poorly paid piecework basis, Shakespeare took a percentage of the box-office income. The Lord Chamberlain's Men constituted themselves in 1594 as a joint stock company, with the profits being distributed among the core actors who had invested as sharers. Shakespeare acted himself—he appears in the cast lists of some of Ben Jonson's plays as well as the list of actors' names at the beginning of his own collected works—but his principal duty was to write two or three plays a year for the company. By holding shares, he was effectively earning himself a royalty on his work, something no author had ever done before in England. When the Lord Chamberlain's Men collected their fee for performance at court in the Christmas season of 1594, three of them went along to the Treasurer of the Chamber: not just Richard Burbage the tragedian and Will Kempe the clown, but also Shakespeare the scriptwriter. That was something new.

The next four years were the golden period in Shakespeare's

career, though overshadowed by the death of his only son, Hamnet, aged eleven, in 1596. In his early thirties and in full command of both his poetic and his theatrical medium, he perfected his art of comedy, while also developing his tragic and historical writing in new ways. In 1598, Francis Meres, a Cambridge University graduate with his finger on the pulse of the London literary world, praised Shakespeare for his excellence across the genres:

> As Plautus and Seneca are accounted the best for comedy and tragedy among the Latins, so Shakespeare among the English is the most excellent in both kinds for the stage; for comedy, witness his *Gentlemen of Verona*, his *Errors*, his *Love Labours Lost*, his *Love Labours Won*, his *Midsummer Night Dream* and his *Merchant of Venice*: for tragedy his *Richard the 2*, *Richard the 3*, *Henry the 4*, *King John*, *Titus Andronicus* and his *Romeo and Juliet*.

For Meres, as for the many writers who praised the "honey-flowing vein" of *Venus and Adonis* and *Lucrece*, narrative poems written when the theaters were closed due to plague in 1593–94, Shakespeare was marked above all by his linguistic skill, by the gift of turning elegant poetic phrases.

PLAYHOUSES

Elizabethan playhouses were "thrust" or "one-room" theaters. To understand Shakespeare's original theatrical life, we have to forget about the indoor theater of later times, with its proscenium arch and curtain that would be opened at the beginning and closed at the end of each act. In the proscenium arch theater, stage and auditorium are effectively two separate rooms: the audience looks from one world into another as if through the imaginary "fourth wall" framed by the proscenium. The picture-frame stage, together with the elaborate scenic effects and backdrops beyond it, created the illusion of a self-contained world—especially once nineteenth-century developments in the control of artificial lighting meant that the auditorium could be darkened and the spectators made to focus on the lighted stage. Shakespeare, by contrast, wrote for a bare platform stage with a standing audience gathered around it in a courtyard in full daylight. The audience were always conscious of themselves and their fellow spectators, and they shared the same "room" as the actors. A sense of immediate presence and the creation of rapport with the audience were all-important. The actor could not afford to imagine he was in a closed world, with silent witnesses dutifully observing him from the darkness.

Shakespeare's theatrical career began at the Rose Theatre in Southwark. The stage was wide and shallow, trapezoid in shape, like a lozenge. This design had a great deal of potential for the theatrical equivalent of cinematic split-screen effects, whereby one group of characters would enter at the door at one end of the tiring-house wall at the back of the stage and another group through the door at the other end, thus creating two rival tableaux. Many of the battle-heavy and faction-filled plays that premiered at the Rose have scenes of just this sort.

At the rear of the Rose stage, there were three capacious exits, each over ten feet wide. Unfortunately, the very limited excavation of a fragmentary portion of the original Globe site, in 1989, revealed nothing about the stage. The first Globe was built in 1599 with similar proportions to those of another theater, the Fortune, albeit that the former was polygonal and looked circular, whereas the latter was rectangular. The building contract for the Fortune survives and allows us to infer that the stage of the Globe was probably substantially wider than it was deep (perhaps forty-three feet wide and twenty-seven feet deep). It may well have been tapered at the front, like that of the Rose.

The capacity of the Globe was said to have been enormous, perhaps in excess of three thousand. It has been conjectured that about eight hundred people may have stood in the yard, with two thousand or more in the three layers of covered galleries. The other "public" playhouses were also of large capacity, whereas the indoor Blackfriars theater that Shakespeare's company began using in 1608—the former refectory of a monastery—had overall internal dimensions of a mere forty-six by sixty feet. It would have made for a much more intimate theatrical experience and had a much smaller capacity, probably of about six hundred people. Since they paid at least six-pence a head, the Blackfriars attracted a more select or "private" audience. The atmosphere would have been closer to that of an indoor performance before the court in the Whitehall Palace or at Richmond. That Shakespeare always wrote for indoor production at court as well as outdoor performance in the public theater should make us cautious about inferring, as some scholars have, that the opportunity provided by the intimacy of the Blackfriars led to a sig-nificant change toward a "chamber" style in his last plays—which, besides, were performed at both the Globe and the Blackfriars. After the occupation of the Blackfriars a five-act structure seems to have become more important to Shakespeare. That was because of artifi-cial lighting: there were musical interludes between the acts, while the candles were trimmed and replaced. Again, though, something similar must have been necessary for indoor court performances throughout his career.

Front of house there were the "gatherers" who collected the money from audience members: a penny to stand in the open-air yard, another penny for a place in the covered galleries, sixpence for the prominent "lord's rooms" to the side of the stage. In the indoor "private" theaters, gallants from the audience who fancied making themselves part of the spectacle sat on stools on the edge of the stage itself. Scholars debate as to how widespread this practice was in the public theaters such as the Globe. Once the audience were in place and the money counted, the gatherers were available to be extras on-stage. That is one reason why battles and crowd scenes often come later rather than early in Shakespeare's plays. There was no formal prohibition upon performance by women, and there certainly were women among the gatherers, so it is not beyond the bounds of possi-bility that female crowd members were played by females.

The play began at two o'clock in the afternoon and the theater had to be cleared by five. After the main show, there would be a jig—which consisted not only of dancing but also of knockabout comedy (it is the origin of the farcical "afterpiece" in the eighteenth-century theater). So the time available for a Shakespeare play was about two and a half hours, somewhere between the "two hours' traffic" men-tioned in the prologue to *Romeo and Juliet* and the "three hours' spectacle" referred to in the preface to the 1647 Folio of Beaumont and Fletcher's plays. The prologue to a play by Thomas Middleton refers to a thousand lines as "one hour's words," so the likelihood is that about two and a half thousand, or a maximum of three thousand lines made up the performed text. This is indeed the length of most of Shakespeare's comedies, whereas many of his tragedies and histories are much longer, raising the possibility that he wrote full scripts, possibly with eventual publication in mind, in the full knowledge that the stage version would be heavily cut. The short Quarto texts published in his lifetime—they used to be called "Bad" Quartos—provide fascinating evidence as to the kind of cutting that probably took place. So, for instance, the First Quarto of *Hamlet* neatly merges two occasions when Hamlet is overheard, the "Fishmonger" and the "nunnery" scenes.

The social composition of the audience was mixed. The poet Sir John Davies wrote of "A thousand townsmen, gentlemen and whores, / Porters and servingmen" who would "together throng" at the public playhouses. Though moralists associated female playgoing with adultery and the sex trade, many perfectly respectable citizens' wives were regular attendees. Some, no doubt, resembled the modern groupie: a story attested in two different sources has one citizen's wife making a post-show assignation with Richard Burbage and ending up in bed with Shakespeare—supposedly eliciting from the latter the quip that William the Conqueror was before Richard III. Defenders of theater liked to say that by witnessing the comeuppance of villains on the stage, audience members would repent of their own wrongdoings, but the reality is that most people went to the theater then, as they do now, for entertainment more than moral edification. Besides, it would be foolish to suppose that audiences behaved in a homogeneous way: a pamphlet of the 1630s tells of how two men went to see *Pericles* and one of them laughed while the other wept. Bishop John Hall complained that people went to church for the same reasons that they went to the theater: "for company, for custom, for recreation . . . to feed his eyes or his ears . . . or perhaps for sleep."

Men-about-town and clever young lawyers went to be seen as much as to see. In the modern popular imagination, shaped not least by *Shakespeare in Love* and the opening sequence of Laurence Olivier's *Henry V* film, the penny-paying groundlings stand in the yard hurling abuse or encouragement and hazelnuts or orange peel at the actors, while the sophisticates in the covered galleries appreciate Shakespeare's soaring poetry. The reality was probably the other way around. A "groundling" was a kind of fish, so the nickname suggests the penny audience standing below the level of the stage and gazing in silent open-mouthed wonder at the spectacle unfolding above them. The more difficult audience members, who kept up a running commentary of clever remarks on the performance and who occasionally got into quarrels with players, were the gallants. Like Hollywood movies in modern times, Elizabethan and Jacobean plays exercised a powerful influence on the fashion and behavior of the young. John Marston mocks the lawyers who would open their lips, perhaps to court a girl, and out would "flow / Naught but pure Juliet and Romeo."

THE ENSEMBLE AT WORK

In the absence of typewriters and photocopying machines, reading aloud would have been the means by which the company got to know a new play. The tradition of the playwright reading his complete script to the assembled company endured for generations. A copy would then have been taken to the Master of the Revels for licensing. The theater book-holder or prompter would then have copied the parts for distribution to the actors. A partbook consisted of the character's lines, with each speech preceded by the last three or four words of the speech before, the so-called "cue." These would have been taken away and studied or "conned." During this period of learning the parts, an actor might have had some one-to-one instruction, perhaps from the dramatist, perhaps from a senior actor who had played the same part before, and, in the case of an apprentice, from his master. A high percentage of Desdemona's lines occur in dialogue with Othello, of Lady Macbeth's with Macbeth, Cleopatra's with Antony, and Volumnia's with Coriolanus. The roles would almost certainly have been taken by the apprentice of the lead actor, usually Burbage, who delivers the majority of the cues. Given that

9. Hypothetical reconstruction of the interior of an Elizabethan playhouse during a performance.

apprentices lodged with their masters, there would have been ample opportunity for personal instruction, which may be what made it possible for young men to play such demanding parts.

After the parts were learned, there may have been no more than a single rehearsal before the first performance. With six different plays to be put on every week, there was no time for more. Actors, then, would go into a show with a very limited sense of the whole. The notion of a collective rehearsal process that is itself a process of discovery for the actors is wholly modern and would have been incomprehensible to Shakespeare and his original ensemble. Given the number of parts an actor had to hold in his memory, the forgetting of lines was probably more frequent than in the modern theater. The book-holder was on hand to prompt.

Backstage personnel included the property man, the tire-man who oversaw the costumes, call boys, attendants, and the musicians, who might play at various times from the main stage, the rooms above, and within the tiring-house. Scriptwriters sometimes made a nuisance of themselves backstage. There was often tension between the acting companies and the freelance playwrights from whom they purchased scripts: it was a smart move on the part of Shakespeare and the Lord Chamberlain's Men to bring the writing process in-house.

Scenery was limited, though sometimes set pieces were brought on (a bank of flowers, a bed, the mouth of hell). The trapdoor from below, the gallery stage above, and the curtained discovery-space at the back allowed for an array of special effects: the rising of ghosts and apparitions, the descent of gods, dialogue between a character at a window and another at ground level, the revelation of a statue or a pair of lovers playing at chess. Ingenious use could be made of props, as with the ass's head in *A Midsummer Night's Dream*. In a theater that does not clutter the stage with the material paraphernalia of everyday life, those objects that are deployed may take on powerful symbolic weight, as when Shylock bears his weighing scales in one hand and knife in the other, thus becoming a parody of the figure of Justice who traditionally bears a sword and a balance. Among the more significant items in the property cupboard of Shakespeare's company, there would have been a throne (the "chair of state"), joint stools, books, bottles, coins, purses, letters (which are brought onstage, read, or referred to on about eighty occasions in the complete works), maps, gloves, a set of stocks (in which Kent is put in *King Lear*), rings, rapiers, daggers, broadswords, staves, pistols, masks and vizards, heads and skulls, torches and tapers and lanterns which served to signal night scenes on the daylit stage, a buck's head, an ass's head, animal costumes. Live animals also put in appearances, most notably the dog Crab in *The Two Gentlemen of Verona* and possibly a young polar bear in *The Winter's Tale*.

The costumes were the most important visual dimension of the play. Playwrights were paid between £2 and £6 per script, whereas Alleyn was not averse to paying £20 for "a black velvet cloak with sleeves embroidered all with silver and gold." No matter the period of the play, actors always wore contemporary costume. The excitement for the audience came not from any impression of historical accuracy, but from the richness of the attire and perhaps the transgressive thrill of the knowledge that here were commoners like themselves strutting in the costumes of courtiers in effective defiance of the strict sumptuary laws whereby in real life people had to wear the clothes that befitted their social station.

To an even greater degree than props, costumes could carry symbolic importance. Racial characteristics could be suggested: a breastplate and helmet for a Roman soldier, a turban for a Turk, long robes for exotic characters such as Moors, a gabardine for a Jew. The figure of Time, as in *The Winter's Tale*, would be equipped with hourglass, scythe, and wings; Rumour, who speaks the prologue of *2 Henry IV*, wore a costume adorned with a thousand tongues. The wardrobe in the tiring-house of the Globe would have contained much of the same stock as that of rival manager Philip Henslowe at the Rose: green gowns for outlaws and foresters, black for melancholy men such as Jaques and people in mourning such as the Countess in *All's Well That Ends Well* (at the beginning of *Hamlet*, the prince is still in mourning black when everyone else is in festive garb for the wedding of the new king), a gown and hood for a friar (or a feigned friar like the duke in *Measure for Measure*), blue coats and tawny to distinguish the followers of rival factions, a leather apron and ruler for a carpenter (as in the opening scene of *Julius Caesar*—and in *A Midsummer Night's Dream*, where this is the only sign that Peter Quince is a carpenter), a cockle hat with staff and a pair of sandals for a pilgrim or palmer (the disguise assumed by Helen in *All's Well*), bodices and kirtles with farthingales beneath for the boys who are to be dressed as girls. A gender switch such as that of Rosalind or Jessica seems to have taken between fifty and eighty lines of dialogue—Viola does not resume her "maiden weeds," but remains in her boy's costume to the end of *Twelfth Night* because a change would have slowed down the action at just the moment it was speeding to a climax. Henslowe's inventory also included "a robe for to go invisible": Oberon, Puck, and Ariel must have had something similar.

As the costumes appealed to the eyes, so there was music for the ears. Comedies included many songs. Desdemona's willow song, perhaps a late addition to the text, is a rare and thus exceptionally poignant example from tragedy. Trumpets and tuckets sounded for ceremonial entrances, drums denoted an army on the march. Background music could create atmosphere, as at the beginning of *Twelfth Night*, during the lovers' dialogue near the end of *The Mer-*

chant of Venice, when the statue seemingly comes to life in *The Winter's Tale,* and for the revival of Pericles and of Lear (in the Quarto text, but not the Folio). The haunting sound of the hautboy suggested a realm beyond the human, as when the god Hercules is imagined deserting Mark Antony. Dances symbolized the harmony of the end of a comedy—though in Shakespeare's world of mingled joy and sorrow, someone is usually left out of the circle.

The most important resource was, of course, the actors themselves. They needed many skills: in the words of one contemporary commentator, "dancing, activity, music, song, elocution, ability of body, memory, skill of weapon, pregnancy of wit." Their bodies were as significant as their voices. Hamlet tells the player to "suit the action to the word, the word to the action": moments of strong emotion, known as "passions," relied on a repertoire of dramatic gestures as well as a modulation of the voice. When Titus Andronicus has had his hand chopped off, he asks "How can I grace my talk, / Wanting a hand to give it action?" A pen portrait of "The Character of an Excellent Actor" by the dramatist John Webster is almost certainly based on his impression of Shakespeare's leading man, Richard Burbage: "By a full and significant action of body, he charms our attention: sit in a full theatre, and you will think you see so many lines drawn from the circumference of so many ears, whiles the actor is the centre. . . ."

Though Burbage was admired above all others, praise was also heaped upon the apprentice players whose alto voices fitted them for the parts of women. A spectator at Oxford in 1610 records how the audience were reduced to tears by the pathos of Desdemona's death. The puritans who fumed about the biblical prohibition upon cross-dressing and the encouragement to sodomy constituted by the sight of an adult male kissing a teenage boy onstage were a small minority. Little is known, however, about the characteristics of the leading apprentices in Shakespeare's company. It may perhaps be inferred that one was a lot taller than the other, since Shakespeare often wrote for a pair of female friends, one tall and fair, the other short and dark (Helena and Hermia, Rosalind and Celia, Beatrice and Hero).

We know little about Shakespeare's own acting roles—an early allusion indicates that he often took royal parts, and a venerable tradition gives him old Adam in *As You Like It* and the ghost of old King Hamlet. Save for Burbage's lead roles and the generic part of the clown, all such castings are mere speculation. We do not even know for sure whether the original Falstaff was Will Kempe or another actor who specialized in comic roles, Thomas Pope.

Kempe left the company in early 1599. Tradition has it that he fell out with Shakespeare over the matter of excessive improvisation. He was replaced by Robert Armin, who was less of a clown and more of a cerebral wit: this explains the difference between such parts as Lancelet Gobbo and Dogberry, which were written for Kempe, and the more verbally sophisticated Feste and Lear's Fool, which were written for Armin.

One thing that is clear from surviving "plots" or storyboards of plays from the period is that a degree of doubling was necessary. *2 Henry VI* has over sixty speaking parts, but more than half of the characters appear only in a single scene and most scenes have only six to eight speakers. At a stretch, the play could be performed by thirteen actors. When Thomas Platter saw *Julius Caesar* at the Globe in 1599, he noted that there were about fifteen. Why doesn't Paris go to the Capulet ball in *Romeo and Juliet?* Perhaps because he was doubled with Mercutio, who does. In *The Winter's Tale*, Mamillius might have come back as Perdita and Antigonus been doubled by Camillo, making the partnership with Paulina at the end a very neat touch. Titania and Oberon are often played by the same pair as Hippolyta and Theseus, suggesting a symbolic matching of the rulers of the worlds of night and day, but it is questionable whether there would have been time for the necessary costume changes. As so often, one is left in a realm of tantalizing speculation.

THE KING'S MAN

On Queen Elizabeth's death in 1603, the new king, James I, who had held the Scottish throne as James VI since he had been an infant, immediately took the Lord Chamberlain's Men under his direct patronage. Henceforth they would be the King's Men, and for the rest of Shakespeare's career they were favored with far more court performances than any of their rivals. There even seem to have been rumors early in the reign that Shakespeare and Burbage were being considered for knighthoods, an unprecedented honor for mere actors—and one that in the event was not accorded to a member of the profession for nearly three hundred years, when the title was bestowed upon Henry Irving, the leading Shakespearean actor of Queen Victoria's reign.

Shakespeare's productivity rate slowed in the Jacobean years, not because of age or some personal trauma, but because there were frequent outbreaks of plague, causing the theaters to be closed for long periods. The King's Men were forced to spend many months on the road. Between November 1603 and 1608, they were to be found at various towns in the south and Midlands, though Shakespeare probably did not tour with them by this time. He had bought a large house back home in Stratford and was accumulating other property. He may indeed have stopped acting soon after the new king took the throne. With the London theaters closed so much of the time and a large repertoire on the stocks, Shakespeare seems to have focused his energies on writing a few long and complex tragedies that could have been played on demand at court: *Othello, King Lear, Antony and Cleopatra, Coriolanus,* and *Cymbeline* are among his longest and poetically grandest plays. *Macbeth* survives only in a shorter text, which shows signs of adaptation after Shakespeare's death. The bitterly satirical *Timon of Athens,* apparently a collaboration with Thomas Middleton that may have failed on the stage, also belongs to this period. In comedy, too, he wrote longer and morally darker works than in the Elizabethan period, pushing at the very bounds of the form in *Measure for Measure* and *All's Well That Ends Well.*

From 1608 onward, when the King's Men began occupying the indoor Blackfriars playhouse (as a winter house, meaning that they only used the outdoor Globe in summer?), Shakespeare turned to a more romantic style. His company had a great success with a revived and altered version of an old pastoral play called *Mucedorus.* It even featured a bear. The younger dramatist John Fletcher, meanwhile, sometimes working in collaboration with Francis Beaumont, was pioneering a new style of tragicomedy, a mix of romance and royalism laced with intrigue and pastoral excursions. Shakespeare experimented with this idiom in *Cymbeline,* and it was presumably with his blessing that Fletcher eventually took over as the King's Men's company dramatist. The two writers apparently collaborated on three plays in the years 1612–14: a lost romance called *Cardenio* (based on the love-madness of a character in Cervantes' *Don Quixote*), *Henry VIII* (originally staged with the title "All Is True"), and *The Two Noble Kinsmen*, a dramatization of Chaucer's "Knight's Tale." These were written after Shakespeare's two final solo-authored plays, *The Winter's Tale*, a self-consciously old-fashioned work dramatizing the pastoral romance of his old enemy Robert Greene, and *The Tempest*, which at one and the same time drew together multiple theatrical traditions, diverse reading, and contemporary interest in the fate of a ship that had been wrecked on the way to the New World.

The collaborations with Fletcher suggest that Shakespeare's career ended with a slow fade rather than the sudden retirement supposed by the nineteenth-century Romantic critics who read Prospero's epilogue to *The Tempest* as Shakespeare's personal farewell to his art. In the last few years of his life Shakespeare certainly spent more of his time in Stratford-upon-Avon, where he became further involved in property dealing and litigation. But his London life also continued. In 1613 he made his first major London property purchase: a freehold house in the Blackfriars district, close to his company's indoor theater. *The Two Noble Kinsmen* may have been written as late as 1614, and Shakespeare was in London on business a little over a year before he died of an unknown cause at home in Stratford-upon-Avon in 1616, probably on his fifty-second birthday.

About half the sum of his works were published in his lifetime, in texts of variable quality. A few years after his death, his fellow actors began putting together an authorized edition of his complete *Comedies, Histories and Tragedies*. It appeared in 1623, in large "Folio" format. This collection of thirty-six plays gave Shakespeare his immortality. In the words of his fellow dramatist Ben Jonson, who contributed two poems of praise at the start of the Folio, the body of his work made him "a monument without a tomb":

And art alive still while thy book doth live
And we have wits to read and praise to give . . .
He was not of an age, but for all time!

SHAKESPEARE'S WORKS:
A CHRONOLOGY

1595–97	*Love's Labour's Won* (a lost play, unless the original title for another comedy)
1595–96	*A Midsummer Night's Dream*
1595–96	*The Tragedy of Romeo and Juliet*
1595–96	*King Richard the Second*
1595–97	*The Life and Death of King John* (possibly earlier)
1596–97	*The Merchant of Venice*
1596–97	*The First Part of Henry the Fourth*
1597–98	*The Second Part of Henry the Fourth*
1598	*Much Ado About Nothing*
1598–99	*The Passionate Pilgrim* (20 poems, some not by Shakespeare)
1599	*The Life of Henry the Fifth*
1599	"To the Queen" (epilogue for a court performance)
1599	*As You Like It*
1599	*The Tragedy of Julius Caesar*
1600–01	*The Tragedy of Hamlet, Prince of Denmark* (perhaps revising an earlier version)
1600–01	*The Merry Wives of Windsor* (perhaps revising version of 1597–99)
1601	"Let the Bird of Loudest Lay" (poem, known since 1807 as "The Phoenix and Turtle" (turtledove))
1601	*Twelfth Night, or What You Will*
1601–02	*The Tragedy of Troilus and Cressida*
1604	*The Tragedy of Othello, the Moor of Venice*
1604	*Measure for Measure*
1605	*All's Well That Ends Well*
1605	*The Life of Timon of Athens,* with Thomas Middleton
1605–06	*The Tragedy of King Lear*
1605–08	? contribution to *The Four Plays in One* (lost, except for *A Yorkshire Tragedy,* mostly by Thomas Middleton)

1606	*The Tragedy of Macbeth* (surviving text has additional scenes by Thomas Middleton)
1606–07	*The Tragedy of Antony and Cleopatra*
1608	*The Tragedy of Coriolanus*
1608	*Pericles, Prince of Tyre,* with George Wilkins
1610	*The Tragedy of Cymbeline*
1611	*The Winter's Tale*
1611	*The Tempest*
1612–13	*Cardenio,* with John Fletcher (survives only in later adaptation called *Double Falsehood* by Lewis Theobald)
1613	*Henry VIII (All Is True),* with John Fletcher
1613–14	*The Two Noble Kinsmen,* with John Fletcher

FURTHER READING
AND VIEWING

CRITICAL APPROACHES

Beiner, G., "The Libido as Pharmakos, or The Triumph of Love: *The Merry Wives of Windsor* in the Context of Comedy," *Orbis Litteraria*, Vol. 43, 1988, pp. 195–216. Examines play's comedic structure in relation to other Shakespeare plays.

Ellis, Anthony, *Old Age, Masculinity and Early Modern Drama: Comic Elders on the Italian and Shakespeare Stage* (2009). Chapter 2, "Old Age and the Uses of Comedy: Bibbiena's *Calenda* and Shakespeare's *Merry Wives of Windsor*," sociohistorical study of Falstaff in early modern context.

Erickson, Peter, "The Order of the Garter, the Cult of Elizabeth, and Class-Gender Tension in *The Merry Wives of Windsor*," in *Shakespeare Reproduced: The Text in History and Ideology*, edited by Jean E. Howard and Marion F. O'Connor (1987), pp. 116–40. Influential historicist reading.

Grav, Peter F., *Shakespeare and the Economic Imperative* (2008). Examines the significance of money in Shakespeare's plays and society; chapter 2 focuses on *Merry Wives*, "Shakespeare's England: *The Merry Wives of Windsor*'s Bourgeois Cash Values," pp. 54–82.

Green, William, *Shakespeare's Merry Wives of Windsor* (1962). Slightly dated but still useful general introduction that covers various aspects of play's historical context, the Order of the Garter, first performance, and text, with some nice illustrations.

Lamb, Mary Ellen, *The Popular Culture of Shakespeare, Spenser, and Jonson* (2006). Cultural studies foray into the importance of fairies, old wives' tales, and hobbyhorses in early modern literature and society; chapter 6 on *Merry Wives*: "Domestic Nationalism and the Refuse of the Realm," pp. 125–59.

Melchiori, Giorgio, *Shakespeare's Garter Plays: Edward III to Merry Wives of Windsor* (1994). Examines all aspects of historical tradition of play and context.

Miola, Robert S., "*The Merry Wives of Windsor*: Classical and Italian Intertexts," *Comparative Drama*, Vol. 27, No. 3, Fall 1993, pp. 364–76. Traces influences on play of comic traditions of Roman New Comedy.

Roberts, Jeanne Addison, *Shakespeare's English Comedy* (1979). Relatively early critical work discussing play's lowly historical position in the canon and arguing for its critical revaluation.

Ryan, Kiernan, *Shakespeare's Comedies* (2009). Excellent introductory account in chapter 7: "Pribbles and Prabbles: *The Merry Wives of Windsor*," pp. 134–63.

Steadman, John M., "Falstaff as Actaeon: A Dramatic Emblem," *Shakespeare Quarterly*, Vol. XIV, No. 3, Summer 1963, pp. 231–44. Iconographic study comparing Falstaff to the Renaissance myth of Actaeon.

Theis, Jeffrey S., *Writing the Forest in Early Modern England* (2009). Ecocritical study exploring the relationship between landscape, culture, and society; chapter 4, "A Border Skirmish: Community, Deer Poaching, and Spatial Transgression in *The Merry Wives of Windsor*."

Wall, Wendy, " 'Household Stuff': The Sexual Politics of Domesticity and the Advent of English Comedy," *English Literary History*, Vol. 65, No. 1, Spring 1998. Ingenious account which argues for the play as an allegory of the gendered formation of English national culture.

THE PLAY IN PERFORMANCE

Holland, Peter, "*The Merry Wives of Windsor:* The Performance of Community," *Shakespeare Quarterly*, Vol. 23, No. 2, 2005, pp. 5–18. Critique of various productions' failure to attend to Shakespeare's precisely detailed rural locale.

Tardiff, Joseph E., ed., *Shakespearean Criticism* 18 (1992). Includes stage history, reviews, and retrospective accounts of selected productions.

AVAILABLE ON DVD

Chimes at Midnight directed by Orson Welles (1965, DVD 2000). Condenses all the Falstaff material from both parts of *Henry IV* plus *Henry V* and *The Merry Wives of Windsor*. Multi-award nominated, with a star-studded cast, as eccentric and brilliant as Welles's own performance as Falstaff. One of the all-time classic Shakespeare films.

The Merry Wives of Windsor directed by David Jones for the BBC Shakespeare (1982, DVD 2006). Stars Richard Griffiths, Michael Bryant, Ben Kingsley, Alan Bennett, with acting honors going to Prunella Scales and Judy Davis as the Merry Wives.

Falstaff directed by Richard Jones (2009, DVD 2010). Fine Glyndebourne Festival recording of Verdi's operatic masterpiece with Christopher Purves as Falstaff.

REFERENCES

1. John Dennis, *The Comical Gallant: or the amours of Sir John Falstaffe. A Comedy* (1702), A2. A famous painting by David Scott, *Queen Elizabeth Viewing the Performance of the "Merry Wives of Windsor" in the Globe Theatre* (1840), captures an imagined version of the first performance, with public figures from across Elizabeth's reign anachronistically brought together to view the play.
2. William Winter, *Shakespeare on the Stage* (1916), p. 383.
3. Samuel Pepys, *Diaries*, 15 August 1667.
4. Dennis, *The Comical Gallant*, p. 49.
5. *London Stage*, Vol. II, pp. 596–97.
6. Winter, *Shakespeare on the Stage*, p. 392.
7. Winter, *Shakespeare on the Stage*, p. 393.
8. *European Magazine*, 17 May 1815.
9. 1824, quoted in Gāmini Salgādo, ed., *Eyewitnesses of Shakespeare* (1975), p. 147.
10. Theodor Fontane, *Shakespeare in the London Theatre 1855–58*, trans. Russell Jackson (1999), pp. 75–76.
11. *New York Times*, 15 January 1886.
12. *Stratford-upon-Avon Herald*, 29 April 1887.
13. *Stratford-upon-Avon Herald*, 29 April 1887.
14. *Western Daily Press*, 3 May 1914.
15. New York *Evening Post*, 16 February 1895.
16. *New York Sun*, 21 March 1916.
17. *Birmingham Post*, 4 August 1919.
18. *Western Daily Mail*, 20 April 1935.
19. *The Times*, London, 20 April 1935.
20. *Birmingham Post*, 25 April 1940.
21. *Birmingham Mail*, 25 April 1943.
22. *Birmingham Post*, 3 April 1945.
23. *Birmingham Mail*, 13 July 1955.
24. *Financial Times*, 13 July 1955.
25. *Guardian*, 21 June 1975.
26. *Shakespeare Quarterly* 14 (1963), pp. 455–59.

27. John Pettigrew and Jamie Portman, *Stratford: The First Thirty Years* (1985), Vol. II, p. 131.

28. *Educational Theater Journal* 28 (1976), p. 407.

29. *The Times*, London, 11 May 1990.

30. *Guardian*, 21 December 1993.

31. *Shakespeare Survey* 49 (2006), p. 262.

32. *Independent*, 28 January 1995.

33. *Time Out*, 9 June 1999.

34. *Guardian*, 29 December 1982.

35. Wilhelm Hortmann, *Shakespeare on the German Stage: The Twentieth Century* (1998), p. 131.

36. Yasunari Takahashi, "Kyogenising Shakespeare/Shakespeareanising Kyogen: Some Notes on *The Braggart Samurai*," in *Shakespeare and the Japanese Stage* (1998), p. 214.

37. Takahashi, "Kyogenising Shakespeare/Shakespeareanising Kyogen," p. 239.

38. Jeremy Kingston, *Punch*, Vol. 248, No. 6845, 23 December 1964.

39. Joseph C. Tardiff, ed., *Shakespearean Criticism* 18, p. 37.

40. Hilary Spurling, *Spectator*, Vol. 213, No. 7122, 25 December 1964.

41. Spurling, *Spectator*, 25 December 1964.

42. *The Times*, London, 18 December 1964.

43. Ronald Bryden, *New Statesman*, Vol. 68, No. 1763, 25 December 1964.

44. Spurling, *Spectator*, 25 December 1964.

45. *The Times*, London, 18 December 1964.

46. *The Times*, London, 18 December 1964.

47. Spurling, *Spectator*, 25 December 1964.

48. Philip French, *New Statesman*, Vol. 75, No. 1939, 10 October 1968.

49. French, *New Statesman*, 10 October 1968.

50. Michael Billington, *Guardian*, 27 March 1976.

51. John Higgins, *Financial Times*, 16 July 1968.

52. B. A. Young, *Financial Times*, 2 May 1968.

53. Young, *Financial Times*, 2 May 1968.

54. Peter Roberts, *Plays and Players*, Vol. 18, No. 11, 11 August 1968.

55. Jeremy Kinston, *Punch*, Vol. 254, No. 6662, 15 May 1968.

56. D. A. N. Jones, *Listener*, Vol. 80, No. 2052, 25 July 1968.

57. Young, *Financial Times*, 2 May 1968.

58. Higgins, *Financial Times*, 16 July 1968.

59. Young, *Financial Times*, 2 May 1968.

60. Irving Wardle, *The Times*, London, 27 March 1976.

61. Tardiff, *Shakespearean Criticism* 18, p. 53.

62. Michael Billington, *Guardian*, 4 April 1979.

63. Benedict Nightingale, *New Statesman*, Vol. 97, No. 2508, 13 April 1979.

64. Thomas Laroque, *Cahiers Elisabéthains* 16, pp. 103–4.

65. Michael Billington, *Guardian*, 4 April 1979.

66. Nightingale, *New Statesman*, 13 April 1979.

67. Billington, *Guardian*, 4 April 1979.

68. Billington, *Guardian*, 4 April 1979.

69. Laroque, *Cahiers Elisabéthains*, p. 104.

70. Michael Ratcliffe, *Observer*, 7 April 1985.

71. Francis King, *Sunday Telegraph*, 7 April 1985.

72. John Barber, *Daily Telegraph*, 6 April 1985.

73. Nicholas Shrimpton, "Shakespeare Performances in London and Stratford-Upon-Avon, 1984–85," *Shakespeare Survey* 39 (1987), pp. 191–206.

74. King, *Sunday Telegraph*, 7 April 1985.

75. Roger Warren, *Shakespeare Quarterly* 37, p. 115.

76. Irving Wardle, *The Times*, London, 6 April 1985.

77. Stanley Wells, *Times Literary Supplement*, No. 4281, 19 April 1985.

78. Michael Coveney, *Financial Times*, 6 April 1985.

79. John Peter, *Sunday Times*, 7 April 1985.

80. Warren, *Shakespeare Quarterly* 37 (1986), p. 115.

81. Shrimpton, "Shakespeare Performances in London and Stratford-Upon-Avon, 1984–85," p. 198.

82. Ralph Berry, *On Directing Shakespeare* (1989), p. 179.

83. Wardle, *The Times*, 6 April 1985.

84. Michael Billington, *Guardian*, 4 April 1985.

85. Wells, *Times Literary Supplement*, 19 April 1985.

86. Kirsty Milne, *Sunday Telegraph*, 6 September 1992.

87. Andrew St. George, *Financial Times*, 4 September 1992.

88. Charles Spencer, *Daily Telegraph*, 6 September 1992.

89. Michael Billington, *Guardian*, 3 September 1992.

90. Benedict Nightingale, *The Times*, London, 4 September 1992.

91. Billington, *Guardian*, 3 September 1992.

92. Paul Taylor, *Independent*, 4 September 1992.

93. Maureen Paton, *Daily Express*, 4 September 1992.

94. Nightingale, *The Times*, 4 September 1992.

95. Irving Wardle, *Independent on Sunday*, 6 September 1992.

96. Michael Coveney, *Observer,* 6 September 1992.

97. Robert Gore-Langton, *Daily Express,* 10 January 1997.

98. Paul Taylor, *Independent,* 21 December 1996.

99. Alastair Macaulay, *Financial Times,* 9 January 1997.

100. Shaun Usher, *Daily Mail,* 20 December 1996.

101. Benedict Nightingale, *The Times,* London, 21 December 1996.

102. Charles Spencer, *Daily Telegraph,* 23 December 1996.

103. Spencer, *Daily Telegraph,* 23 December 1996.

104. David Nathan, *Jewish Chronicle,* 27 December 1996.

105. Gore-Langton, *Daily Express,* 10 January 1997.

106. Macaulay, *Financial Times,* 9 January 1997.

107. Charles Spencer, *Daily Telegraph,* 2 November 2002.

108. Ian Shuttleworth, *Financial Times,* 1 November 2002.

109. Shuttleworth, *Financial Times,* 1 November 2002.

110. Lyn Gardner, *Guardian,* 5 November 2002.

111. Michael Coveney, *Daily Mail,* 1 November 2002.

112. John Gross, *Sunday Telegraph,* 3 November 2002.

113. Spencer, *Daily Telegraph,* 2 November 2002.

114. Jeremy Kingston, *The Times,* London, 2 November 2002.

115. Shuttleworth, *Financial Times,* 1 November 2002.

116. Kingston, *Times,* 2 November 2002.

117. Spencer, *Daily Telegraph,* 2 November 2002.

118. Gardner, *Guardian,* 5 November 2002.

119. Sheridan Morley, *Punch,* Vol. 290, No. 7572, 5 February 1986.

120. Nicholas de Jongh, *Evening Standard,* 13 December 2006.

121. Sheridan Morley, *Daily Express,* 13 December 2006.

122. Michael Billington, *Guardian,* 13 December 2006.

123. Paul Taylor, *Independent,* 13 December 2006.

124. Quentin Letts, *Daily Mail,* 13 December 2006.

125. Benedict Nightingale, *The Times,* London, 13 December 2006.

126. Charles Spencer, *Daily Telegraph,* 13 December 2006.

127. Morley, *Daily Express,* 13 December 2006.

128. Macaulay, *Financial Times,* 9 January 1997.

129. Christopher Hart, *Sunday Times,* 17 December 2006.

130. Macaulay, *Financial Times,* 9 January 1997.

ACKNOWLEDGMENTS AND PICTURE CREDITS

Preparation of "*The Merry Wives* in Performance" was assisted by a generous grant from the CAPITAL Centre (Creativity and Performance in Teaching and Learning) of the University of Warwick for research in the RSC archive at the Shakespeare Birthplace Trust.

Thanks as always to our indefatigable and eagle-eyed copy editor Tracey Day and to Ray Addicott for overseeing the production process with rigor and calmness.

Picture research by Michelle Morton. Grateful acknowledgment is made to the Shakespeare Birthplace Trust for assistance with picture research (special thanks to Helen Hargest) and reproduction fees.

Images of RSC productions are supplied by the Shakespeare Centre Library and Archive, Stratford-upon-Avon. This library, maintained by the Shakespeare Birthplace Trust, holds the most important collection of Shakespeare material in the UK, including the Royal Shakespeare Company's official archive. It is open to the public free of charge.

For more information see www.shakespeare.org.uk.

1. Directed by Augustin Daly (1886) Reproduced by permission of the Shakespeare Birthplace Trust
2. Directed by Glen Byam Shaw (1955) Angus McBean © Royal Shakespeare Company
3. Directed by Terry Hands (1968) Tom Holte © Shakespeare Birthplace Trust
4. Directed by Trevor Nunn (1979) Joe Cocks Studio Collection © Shakespeare Birthplace Trust
5. Directed by David Thacker (1992) Malcolm Davies © Shakespeare Birthplace Trust

6. Directed by Rachel Kavanaugh (2002) Manuel Harlan © Royal Shakespeare Company
7. Directed by Bill Alexander (1985) Joe Cocks Studio Collection © Shakespeare Birthplace Trust
8. Directed by Gregory Doran (2006) Stewart Hemley © Royal Shakespeare Company
9. Reconstructed Elizabethan Playhouse © Charcoalblue

MODERN LIBRARY IS ONLINE AT
WWW.MODERNLIBRARY.COM

MODERN LIBRARY ONLINE IS YOUR GUIDE TO CLASSIC LITERATURE ON THE WEB

THE MODERN LIBRARY E-NEWSLETTER

Our free e-mail newsletter is sent to subscribers, and features sample chapters, interviews with and essays by our authors, upcoming books, special promotions, announcements, and news. To subscribe to the Modern Library e-newsletter, visit **www.modernlibrary.com**

THE MODERN LIBRARY WEBSITE

Check out the Modern Library website at **www.modernlibrary.com** for:

- The Modern Library e-newsletter
- A list of our current and upcoming titles and series
- Reading Group Guides and exclusive author spotlights
- Special features with information on the classics and other paperback series
- Excerpts from new releases and other titles
- A list of our e-books and information on where to buy them
- The Modern Library Editorial Board's 100 Best Novels and 100 Best Nonfiction Books of the Twentieth Century written in the English language
- News and announcements

Questions? E-mail us at **modernlibrary@randomhouse.com**.
For questions about examination or desk copies, please visit the Random House Academic Resources site at
www.randomhouse.com/academic